# FabJob® Guide to

# BECOME A MAKEUP ARTIST

JENNIFER JAMES

# FABJOB® GUIDE TO
# BECOME A MAKEUP ARTIST
## Editor: Jennifer James

ISBN 1-894638-64-6

Library and Archives Canada Cataloguing in Publication

James, Jennifer
FabJob guide to become a makeup artist / Jennifer James.

Accompanied by CD-ROM.
Includes bibliographical references.
ISBN 1-894638-64-6

1. Makeup artists—Vocational guidance.    I. Title.
PN2068.J34 2005      646.7'26'023      C2005-902752-5

**Important Disclaimer:** Although every effort has been made to ensure this guide is free from errors, this publication is sold with the understanding that the authors, editors, and publisher are not responsible for the results of any action taken on the basis of information in this work, nor for any errors or omissions. The publishers, and the authors and editors, expressly disclaim all and any liability to any person, whether a purchaser of this publication or not, in respect of anything and of the consequences of anything done or omitted to be done by any such person in reliance, whether whole or partial, upon the whole or any part of the contents of this publication. If expert advice is required, services of a competent professional person should be sought.

**About the Websites Mentioned in this Guide:** Although we aim to provide the information you need within the guide, we have also included a number of websites because readers have told us they appreciate knowing about sources of additional information. (**TIP:** Don't include a period at the end of a web address when you type it into your browser.) Due to the constant development of the Internet, websites can change. Any websites mentioned in this guide are included for the convenience of readers only.  We are not responsible for the content of any sites except FabJob.com.

FabJob Inc.
19 Horizon View Court
Calgary, Alberta, Canada T3Z 3M5

FabJob Inc.
4603 NE University Village #224
Seattle, Washington, USA 98105

To order books in bulk phone 403-949-2039
For media inquiries phone 403-949-4980

# www.FabJob.com

## About the Editor

**Jennifer James** leads the Editorial Department at FabJob Inc., the world's leading publisher of information about dream careers. She has edited, researched for, and contributed to more than 30 FabJob career guides, including the *FabJob Guide to Become a Fashion Designer*, and the *FabJob Guide to Become a Celebrity Personal Assistant*, as well as the forthcoming book *Dream Careers* by Tag and Catherine Goulet. A business communications consultant specializing in music and fashion, she has advised and prepared marketing materials to launch businesses and individual careers in these industries.

## About the Authors

**Eva Jane Bunkley** is a two-time Emmy Award-winning makeup artist. In her more than ten years as a professional makeup artist, her talent has been viewed in television, videos, film projects, runway and print. Eva (shown in photo with husband Terence after winning her first  Emmy) earned her two Emmy awards while spending seven years doing makeup for television news in Atlanta. Celebrity faces she has worked on include Hugh Grant, Stephen Baldwin, L.L. Cool J, Evander Holyfield, Larry King, Chris Tucker, former President and First Lady Jimmy and Rosalyn Carter, Usher, Ed McMahon, Danny Glover, Jasmine Guy, Jeff Foxworthy, Judge Glenda Hatchett (the *Judge Hatchett* TV show), The Rock, Johnny Cochran, David Copperfield, former Secretary of State Madeline Albright, Jermaine Dupree, Donnie Osmond, Creflo and Taffi Dollar (the *Changing Your World* Broadcast), and Bishop T.D. Jakes, to name just a few. Eva holds a Bachelor of Science degree from Ohio State University, where she studied fashion. Eva currently resides in the Atlanta, Georgia area, and is available for Atlanta as well as travel bookings. She can be contacted through her website at **www.anointedhands.com**.

**Caryne Brown** is an editorial consultant and business planner based in Los Angeles. As Senior Editor of *Entrepreneur Magazine*, she wrote or supervised editing of more than 60 how-to books, and developed distance-learning courses in business planning and entrepreneurial management. Topics of business manuals she has written include image consulting, start-up basics, and increasing sales. As the "Ask the Experts" columnist for *Income Opportunities Magazine*, she answered reader inquiries on small business management. She was a founding editor of *Woman's Enterprise*, and her numerous other writing credits include *American History*, *Architectural Digest*, *Bon Appétit*, *Ironman*, and *Shape*.

**Alisa Gordaneer** is the author of the *FabJob Guide to Become a Florist*, and the editor of *Monday Magazine*, an alternative weekly newspaper in Victoria, B.C., where she writes a weekly column on current events and social trends, and covers numerous aspects of contemporary lifestyles. She has worked in various creative industries, from floral design to photography to publishing. A professional editor and writer, she has contributed to the *FabJob Guide to Become a Fashion Designer*, and to the anthologies *Women Who Eat*, *Three Ring Circus*, and *Breeder* (all from Seal Press).

**Todra Payne** has been a professional makeup artist for more than ten years; six of which were spent in the highly competitive world of New York fashion. Her artistry has been featured in national and international fashion & lifestyle magazines such as *Elle*, *Harper's Bazaar*, *O*, *Redbook*, *Martha Stewart's Living* and *W*, as well as on designer's runways and television.  Celebrity clients such as Sigourney Weaver, Leelee Sobieski, Donna Karan, Soledad O'Brien and Anna Kournikova have used Todra to polish their looks. She writes beauty articles for magazines, conducts workshops on makeup techniques, and runs a bridal beauty service. At her blog at **www.crushedberries. blogspot.com**, Todra highlights beauty trends and chronicles her adventures in opening her own cosmetic studio. She and her husband and cat reside in Pennsylvania.

**Penny Ruekberg** is a professional writer and actress, currently residing in Dallas, Texas. For many years she worked in the cosmetics and beauty industry as an in-house copywriter for Mary Kay Cosmetics, Inc. In addition, she wrote website and marketing materials for Polished, Inc., a "new-concept" spa and beauty supply store. Her writing on various topics has appeared  in regional and national magazines, including *Beauty* magazine and *Dallas Home Living*. She is currently at work on a book debunking myths and misconceptions about a career in acting.

**Rennay Craats** is a freelance writer and editor in Calgary, Alberta. Trained in journalism and communication, she has written and edited newspaper and magazine articles on a wide variety of topics ranging from archaeological digs to profiles of humanitarians. Her writing includes a feature on the men's spa experience for *American Health and Fitness*, and articles on cosmetic dentistry and other topics for a daily newspaper. She has written career profiles for a website maintained by the Government of Michigan, and prepares promotional material through her company, Boomerang Communications.

**Susan Wessling** is an award-winning writer and editor whose work has been recognized by the National (U.S.) Newspaper Association and The New England Press Association. Her articles have appeared in a number of newspapers, U.S. and international magazines, and numerous education, health, and sports websites including Encyclopaedia Britannica's online encyclopedia. She has interviewed some of the top makeup artists in the world. Wessling lives in central Massachusetts with her partner, Pat, their son Stephen, and Irish Setter Clancy.

# Acknowledgments

The authors thank professional makeup artists **Dyana Aives**, **Tara Anand**, **Tobi Britton**, **Thecla "TC" Luisi**, and **Davida Simon** for providing details about their career paths for this guide, as well as the following professionals in the makeup and entertainment industry for their advice and guidance:

- **Whitney Adkins-Mvondo**, makeup artist and hairstylist

- **Marie Augustine**, makeup artist, Alex Roldan Salon, West Hollywood, CA

- **Jeremy Gordaneer**, theatrical props designer

- **Mary Goodman**, talent agent, Celestine Agency, www.celestineagency.com

- **Jim Hedge**, Director Student Services, Studio Makeup Academy, www.studiomakeupacademy.com

- **Florence Johnson**, makeup artist

- **Robert Jones**, makeup artist, author of *Simple Beauté* and *Beauté Occasions*, beautemadesimple.com

- **Michael Key**, *Make-Up Artist Magazine*, www.makeupmag.com

- **Anthony Pepe**, owner of Demonic Pumpkins FX, New York, NY, www.demonicpumpkins.com

- **Timothy Priano**, Artists by Timothy Priano, www.artistsbytimothypriano.com

- **Jesse Valentine**, De Facto agency, New York, NY, www.defactoinc.com

- **Marvin Westmore**, Westmore Academy of Cosmetic Arts, Hollywood, CA, www.westmoreacademy.com

- **Andrew Zahn**, stage actor

# Contents

# 1. Introduction

As a makeup artist, you will get paid to help people look drop-dead gorgeous and feel great about how they look. You will use your sense of style and creativity to select the right colors and types of makeup, and apply it to your clients. You may find yourself working on movie stars one day, and runway models the next, or you may put the perfect touch on weddings and other special occasions.

A career in makeup artistry gets people excited, and for good reason. The hours are flexible, the job is fun and creative, and top makeup artists command hundreds or thousands of dollars a day for their services. Behind many beautiful faces is a makeup artist who transformed it into what you see. Some makeup artists come into contact with celebrities on a daily basis, to the point where certain stars will only have their faces made up by one chosen individual.

No matter if you work with beauty queens or brides, you will be helping people achieve their dreams by enhancing their image. With the right makeup, you can take people back in time, make fantasies believable, and make everyday life shimmer with excitement—if only for one enchanted evening. This is a gift that makeup artists share with the world: touching lives with beauty and glamour.

The *FabJob Guide to Become a Makeup Artist* will show you how to get started and succeed in this fabulous job. It is loaded with the kind of insider information that helped established makeup professionals get to where they are today.

The next few pages will introduce you to makeup and makeup artistry. You will learn what role makeup plays in a modern world, and how you can apply your makeup talents in a variety of ways to find a career path that suits you and your lifestyle. You'll also learn about the benefits of this career that is growing in popularity. If you have a desire to be the real reason people look "naturally beautiful," then read on.

# 1.1 Makeup in Society

Cosmetics, including makeup and personal hygiene products, have been in use since ancient times. As early as 4000 BC, the Egyptians were using cosmetics made of iron oxide, black kohl, powdered green malachite, and ochre. Modern cosmetics saw significant growth at the turn of the 20th century. The sudden absence of men during World War I led to increased social and financial independence for women, and many spent their newly found money on lipstick, powders, and other personal items.

The emergence of color cinema and movie stars who wore bright red lipstick and other makeup during the 1930s, '40s, and '50s resulted in an increase in cosmetic use as well. From that time until today, North Americans have continued to be influenced by celebrity trends in makeup and by the styles depicted on the pages of fashion magazines such as *Vogue* and *Glamour*.

## The Importance of Image

Although standards of beauty vary around the world, looking the best you possibly can is important everywhere. Self-presentation often determines a person's success or failure in the business world as well as in social settings, particularly in North America.

True, how a person talks or acts over the long term makes an impression on people. But it's that all-important first impression that counts the most, and first impressions often depend on how a person looks.

The media and social pressures reinforce the attitude that "image is everything." How else can we explain the explosion in makeover shows—complete with through-the-roof viewer ratings—such as *Queer Eye for the Straight Guy, Extreme Makeover, Style Court*, and *What Not to Wear*?

The strong interest in personal appearance is backed up by annual sales figures for cosmetics. A 2003 report by the UK market-research firm Snapshots International puts the annual sales of color cosmetics in the United States at $3.82 billion in 2003. Three companies, namely L'Oreal, Revlon, and Procter & Gamble, control more than 32 percent of the multibillion-dollar cosmetics market, although there are many other low- and high-end manufacturers.

## Why Makeup Consultation Matters

While proper makeup application can help people make a positive impression on others, improper makeup application can result in a negative impression that may never fade.

For instance, in a 2001 Cosmetic, Toiletry and Fragrance Association survey, 82 percent of those surveyed said that light makeup is a good idea for women in the workplace, but 80 percent of those surveyed believe that heavy makeup is a definite workplace faux-pas.

That's all well and good, but who decides the difference between light makeup and heavy makeup? And are there times—say, outside the workplace—when heavy makeup is a good thing? Understandably, many women are intimidated by the selection of cosmetics out there, and are confused about the latest and greatest techniques to apply them.

That's where the makeup artist comes in. A makeup artist is a professional whose training and experience can prepare him or her for helping others select and use makeup appropriately. It's a creative profession that can literally help people transform the way they see themselves.

According to a 2002 survey conducted by Market Research Pro for *Soap, Perfumery & Cosmetics Magazine*, 75 percent of all women seek advice about cosmetics from some source, and 5 percent report having difficulty in getting good information. While women reported that they do consult magazines and books, product packages, and online sources, nearly half of all women surveyed asked friends and family for cosmetics advice.

To an aspiring makeup artist, this means that women value the opinion of others when it comes to cosmetics. They want to be good at using cosmetics and want their makeup results to make a good impression. As a makeup artist, you will be uniquely positioned to assist women in optimizing their personal appearance.

## 1.2  A Career in Makeup Artistry

Essentially, a makeup artist has two career paths to choose from (or combine): you can work with individuals who hire you to enhance their image, or you can work with other professionals who hire you to help them do their work.

### Work with Individuals

If you work with individuals, your clients will generally be women, although some men in the public eye, such as politicians and high-level executives, hire makeup artists as well. Your clients might include brides, wedding parties, and their families, as well as people who need to look their best for a special occasion, such as an awards dinner, beauty pageant, Christmas party, or prom night.

You might do a makeup consultation (as opposed to application) for women who want a new look or who have had plastic surgery, young girls who are just learning to use makeup, or for a group of friends at a makeover party. You will usually be applying powder, lipstick, mascara, and other basic products to the face, but in some cases, you could be using body glitter, body paint, or shimmer powder on your clients' bodies to complement the look you have created.

Makeup artists who enhance the look of regular people can work for a company, or be self-employed. You might find full-time work in a busy beauty salon or spa, with customers coming to you with the frequency they come to hair stylists. Full-time work is also offered by department stores and cosmetics companies looking for makeup artists to do consultations to sell their products.

Self-employed makeup artists work out of their own home or visit clients' homes, or they might rent space out of a salon or spa. They also find work with private clients by partnering with wedding planners, image consultants, PR firms or portrait studios for referrals, on a part-time or full-time basis.

## Work with Professionals

When you work with other professionals, you will be hired by photographers, videographers, theater directors, production companies, fashion designers, TV producers and filmmakers to design and execute a look for print models, actors, TV reporters and personalities, and other people in the public eye. You will take direction from whoever hired you, and add your own creative flair.

Most makeup artists working with professionals are self-employed and hired on a contract basis, although longer-run engagements like TV shows might provide full-time employment. Makeup artists who work with professionals will do their job "on-site," meaning a foreign or local film location, TV studio, or runway show, for example. They are usually required to work quickly in an industry where "Time is money, people!" The makeup artist has to be on hand in case changes or touchups are needed, so some work days may be long, but there will likely be several days between assignments for you to relax.

Experienced makeup artists with more technical expertise are hired by filmmakers to do special-effects makeup, in which case you would be working with latex, fake beards, and prosthetics to dramatically alter the look of the actor. You've seen special effects makeup in movies such as *The Lord of the Rings*, *The Nutty Professor*, and the *Star Wars* films.

Another area of makeup specialization is the theater, where makeup must be visible even from the balcony, and hold up under hot lights and activity. The type of makeup used in theater is very different from everyday makeup, and because most stage actors will apply their own makeup, this specialty is focused more on designing a look than the actual application.

## Industry Terminology

Let's start with a few definitions that will help you as you read this guide. You will see the words "makeup" and "cosmetics" used somewhat interchangeably, as both are used to describe the makeup artist's tools of the trade. The term "cosmetics" applies to a broader range of beauty products applied to the face, hair, hands, and body, while "makeup" is specific to products applied to the face.

Makeup products include foundation, concealer, blush, lipstick, lip gloss, lip liner, eyeliner, eyebrow pencils, eye shadow, and finishing powder. Certain types of makeup artistry, such as special effects or theater, include a broader range of products than these, and will be referred to as "special effects makeup" or "stage makeup".

Some other types of makeup application include "straight makeup", which is makeup for actors, models, celebrities, etc. that is supposed to look like everyday wear—or perhaps slightly more glamorous or handsome. Straight makeup is meant to enhance the actor's looks, but not to make him look otherwise different, though it could be used to slightly alter the shape of his face, for example, to make him look more attractive.

"Character makeup" is used in TV, film, video and theater work to make actors look like the character they are trying to portray—older, younger, downtrodden, or even like another species. Character makeup takes advantage of all the tricks in a makeup artist's bag, from false hair used to create beards, to extravagant makeup effects to create gory and frightening injuries.

"Fashion, beauty or glamour makeup," is applied to models and women wanting to look stunning for an event. "Corrective makeup" is used to cover scars, burns, and other skin problems or physical disfigurements.

A makeup artist is anyone who applies makeup professionally, and is not a cosmetologist or an esthetician, which both require licenses in many jurisdictions. While a makeup artist can be a licensed cosmetologist or esthetician, this training is not required to call yourself a makeup artist, although it is required to collect a fee for personal makeup services in some states like New York.

- A cosmetologist's job is likely to include cutting and dying hair, and shaping eyebrows, as well as doing manicures and pedicures.

- An esthetician may apply makeup, but will also do skin treatments, facials, and hair removal.

To become a licensed cosmetologist or esthetician, your state may require you to be of a certain age, have a certain number of hours worked or type of training, and pass a written test. Requirements vary from state to state, so check with your state's professional licensing board if you plan to pursue this type of training. Contact information for these boards is provided in section 3.3.4.

As custom and practice have evolved in this line of work, providing "makeup services" means that you provide the makeup as well. Makeup artists routinely keep a stock of cosmetics on hand that they use for their clients, and they may purchase client-specific products. Some makeup artists charge for the use of cosmetics, or build this cost into their fees.

"Hygiene management"—that is, making sure you don't spread germs by using the same makeup applicator on more than one subject—is an important part of makeup service professionalism, and the trade offers palettes, sponges, brushes, and other devices to help with that.

## The Makeup Artist's Day

A makeup artist's day might include any of the following:

- Preparing clients' skin for makeup application

- Applying and retouching makeup as needed

- Redoing makeup if the look is not working

- Researching historical makeup for a period piece

- Brainstorming ideas with costume designers, directors, producers, etc.

- Shopping for and maintaining an inventory of supplies

- Consulting with clients for weddings, proms and other special events

- Keeping up with trends in the industry

- Evaluating lighting or scripts in advance for appropriate makeup

- Networking with other professionals to promote your services

- Building special effects pieces by hand

# 1.3  Benefits of the Job

So what are the perks of being a makeup artist, besides having all the latest cosmetics at your disposal and loving what you do? There are many, so read on.

## It is Flexible

Being a makeup artist is a career that offers a lot of flexibility in terms of how much and when you want to work. Many makeup artists start their career part time, and can keep another job if they want. Makeup artists might work only a few days a week, or work for a few weeks and then have some time off. You are the author of your own career progression, and can take things at your own pace.

A self-employed makeup artist can choose which projects he or she wants to take on, and can schedule themselves around personal commitments and family time. Of course, once you have accepted a job, you need to show up on time, but there is no office to drag yourself into Monday morning, or business suits to wear.

## You Can Travel

The career of a professional makeup artist usually involves a certain amount of travel, particularly if you are working on film or exotic photo shoots. For example, if you are filming a movie set in Dublin, Ireland, chances are a good part of the film will be shot "on location", so pack your bags!

A makeup artist who works with private clients might be expected to travel as well, for example to a Vegas wedding to do makeup for the bridal party, or just a few hours upstate to the bride's hometown. At any rate, your expenses, or at least a portion of them, should be covered, and you'll get to see more of the world.

## An Exciting Environment

A makeup artist is intimately involved in the most important and exciting events of people's lives, from weddings, to political campaigns, to accepting Academy Awards. You are on-hand at the big events amid the flurry of excitement, trying to keep perspiration to a minimum as you do your work.

Makeup artists get up-close-and-personal with models, actors, politicians, and musicians, and can develop relationships that go beyond the professional. You get to see what celebrities are really like, and help them do what they do best—present a glamorous, exciting image, courtesy of you and all the other people behind the scenes. Their appreciation of your art might include invitations to parties, admission to exclusive restaurants and clubs, or recommendations to other celebrities you admire.

## It is Social

Whatever the type of makeup artistry you choose, you will always be working with people. You will need to communicate and find out what look they (or the people they work for) are trying to achieve, and help create it.

You will work in close physical contact with people, and will often be a key factor in helping them relax before the shoot or big event by chatting with them and taking their mind off things. The nature of the job is that you will meet different people all the time, as not many people need a glamorous makeup job every day.

## It is Creative

A makeup "artist" is exactly that: an artist who uses human faces as a canvas for creating innovative and exciting artwork. You will be on the cutting edge of the latest trends in cosmetics, perhaps even getting "previews" of new products to test for the big cosmetics companies. You will get to express your makeup ideas for the world to see.

The job will challenge you to use your most creative ideas to solve problems, create illusions, and bring out a beauty that you can see is hiding, just waiting to be exposed. And when you are at the top of your game, you will have the satisfaction of seeing other people imitating your makeup artistry in their own lives, and possibly inspiring young people to pursue the same dream you once had of becoming a makeup artist.

## The Earning Potential

The salary for this job varies depending on the type of clients and frequency of work, but there is potential to be very well paid, especially if you are self-employed. A part-time makeup artist doing bridal or prom makeup may charge $30 to $75 per application, or sometimes more. You might also anticipate tips for a job well done.

According to the U.S Department of Labor and Statistics, the mean annual wage for makeup artists in the field of performing arts (theater) is about $30,000 per year. In the film and video industry, the mean annual wage for makeup artists is about $88,000. A freelance makeup artist working for film or television may earn around $500 per day, and a highly experienced makeup artist working in these industries can command as much as $2,000 to $5,000 per day.

Some notable makeup artists, such as Bobbi Brown, have parlayed their careers as makeup artists into multimillion-dollar cosmetics enterprises. Brown started her career in 1979 as an assistant to a New York makeup artist, but she quickly worked her way up to doing makeup for models at photo shoots for *Glamour* and *Vogue*. In 1990, she and a friend put $10,000 each into manufacturing and marketing a limited lipstick line. Within four years, the company was doing $20 million in sales.

## You Can Start Right Now

You don't need $100,000 in start-up capital to start a makeup artistry business, or a bunch of large equipment, or even much of an inventory. You don't need years of specialized training, or any particular licenses or certification to start out. You can start this career part time, from your home, or whatever your needs dictate.

What you do need is a drive and determination to succeed, a start-up kit of cosmetics, and an eye for making people look their best. This career is open to you starting today, and you can call yourself a professional makeup artist as soon as you beautify your first client.

# 1.4 Inside This Guide

The *FabJob Guide to Become a Makeup Artist* is arranged to take you step-by-step through the process of getting started and succeeding as a makeup artist.

Chapter 2, How to Do the Job, explores how makeup artists apply their knowledge and expertise. You'll learn about the tools of the trade and how to use them, including information about the contents of your makeup kit. We'll give you practical information on how to do a typical application, and go over how makeup type and application varies in other branches of the profession, including TV, theater, and film.

Chapter 3, Getting Ready, covers the skills you'll develop to succeed in the industry. We'll explore all sorts of different ways you can get the training and experience you'll need to get hired in whatever type of makeup artistry you choose. From working (or interning!) for a cosmetics company to apprenticing with a working makeup artist to attending a training program, you'll get all the information you need to figure out what preparation is right for you.

Chapter 4, Getting Hired, will tell you who employs part-time and full-time makeup artists, where to find out about job openings, and what employers are looking for on your resume and cover letter. We'll also make sure you're fully prepared for an interview, and tell you what you need to know to get ahead once you're hired.

Ready for the next step? You will find advice on Starting Your Own Business in Chapter 5. This section provides practical information on what you need to do to start up a makeup application and/or consulting business where you live, including creating a business plan, choosing a name, and where to locate. We'll also give you examples of how independent makeup artists set their fees, and innovative ideas on how to market your service to clients and spread the word about your business.

Chapter 6 looks at working in the big leagues: Freelancing as a Makeup Artist for professional media. We'll take you through the process involved in building a professional portfolio of work (including what not to include!) and how new makeup artists get great samples of work through "testing" or working for free. Then we go through where the jobs are: print, runway, TV, film, commercial, etc. The guide has insider advice from those who have succeeded about the true windows to working with celebrities, actors and musicians: getting hired by an agency, and getting into the union.

Chapter 7 rounds out the guide with Success Stories of several working makeup artists—to inform you, inspire you, and give you a realistic idea of how a career path develops. You'll also find a helpful list of Resources for learning more about all aspects of makeup artistry.

By the time you are finished with this guide, you will have a realistic picture of your entry point into the trade. By applying what you learn, you'll be on your way to a fabulous new career as a makeup artist! Let's get started.

# 2. How to Do the Job

This chapter will introduce you to the art of applying makeup professionally. First we'll explain the tools and supplies you'll use, and how to store them. We'll give you an idea of how much your kit will cost to put together, go over the basic items every kit should have, and explain how to care for and clean your reusable items.

Next we'll take a look at the steps of a basic makeup application, from foundation to finishing powder. You'll see how a makeup artist evaluates a face, and then creates dimension in a face with special highlighting and contouring techniques. Even if this is an area you are already knowledgeable in, you may still pick up a trick or two from our experts.

The makeup used for a wedding or prom will quite naturally be different from makeup done for a stage production performed in an enormous theater. The basics are the same: both are applied to the skin, and both are meant to change the client's appearance in some way. How they're used, though, and how they work are a bit different. The chapter rounds out with some of the nuances of makeup in different environments, to help you choose a specialty that suits your interests and talents.

## 2.1 Supplies and Tools

In this section, we'll discuss the tools and supplies you'll use as a makeup artist—both the physical tools, such as brushes and applicators, and all the various substances you'll apply with those tools.

A good way to build your kit is to shop as you pick up gigs or jobs. It is especially helpful if you know what the person that you are going to work on looks like and what type of look will be required. That way you can invest part of the money that you will earn through that job into building your supply of makeup.

If you work at a salon, spa, or for a cosmetics company, all these items will be supplied for you. In some cases a school will also supply you with a kit as part of your training. However, if you are striking out on your own, you will need to build up your own collection. Here's what you'll need.

## 2.1.1 Your Kit

Every makeup artist needs a kit to carry all their tools and supplies. Naturally, the more tools and supplies you accumulate, the larger this kit will need to be. You might choose to have several makeup kits to accommodate your different projects. For example, you could devote one kit to live events, one to stage work, and another to special effects. The kind of work you do most often will dictate which of your kits should be the largest and most elaborate.

You can buy an empty makeup kit from a makeup supply company, in person or online. These cases are usually boxy-looking aluminum cases (also called train cases) with drawers, compartments and places to store your brushes and bottles. These days you can get enormous ones that are like pull-along luggage, with a handle and wheels for getting around, or you can put smaller cases in a practical, all-terrain rolling suitcase that you can pick up at Wal-Mart.

You can look at some train cases for sale from Cases by Source at **www.casesbysource.com/makeup/pro_makeup_cases.htm**.

When buying a case, check the overall dimensions as well as the weight. The lighter and smaller ones that magically hold lots of stuff are better, since you will be filling it with makeup and lugging it around to photo shoots, film sets and hotel rooms. Look for strong handles and sturdy hinges. On average, a pro makeup case will cost between $40 and $100, depending on how large and fancy you want it to be.

> **TIP:** You can use white tape and a permanent marking pen to label the front of the kit's drawers with "eye colors", "foundations", etc. so you don't have to search for what you need.

### Makeup Kit Checklist

On the next two pages you'll find a handy checklist of what you'll need to start off a makeup kit. You will need to monitor these supplies in order to ensure you're not running low—there's nothing worse than running out of an essential item while you're in the middle of an application! Make a weekly check of everything, and replenish any items you know you have less than a week's supply of.

# Makeup Kit Checklist

- ❏ Foundation in many shades and consistencies
- ❏ Blushes in pinks, peaches and reds
- ❏ Eye shadows (look for palettes that contain a number of shades in one tray)
- ❏ Eyeliners in a range of shades including black, browns and white
- ❏ Eyebrow pencils in black and brown
- ❏ Normal concealer in tones a bit lighter than foundations
- ❏ Heavier "camouflage" concealer in a variety of tones to match foundations
- ❏ Lip colors including reds, pinks, peaches and browns
- ❏ Lip pencils to complement lip colors
- ❏ Lip gloss in clear and a variety of finishes (sparkling, tinted, metallic, etc.)
- ❏ Lip moisturizer in a pot (e.g. Carmex or Blistex)
- ❏ Loose powder in light to dark and translucent
- ❏ Mascara in black and brown-black
- ❏ Brushes: (at least two of each) powder brush, blush brush, sponge brush, blending brush, contour brush, eyeliner brush, angled eyebrow brush, lip brush, concealer brush, eye shadow brush, detail brush
- ❏ Sponges: many cosmetic wedges and some natural sea sponges
- ❏ Large cotton cosmetic puffs
- ❏ False eyelash strips and clusters, and application glues for each type
- ❏ Eyelash curler
- ❏ Makeup pencil sharpener
- ❏ Tweezers
- ❏ Scissors
- ❏ Tissues
- ❏ Makeup removal cream

- ❏ Astringent and toner/freshener
- ❏ Hand sanitizer
- ❏ Cotton balls, pads and swabs
- ❏ Disposable cosmetics applicators (eye shadow and mascara wands)
- ❏ Moisturizer
- ❏ Anti-shine (e.g. Neutrogena shine control gel or Super Matte Anti-Shine)
- ❏ A makeup cape
- ❏ Paper towels
- ❏ Quick drying cosmetic brush cleaner
- ❏ Hair clips

**You may also want to add:**

- ❏ Airbrush makeup and compressor (see the section on Airbrush Makeup for more about this tool)
- ❏ Metal makeup palette and spatula (for mixing foundations or lip colors)
- ❏ Shimmering body powder
- ❏ Vaseline and baby oil
- ❏ Facial wipes
- ❏ Atomizer of water (Evian Spray)
- ❏ Small plastic cup for water to dip sponges or brushes into
- ❏ Hip apron to carry cosmetics on set
- ❏ Facial hair bleach
- ❏ Razor brow shapers
- ❏ A personal battery-operated fan
- ❏ A monocular or binoculars (for viewing faces on sets from afar)
- ❏ A small portable chair for you to sit on for long waits out on location
- ❏ A portable professional lighted mirror station (see them at **www.makeupstation.com**)
- ❏ A tall director's chair

# A Set Bag

After you have finished a face, to keep your "talent" (actor, model, or performer) from having to return to the makeup area for touch-ups, having a set bag with you on the sidelines is essential. This is especially needed if you do a lot of work on location.

Your set bag should contain smaller containers of the most essential products in your main makeup kit. Some general items can remain in your set bag but you will add items specific to the particular talent, such as the lipstick, gloss, powder, etc. that you used that day to take to the set with you for quick touch-ups in between shots.

Set bags can be found at costume shops and art supply stores. They are usually made of heavy canvas and leather and have a sturdy strap and lots of easy-access pockets for brushes, sponges, powders, etc. You can even find ones that are made of transparent plastic, which makes locating an item in the many pockets easier.

A typical set bag might contain:

- Blush and eye shadow palette

- Hairbrush/comb

- Blotting paper

- Travel-size hair spray

- A few brushes and sponges

- Lipstick palette and gloss

- Foundation palette

- Tissues and a cosmetic puff

- Pressed powder

# A Hair Kit

If you are doing hair as well, you will need a separate kit containing:

- Brushes and combs (a wide bristle brush, a round curler brush, a pik, and a straight comb are a good combination)

- Curling iron or hot rollers

- Hair dryer

- Hair "bodifiers," such as mousse or gel

- Styling gels or lotions

- Hairspray

- Clips

- Bobby pins and hair pins

- Barrettes

- Hair elastics

- Hair nets

If you do a lot of period hair work, you may need:

- Hair pieces, such as braids and falls

- Wigs

- Wig stands

- Wig pins

- Bald caps (latex caps that make actors appear bald)

# 2.1.2  Your Makeup

There are hundreds of brands of makeup from cosmetics companies large and small. Which brands you choose will depend on price, the type of makeup you are doing, and personal preference. Makeup artists usually have a preferred company for different products they use, and that company varies depending on the product.

You can find great items in the drugstores as well as department stores, and then the stores that are somewhere in between such as Wal-Mart, Ulta and Sephora. Some of the department store lines offer industry discounts to makeup artists.

Working for a makeup line is a great way to build your kit and get huge discounts on supplies as well. Some stores even offer discounts to industry professionals such as costume shops or makeup stores. Ulta has a great rewards program, where you earn points towards free cosmetics by buying from them. You can find a list of cosmetics companies at the end of this guide.

> **TIP:**  Check the local Yellow Pages under the headings of "beauty supplies," "cosmetics" or "theatrical supplies" to find suppliers of makeup or cosmetics in an unfamiliar area. The advantage of a local supplier is that you can quickly access anything you might need should you suddenly run low. The disadvantage is that it might not carry your preferred brands.

We'll look briefly at the brands on the market, and then below is a list of all the makeup you will use regularly, plus a quick definition of what the product is, what it is used for, and an approximate price for one standard unit.

## Choosing a Brand

You will discover through working with various makeup lines which ones you are most comfortable with that also provide a good value. Experiment with a range of brands, especially when it comes to foundations. Max Factor makes some wonderful foundations just as MAC does as well. The key is to be prepared with enough makeup in the appropriate tones and formulations for all the models or actors on the job!

## Salon and Everyday Makeup

Some of the popular makeup brands for everyday makeup are MAC, Bobbi Brown, Sacha, Stila, and Sephora. When clients want a more unusual or outrageous look, you will want to use a brand that features bolder colors, such as Shiseido or Manic Panic. Some cosmetics are hypo-allergenic (non-allergy-causing), such as Clinique; some are non-comedogenic (non-acne-causing), such as Almay, Clinique and Lancôme.

If you work in a salon, spa, or cosmetics company, your employer may prefer you to use one in particular; Aveda, for example. Most clients will be happy with any type of makeup as long as it makes them look great, although others may prefer to use only one line. Again, you will find a list of the more recognizable brands and retailers at the end of this guide in the resources section.

## TV and Film Makeup

The old days of TV and film when thick makeup or pancake makeup was applied with a heavy hand are gone. Television cameras today are more sophisticated and take much of the hassle out of makeup application. In addition, television studios, unlike theater stages, are normally cold. So even though the performer is under lights, the temperature of the room keeps the makeup from melting. Consumer brands like MAC or even Bobbi Brown work on television if there's no need for special effects. For film work, the brands most often mentioned among makeup artists interviewed for this guide were MAC and Cinema Secrets.

## Print Makeup

Professional makeup artists will agree that drugstore brands don't cut it on professional shoots, with the exception of the famed Great Lash mascara by Maybelline. Stick with brands developed by a makeup artist such as Lorac, Laura Mercier and Shu Uemura to get the kind of look that will be consistent from behind the lens of a camera.

## Stage Makeup

Certain types of makeup artists use stage makeup that is designed to hold up under hot lights and extreme conditions. Alcone, Kryolan, Ben

Nye, Joe Blasco, and Mehron are some well-known brands. A more complete list and contacts are at the end of the guide.

Compared with cosmetics, they're formulated to be more vivid in color in order to be seen under bright lights, which can wash out the appearance of ordinary cosmetic colors, and from a distance. The trade-off is that up close, stage and studio makeup can look thick and unnatural, which is why it's not used for anything with a close up.

Theater, opera, ballet, circuses, and live gymnastics, music or dance performances are the types of events that would most likely require stage makeup.

## SFX Makeup

Even a "straight makeup" artist may be called upon to create special effects in a pinch, such as making a young actor look older, or making a performer appear as though he's been injured. This also requires different types of materials such as latex and glue, as you'll find out in section 2.4 on special effects.

# Types of Makeup

## Foundation

Foundation is the base you will spread on the face to even out skin tones and provide a smooth look to the skin. Foundation is arguably the most important part of any makeup application, as it is extremely noticeable when applied in the wrong shade or not properly blended, and can ruin an otherwise perfect application.

Foundation comes in a range of colors meant to match every possible skin tone, from very light to very dark. For general use, foundation comes in several types: liquid, souffle, cream, or powder. For stage use, you can also get pancake foundation, a heavier base makeup which is applied with water and a cosmetic sponge.

A liquid foundation will cover evenly and fill dips and folds in the skin. A souffle gives a heavier coverage but still feels very light weight when worn. Cream foundations come in both stick and cake form and will go on thicker in most cases, but also can come in sheer finishes. Powder foundation is good when you want to skip the step of applying a liquid foundation or when you need a heavier coverage than the typical powder would give over foundation. If used alone it may be too powdery for dry skin.

There are oil-free foundations for oily skin, and moisturizing formulas for dry skin. You can even use a tinted moisturizer to simplify things, if you are looking for light and even coverage on relatively flawless skin. Foundations also offer different finished looks, from "dewy" to "matte".

As a makeup artist you will want to have a wide selection of foundation types available. Cosmetics companies will often provide free samples to working makeup artists that you can test out until you settle on a brand and type that suits your application needs.

*Cost per unit: $5 to $35*

## Concealer

Concealer comes as a cream, in sticks, small jars and tubes. It is available in a variety of skin tones, as well as in pale yellow for counterbalancing pinkish skin tones, pale lilac for counterbalancing rosy skin tones, pale green for counterbalancing reddish skin tones, and in white for highlighting areas of the face. It is typically used under foundation to offer extra coverage under the eyes, on blemishes or freckles, and other skin imperfections.

*Cost per unit: $4 to $12*

## Eyeliner

Eyeliner is used to emphasize and frame the eyes. Eyeliner is available in pencils, creams, cakes and liquid, and comes in a wide range of colors, from blacks and browns to blues, purples, and even pinks. Eyeliner pencils are drawn around the edges of the eyes to define and enhance them. Liquid eyeliners are painted onto the eyelids and sometimes under the eyes close to the lash line, with a small, narrow brush that comes with the product.

*Cost per unit: $1 to $12*

## Eyebrow Color

Eyebrows that are light-colored, thin, or patchy can be evened out and defined with eyebrow color, which is available as a pencil or as a powder. Both are available in browns and blacks and are used to enhance the shape and appearance of the eyebrows. Eyebrow powder must be applied with an eyebrow brush, while eyebrow pencil may be drawn directly onto the skin. A thin angled brush moistened with water can be used to give a more defined and stronger application.

*Cost per unit: $1 to $12*

## Eye Shadow

Eye shadow is used to complement or contrast the natural eye color, or coordinate the face with an overall look. It is available in powder, cream, and wide pencil form. It is applied with an applicator (in the case of powders or creams) or directly from the tip of the pencil and comes in virtually every color and finish, from matte to frosted (shiny). It is wise to invest in a reputable brand that is least likely to cause a reaction in this sensitive area.

As a makeup artist, you will need to have a range of colors on hand. Eye shadows vary in the intensity of pigment. You mostly want to have shadows that have more concentrated pigment, so that you will be able to use less product to achieve the desired look, and preserve your shadows longer.

One way to keep your eye shadow organized is with a palette, which allows you to keep many different colors together in one place. This is also an economical way to build your collection of colors, as a palette tends to cost less than buying each individual color separately. Many companies will also let you mix and match the colors in a palette to create your own unique collection of colors.

*Cost per unit: $3 to $12*

## Mascara

Mascara is applied to the eyelashes to create bolder lashes by making them darker and longer or thicker, for a more defined eye. Mascara is available either as a block, which must be applied with a separate eyelash brush, or in a tube already equipped with a brush. It is available in black, brownish-black, brown, and a variety of fashion colors—however, blacks and browns are appropriate for most circumstances.

*Cost per unit: $3 to $10*

## Powder

Powder is used to set foundation, control shine, and to finish a makeup look once it is applied to protect it from heat and perspiration. Powder comes "pressed" in cakes, enclosed in small compacts, and "loose" in containers. The advantage of loose powder is the light, grainy consistency and therefore versatility in application. Pressed powder is handier than loose powder; it is compact and easy to carry for touch-ups or on location. Both can be applied with a wide, fat brush and come in a variety of colors to match foundations, and in translucent as well.

*Cost per unit: $15 to $30*

## Blush

Blush (also known as "blusher" or "rouge") is used to give a healthy flush to cheeks and is available as a powder, cream, or gel. Powder blush is brushed onto the cheeks with a wide brush, and is usually applied after the foundation and powder are already in place. Cream and gel blush are applied on top of the foundation but before the powder. Blush is dabbed with the fingers in spots along the cheeks (following the line of the cheekbone) and is blended in with the fingertips or with a cosmetic sponge.

*Cost per unit: $3 to $12*

## Lip Color

Lip color is available as lipstick, cream, or lip pencils, and comes in a wide range of colors from palest whites and pinks to deepest plums and browns. It is applied following the natural contours of the lips, or can be applied beyond the natural lips to emphasize or enhance the lip size and shape.

*Cost per unit: $1 to $15*

## Lip Gloss

Gloss is a shiny, clear, glittered or tinted product meant to add a sheen and sparkle to the lips after (or instead of) the application of lip color.

*Cost per unit: $1 to $10*

# 2.1.3 Your Tools

Every artist has a set of tools that they use, and as a makeup artist, your tools are the brushes, sponges, applicators and other gadgets that you use to apply makeup.

"Your tools are the most important part of your makeup kit," says professional makeup artist Robert Jones. "You need to have the right brushes, sponges, and [other] implements to work with. If you are good at what you do, you can work with almost any line of makeup."

A professional makeup artist will invest in a good set of tools because he or she knows that they are just that—an investment. If you are self-employed, as many makeup artists are, you will be able to deduct all or part of the cost of your equipment from your income taxes.

Expect to spend a few hundred dollars on your tools, depending on the quality you choose and what you already own. You will also replace them as time goes on, so that cost should be built into your fees. Here are some of a makeup artist's most important tools and supplies.

## Brushes

Makeup brushes come in a variety of sizes, from extremely narrow for applying liquid eyeliner, to slightly wider for lip color and eye makeup, to about one inch wide at the base for applying blush and powder, to more than an inch wide for applying powder.

Expect to pay between $5 and $30 for each good brush, depending on the quality and size. A small eyeliner brush, naturally, will cost less than a large, wide one. A good quality brush can last five years or more, even as many as ten with proper care.

## Eyelash Curler

This device is used to create a slight curl in eyelashes that are somewhat flat. There are several types of curlers available, but they all work on the same principle, which is to bend the hairs of the eyelashes so that they turn upwards.

## Sharpener

You'll need a good quality sharpener to ensure your cosmetic pencils are fine enough to create the type of lines you desire. In addition, it is good hygienic practice to sharpen eyeliners and lip liners between clients to remove any germs. Choose a sharpener with several sizes of holes so that you can sharpen both narrow and wide pencils with the same tool.

## Sponge Wedges

These are one- or two-inch pieces of sponge used for applying and blending makeup and cosmetics. They come in wedge shapes, which allow you to blend small or large areas with the same sponge. They are cheap and disposable. They come made of latex and also in a non-latex material.

You can achieve a heavier amount of coverage when using a wedge to apply powders to the face, because it is a more concentrated application than with a brush or puff. You are also not incorporating air into the process as you would be with a powder brush, so more product goes on the face instead of in the air. Using a sponge is also good for a first application of eye shadow, and then you can use a shadow brush for blending.

## Tweezers

These devices are useful for plucking stray hairs, picking up and holding false eyelashes, and holding small or delicate items like false hair before applying it. There are several different lengths and styles of tweezers, depending on their intended use (study the tip before you grab a pair). One of the most popular brands is Tweezerman, available at commercial pharmacies, beauty supply stores, and online (see a list of suppliers at the end of this guide).

Tweezerman also makes a mini-version of their tweezers called "tweezerette" that work great and cost much less than their standard-sized pairs. You can find them online at **www.tweezerman.com/home**.

## Mixing Palette and Spatula

A mixing palette is a small flat piece of metal that you can use to mix different colors of makeup on. The spatula (or "palette knife") is used to mix the colors on the palette. These tools come in handy when you don't have an exact foundation match and you need to combine two or more colors to match a client's complexion, or perhaps to change the color or consistency of a lip color by adding a gloss.

## Astringent and Toner/Freshener

These products are used to remove natural oil and dirt from the face and neck before beginning a makeup application. It is an essential step, both to ensure a smooth application and to ensure that the client's skin is not overly damaged by clogged pores. After applying the astringent, use a skin toner for oily to medium skin, or freshener for medium to dry skin, to catch any oil or dirt the astringent missed.

## Cotton Balls or Pads

You'll need these for applying astringent and wiping away moisture, and any other time you need a disposable, absorbent material. A big bag of several hundred will cost you about a dollar. Cotton pads are easier to use because they are quilted and create less mess when used on male clients, whereas traditional cotton balls are more likely to snag on beard stubble.

## Cotton Swabs

These can be used to apply small dabs of makeup, and to correct mistakes if your hand has slipped. You can dip the end of a cotton swab in a small amount of makeup removal cream, for example, and use it to correct just the area where a spot of mascara has fallen on your client's cheek.

## Disposable Makeup Applicators

Disposable makeup applicators are useful for when you need to apply eye makeup to a number of clients (at a cosmetics demonstration or makeover party, for example), or when you are concerned about the possibility of spreading eye infections from one client to another.

Disposable eye shadow applicators give a very concentrated application. They have a sponge-like tip which is good for a strong initial application to say, an eyelid, but they don't work as well for blending. Disposable mascara wands are great for brushing away excess powder from brows, as well as a more sanitary means of applying mascara from a tube.

## Facial Tissue

Choose a lint-free but soft facial tissue for wiping away makeup removal cream, dabbing at makeup spills, and blotting up excess moisture wherever it occurs. Many cheaper brands will tear and disrupt your makeup application. Facial tissues are also extremely helpful when you have to blot excess oil. A great trick of the trade is to wrap a facial tissue around a cotton cosmetic puff to blot a shiny nose or add a touch of powder; especially when you are on a set with a lot of extras that you have to touch-up in between takes.

## Makeup Removal Cream

You may have to redo a makeup design from scratch, or remove a portion of it to start over. Some cosmetics wash away with soap and water, while others, particularly the waterproof ones and theatrical cosmetics like greasepaint, need to be removed with makeup removal cream or "cold cream". Be sure to choose a non-irritating brand of removal cream, such as Clinique.

## Moisturizer

A good moisturizer is a finishing touch to use after the makeup has been removed, or even before on especially dry skin. Choose a light, non-comedogenic one, and smooth it gently over your client's face, concentrating on the cheeks and the eye area. Some moisturizers come with sunscreen in them. If you choose these types, it is essential to smooth them over the entire face in order to benefit from the protective properties. An oil-free moisturizer is usually the best bet all around if a moisturizer is needed. They add the suppleness needed without unwanted oils.

## Anti-Shine

On a face that has a tendency to get oily, especially under the hot lighting environments on sets, a shine control agent such as SuperMatte Anti-Shine by Make-up International, (a staple of the film industry) is a must-have addition to your kit. This will save you from having to run to re-set the look with powder so frequently. You can find the Make-up International Catalog online at **www.make-upinternational.com/catalog/index.php**.

It must be used very sparingly—if not, it can leave a chalky streak on the face that makeup will not conceal. It is usually less costly to order online directly from the manufacturer in Canada. It comes in light, medium and dark tints. Neutrogena also makes a "shine control gel" that comes in clear and can be found in drugstores. It doesn't work as well, but it is a good back-up.

## 2.1.4  Proper Hygiene

Bacteria can live on makeup application tools and can cause blemishes and infections. As a makeup artist, you are responsible for ensuring that your clients' skin is protected. If you cleanse each client's skin and your brushes thoroughly before applying any makeup, you will help minimize this risk. Not sharing applicator tools between clients can also help, though this is less necessary for items like powder brushes than for eye makeup applicators and lip makeup applicators.

Use a metal makeup palette for items that you can scrape into with a spatula or pour out, such as foundations, lipsticks and lip glosses. That keeps you from contaminating your cosmetic supply. You can clean your reusable tools by wiping them with rubbing alcohol, and clean your brushes in between clients in specially formulated brush cleaner, available from companies like Cinema Secrets and Ben Nye, which you can order from the suppliers listed at the end of this guide, or in warm, soapy water. Using rubbing alcohol on your brushes works as well, but should only be done in a pinch as it can dry out the hairs.

## How Long Does it Last?

According to *Essence* magazine's September 2002 edition, here is the general shelf life of each of the following cosmetic products:

| | |
|---|---|
| **Powders** | 8 to 12 months |
| **Eyeliners** | 3 to 6 months |
| **Eye shadows** | 3 to 12 months |
| **Mascara** | 3 months |
| **Concealer** | 4 to 6 months |
| **Lipstick** | 1 year |

On a set where you have to do several faces and must reuse your brushes on different faces, Ben Nye offers an excellent quick-drying cleaner. Do not let any of these chemicals get into the bases of the bristles of your brushes as the solvents can dissolve the glue and cause your bristles to shed. Let your tools air dry.

If a client has an eye infection, do not use reusable tools on them. Squirt a small supply of liquid makeup onto a palette, and use this supply for that client only. For eye makeup, use the client's own, or scrape small amounts of yours onto the palette. You can buy disposable mascara and eyeliner brushes. Do not put these back into your products after they have touched the client's face, and do not use the same applicators on different clients.

To keep all your products in top condition so you are always ready to work, store your makeup kit somewhere cool and out of direct light. This helps the preservatives in the cosmetics remain effective in fighting off bacteria.

Liquid cosmetics should be replaced at least every 6 to 12 months. If any of your cosmetics change in color, smell or consistency, whether they have reached their supposed life span or not, get rid of them. If you are working steadily, you will probably go through your cosmetics quickly, but you should review the contents of your entire kit once a month to be sure everything is still fresh.

# 2.2 Steps of Applying Makeup

Applying makeup is a matter of building up layers until you've achieved the desired effect. Working from the bottom layer to the top is important because each layer is designed to work with the next.

For example, foundation helps powder adhere to the skin, and powder helps to keep foundation from creasing. The two work together in harmony when used properly. You should also work from top to bottom of the face when applying the makeup, because it prevents your hands from smudging your own work. For instance, you would finish the eyes before starting the lips.

Here are the general steps of a makeup application. Of course, every situation will vary depending on the reason you are applying makeup, and the overall look the person or professional is looking for, as explained later in this guide. After going over the basics, the rest of this chapter will break down makeup application for different types of private and professional clients.

## 2.2.1 Assess the Look

*"I've had the opportunity to work with every living beauty icon. I've learned to appreciate idiosyncrasy. The fact is, there really is no such thing as normal—everybody's different, and that is the essence of his or her beauty."*
—Makeup Artist Kevyn Aucoin, in his book *Making Faces*

Understanding the beauty of people's idiosyncrasies is the essence of applying makeup. Once you know the environmental parameters, your job is to use makeup to bring out the natural beauty of your subject's face. The makeup you choose for a particular client or subject should be based on several different factors, such as their:

- Coloring (skin, eye and hair)
- Skin Type
- Face Shape
- Features
- Wardrobe

Once you have assessed the face and have a vision in mind, you can begin preparing the face for makeup application.

# Skin, Eyes and Hair

You will need to determine what cosmetic colors and shades will best complement each other and the client's look. Usually this is done using a system of color analysis, which is based on the idea that everyone has a dominant color in their skin that is either a cool color (blue tones) or a warm one (golden tones). To determine if someone is cool or warm, you will examine their skin tone, eye color, and hair color.

## Skin Tone and Undertone

Skin is usually classified into light, medium, or dark shades, although there are actually hundreds of variations in tone. Beyond that, though, people of all skin colors have either warm (yellowish) or cool (bluish) undertones. The foundation color you select should match the natural color of the skin. Eye, cheek and lip colors should complement the face. Anyone can wear any color, but the colors chosen must have the right intensities and the right undertones.

## Hair Color

There are only three or four basic hair colors, but there are hundreds of shade variations in between, and one person may have several shades going on. In general, cooler hair colors have a blue or ashy undertone, while warm hair colors have a golden or reddish tone.

## Eye Color

Cool-colored eyes are cool dark brown, grey-blue, grey-green, blue, hazels (brown and green mixes with some grey effects), grey, soft brown, aqua, clear blue, and taupe. Warm-colored eyes are golden-brown, rich dark brown, warm hazels (combinations of gold, moss-greens, browns, yellows) greens, and light golden brown.

Although you have some room for creativity when it comes to choosing makeup colors, you want to stay within general ranges of colors that work well with the person's own coloring. You can enhance using tones similar to the natural colors they already have, or in some cases like eye shadow, use colors that bring out the color of the eye by contrasting it. For example, a salmon tone can bring out the "green" in a hazel-colored eye, possibly to complement a green dress.

For print or runway work, you may decide to follow the color choices recommended by current fashion magazines. Follow the direction of the artistic director of the production you are working on if you're doing the makeup for stage or screen.

Also, when choosing makeup for different parts of the face, remember that some colors look better together than others. To create beautiful combinations, be consistent with your undertones. If you do the eyes in cool colors such as sky blue and navy don't put a rust-colored lip color on the lips.

You will also want to consider the person's contrast level, meaning the difference between a person's skin tone and their hair color and eye color. Someone with pale skin and dark eyes and hair has a high contrast level. A person with medium-toned skin, brown eyes and brown hair has a low contrast level.

People with higher contrast levels can usually wear more dramatic makeup shades, whereas people with low contrast levels look best with warm neutrals that don't "jump out" and overpower their natural coloring, unless drama is desired for a fantasy or runway look. For classic beauty makeup, work along with nature.

## Skin Type

Skin can be dry, oily, or "combination," with some dry and some oily spots. Some people have dry skin on their cheeks, but oily skin on their noses and foreheads (called the T-zone, to describe its shape). Skin type determines the kind of foundation you will choose, be it oil-control, moisturizing, or normal. You'll want to eliminate any excess oil or dryness so that the makeup application will be easier and require fewer touch-ups.

If you can't tell which type of skin your client has by looking, just ask. Most people know what skin type they have because of the soaps and moisturizers they normally use. As mentioned earlier, using an anti-shine agent under foundation can decrease the need for frequent touch-ups.

# Ethnicity

Women of different ethnic origins may have specialized needs for their skin color and type. You will have to consider the unique features and colors of Latin-Americans, African-Americans, Asian-Americans, and a range of other ethnic origins when you stock your makeup kit. For example, a powder or foundation that looks perfect on a Caucasian woman can make an African-American's skin look flat or ashy-colored, without any sheen.

Here are a few general tips for making up women of non-Caucasian background, although every face you make up will have its own nuances and uniqueness.

- African-American women are most likely to have a complexion that is more oily than dry, at least where the face is concerned. Try to find foundations and powders that control oil, but don't contribute to an ashy look, which is a common pitfall in making up women with brown skin.

- When choosing a palette of color for eyes, cheeks and lips, choose not only according to the color of the skin, but the undertones as well. Darker or ebony-type complexions are likely to have cool undertones, and light brown or caramel colors tend to have golden undertones. You can either choose to use shades that blend with the overall coloring, such as coppers, rusts, plums, cinnamons, and honey shades, or you may choose to go with cool tones which will stand out more against their warm background. You will also need products that are more heavily pigmented to get them to be noticed against a darker background, rather than sheer consistencies which may tend to give an ashen appearance.

- Choosing the right foundation can be tricky with women of any skin color. In general, Asians should use a foundation that has yellow undertones, and Latinos look best with a yellow-to-orange base. African-Americans tend to have more yellow, orange and red undertones, but some darker complexions can be cool rather than warm. Also, women with such pigmentation tend to have more noticeable variations and discolorations in skin color and tone.

- Women with less pigment in the skin and a pale or "porcelain" look are more prone to noticeable blemishes, as there is more of a contrast between the blemish and their skin. These complexions are also more sensitive to the sun, and will need a product with sunscreen for outdoors.

Prescriptives (**www.prescriptives.com**) has a good reputation for offering a variety of foundations to match skin tones, and will also custom-blend colors for you if you will be making up the same person, such as a celebrity, every time.

Supermodel Iman developed her own line of cosmetics when she couldn't find anything to match her unique complexion. She now has two lines, "Iman" and "I-Iman", which can be purchased online at **www.i-iman.com/cosmetics**. The original Iman line can also be found in Wal-Mart and Target stores, while I-Iman is available at Sephora stores.

There are some well-respected books to help you get accustomed to working with a range of ethnicities on the job. They include the following books which can be found at **www.amazon.com**: *Brown Skin*, by Dr. Susan Taylor, *Asian Beauty*, by Margaret Kimura, and *Latina Beauty*, by Belen Aranda-Alvarado.

## Face Shape

Looking at the shape of your client's face will also help you decide what makeup to use. If she has prominent cheekbones or eyes, you will need to do less to accent these features than you would for someone with a softer, rounder face or less dramatic eyes.

You can determine the shape of a person's face by looking at the person with his or her hair pulled back, and imagining which shape would fit most neatly around the edges of the face.

You can change the way the face is perceived by using subtly different colors of foundation to create shadows and highlights. Correct use of highlighting and shadows can make a long face seem shorter, or a round face more drawn out. More about this technique will be explained in the upcoming section on foundation.

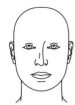

**Oval** is considered the ideal face shape. This face shape is about one and a half times longer than it is wide. An oval doesn't require any corrective highlights or lowlights. In fact, it's the shape the others are corrected to look like. See the illustration at left.

**Round** faces are just about as wide as they are long. They benefit from lowlights under the cheekbones and highlights above them applied in more vertical than horizontal strokes, with blush immediately along the bottom edge of the cheekbones. Use a dash of highlight on the chin, too.

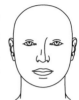

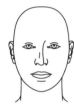

**Heart**-shaped faces have a narrow jaw line, and become gradually wider up to the temples. They benefit from lowlights at the temples and on either side of the forehead, as well as on the chin. Use highlights just above the client's cheekbones, and blend the blush all the way from the cheekbones to the temples.

**Square** faces have a forehead, cheekbone and jaw line that look almost equal in width. They can be shaded at the corners (imagine the four corners of a square), which means the jaw and sides of the forehead. Blush goes on the cheekbones, and highlights go above them.

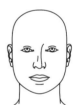

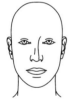

**Long** faces should be shaded at top and bottom—the jaw line under the chin and the forehead near the hairline. Highlights go above the cheekbones, and blush goes immediately under the highlights.

**Diamond** faces are widest at the cheekbones, with a narrow forehead and jaw line. Highlights go on the jaw line, and shading goes on the tip of the chin, the cheeks and the temples. Blush should go right on the apples of the cheeks, in a fairly neutral color.

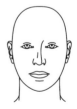

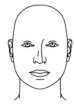

**Triangle** or "pear-shaped" faces have a narrow forehead and a wider jaw line. You will shadow or contour the sides of the jaw and neck, and highlight the center of the nose, cheeks and temples.

# Features

As a professional makeup artist, you must know how to pick out the client's best facial features and call attention to them with color and drama, and understand how to use makeup to downplay less desirable ones using contouring and shading.

Perhaps the person has features that will benefit from highlights, such as beautiful eyes, high cheekbones, or shapely lips. You can accentuate these features with extra color, highlighting cream or light-colored foundation, or heavier makeup application.

You will also want to notice, but not comment on, the client's less-flattering features. Does the person have a prominent nose, a blotchy complexion, an unevenly shaped face, or a noticeable pimple or scar? While you can't make these characteristics vanish completely, you can do your best to subtly minimize them.

# Wardrobe

Also, in assessing which makeup colors to use on a face, wardrobe will play a part. Of course, this would not affect what foundation and powder colors you would pick, but it could affect how much foundation and powder that you apply.

For instance, if it is an outfit that is going to be shot in a very natural setting, such as a swimsuit on the beach, heavy makeup would look out of place. You would make sure that the "application hand" was lighter, and possibly use less if the client's skin is extremely clear. Alternately, you could use as much foundation and powder as you wanted with a more dramatic outfit, like a fantasy outfit for a runway show.

As far as eye, lip and cheek colors are concerned, you want to make sure that the colors that you choose match the undertones of the outfit (warm or cool), and that the intensity that you use works with the wardrobe as well. If you have a dark outfit, you probably wouldn't want to use pale or soft colors on the face, which could tend to give a washed-out look when compared to the wardrobe and could make the outfit seem overpowering.

Use colors that match the "feel" of the outfit. They don't have to "match" by being the exact shade of the outfit, like green eye shadow with a green outfit, but perhaps a cool brown-and-cream-colored shadow to complement a forest green dress, for example.

## 2.2.2  Prepare the Face

Before you begin any makeup application, you must first prepare the client's face. These steps are extremely important both to ensure that your makeup application lasts as long as possible (because it adheres better to clean skin), and to protect your client's skin from blemishes or acne outbreaks that can happen as a result of oil or old makeup remaining on their skin and clogging their pores.

### Remove Oil and Makeup

You begin by applying astringent to the client's face. To do this, wet a cotton pad with a squirt of astringent, then gently wipe it over the client's entire face, beginning at the top and working in short strokes downward and outward, towards the chin and jaw line. If the pad gets soiled in the process of doing this, wet a fresh one and continue. Keep wiping downwards and outwards to beneath the client's chin and down the neck as far as the collar. Be cautious around the eyes, as they can be sensitive to astringent.

Next, do the same with toner or freshener to remove any last traces of oil or makeup that might have remained after the astringent. Apply toner or freshener in the same manner as the astringent, smoothing out and down and avoiding the eye area. Apply some moisturizer sparingly if needed, avoiding any oil-prone areas.

### Eyebrows

Eyebrows are very important to the overall "mood" of the face. For a clean makeup look, brows must be neat and shaped—although brows do not necessarily need to be thin to look clean. The shape of the brows will be determined by client preference, natural shape and your expert opinion.

Before any makeup is applied to the face, you must shape and clean up the brows. Because makeup is going to immediately follow, waxing is not the technique to use, as there will be residue from the wax, and possible swelling and skin irritation. Tweezing and shaving are the methods of choice on set.

A way to find the perfect shape for an individual is by using one of your skinnier cosmetic brushes as a guide. Hold one end of the brush on the outside edge of the nostril, and align it with the outside corner of the eye on the same side of the face. The extension of the brush will mark the maximum length the brow should extend towards the temple. Keeping the brush on the edge of the nostril, shift over to the inside corner of the same eye. Your brow should not extend any further to the center of the forehead than the point marked by your brush.

Where to place the arch (where the brow will reach its highest point) should be easily visible, but if not, have the person you are working on look straight ahead and shift your brush from the same point on the nostril to the pupil of the eye. That will mark where the highest point of the brow should be.

Using tweezers is an effective way to remove errant eyebrow hairs. Pull the skin taut, grab the hair firmly and pull quickly in the direction of the hair growth. If brows are long or unruly, just trim them. Be careful not to cut them too short or you may end up with patchy brows.

There are also "brow shapers" available, which are razor blades with guards on them that can be purchased at beauty supply stores for under a dollar. However, if you are unskilled in using a razor, you shouldn't experiment on anyone's face but your own!

## Facial Hair

Some women may have a moustache or longer dark hairs on the corners of the mouth (commonly referred to as a "Fu-Man-Chu") that will be visible even under makeup. Explain to them that it will look better if they are removed and discuss the best way to proceed.

If there are only a few, tweezing is a good option: it can be a bit painful, but bearable. Short dark hairs can be bleached, but if they are coarse, then shaving is usually a better option. Stray hairs on the chin and neck can be pulled out relatively painlessly with the tweezers.

# Concealer

Concealers are used in two ways: either to camouflage or to highlight. This section will look at the camouflaging use, while the highlighting will be discussed in the section on contouring the face.

Let's face it: no one has truly perfect skin past the age of twelve. It is your job as a makeup artist to skillfully camouflage skin imperfections such as dark circles, acne, blemishes, scars, redness, and age spots. While you can't make these skin flaws vanish completely, the eye can be fooled by the application of makeup.

Concealer usually comes in a rather small container which would suggest that it is to be used sparingly. One trick to get more mileage out of your "concealer" is to use foundations as concealers. To do this, just use a foundation color that is a shade or two lighter than the foundation that you will use. You will spend less because foundations come in larger containers.

For minor problems, application of a standard concealer should do the trick. If freckles are present, ask the client if they want them to be visible or not, as they might be part of his or her "look". The color you choose is dependent on what area of the face you are working on. For example, under the eye the concealer should be a shade or two shades lighter than the foundation you plan to use. It can be applied with the fingers, a concealer brush, or a sponge wedge.

As mentioned earlier, colored concealers (lavender, mint green, etc.) can be used to counterbalance skin discolorations on fairer complexions. The color you choose should counterbalance the color of the flaw. A red spot, for example, can be neutralized by putting a small dab of pale green concealer on it. Dab a spot of concealer directly on the blemish using a fine tipped brush. Be careful—using a concealer that is too light will actually highlight and draw attention to the area instead of minimizing it.

> **TIP:** For an extremely red blemish, try dabbing it with a drop of Visine (an over-the-counter remedy for red eyes) and letting it dry before applying foundation or concealer.

To hide a dark under-eye circle, choose a color of concealer that is one shade lighter than the foundation. Dab the concealer directly onto the dark circle, and blend it in to just beyond the edges of the circle, and continue with the foundation application, gently dabbing foundation directly over the concealer. You want to achieve a gradual transition between the concealer and the foundation. Blending is the key, as you don't want to see any hard lines.

More dramatic problems may require corrective cosmetics such as DermaBlend, which is formulated to be thicker than traditional makeup and can successfully cover large birthmarks, rosacea, and other skin problems. See section 2.3.5 on corrective makeup for more details on these types of products.

## 2.2.3  Foundation

As its name implies, foundation, or base, is the first layer in a makeup look. You will apply and blend foundation over the face, and sometimes even the neck, to give the skin an even and smooth look. You can also use slightly darker and lighter shades of foundation to bring attention to some areas, and draw attention away from others, as will be explained below.

Choosing the right foundation to use depends on the type of coverage you are looking for, and the subject's skin type. You will also match the foundation to the event and lighting, as we'll explain later.

> **TIP:** If the client will be wearing the makeup outdoors on a sunny day, you may want to use one of the brands of foundation that include sunscreen. If you do use this type of product, you'll need to be sure it is used in conjunction with a traditional sunscreen that has been applied to the client's ears and any parts of their neck that will be exposed to the sun.

For the main foundation you will apply, choose a foundation color as close as possible to your client's natural skin tone. Aim to match the color of their neck, as this is likely to be the part of the skin that is least affected by tanning or blushing and is therefore the truest representation of the person's natural color.

You can also mix foundation colors to get the perfect match. This is where the palette and spatula come in. For liquid foundations you can do your mixing with a brush, for heavier foundations you will use your spatula. Mix until you have the desired color.

For foundation, blending is the most important step of all. Foundation should be blended down below the jaw line onto the neck with no harsh lines of demarcation showing. Different shades of foundation should blend evenly with each other.

## Liquid Foundation

To apply liquid foundation, pour a small amount of foundation onto a palette or any small, flat surface. To apply, you can either make dots of foundation with your finger evenly over the client's face, including the eyelids and just beneath the jaw line, or you can apply the foundation directly to the face by dipping a sponge directly from your palette. Use the sponge to gently blend the foundation over the client's whole face.

Begin at the hairline, and work downwards, from top to bottom, moving from the center outward. Be gentle around the eyes, and avoid the lips. Smooth the foundation down beyond the jaw line and into the neck, if needed. It is generally not necessary to apply foundation to the client's neck unless there is some reason to do so, such as a blemish or razor burn.

When you have finished this process, the client's face should look smooth and clear. If there are any areas that need additional concealer or foundation, you may add another dot of foundation to that area and gently blend it into the surrounding area with the same technique.

## Cream Foundation

If you choose to work with a cream foundation, it will provide a slightly thicker layer of coverage in a single stroke. To apply cream foundation, use your spatula to scrape off a small amount onto your palette. Use only a little; if you need more later, scoop out more. This helps eliminate waste and is more sanitary than dipping from the container or applying the stick directly to the client's face. Use a sponge wedge to smooth the foundation out over the client's face.

Again, begin at the top and work from top to bottom, nose to ears. It is better to go with a little rather than too much, as cream foundation tends to be heavily pigmented and can appear unnatural. If there are areas that need more foundation after your initial blending, you can add a small amount after.

## Powder Foundation

There are also cream-to-powder and powder foundations to choose from, which are best for skins types in the normal range. You can apply pressed powder foundation with a sponge or enclosed puff, either wet or dry. You will get heavier coverage applying it wet, but the dry look will be more sheer. Cover the face with a base layer, and then add more wherever you think it is needed.

## Highlights and Contouring

Applying highlights and contours to the skin is the process of using lighter colors to draw out certain aspects of the face and darker colors to minimize them. For print and television makeup, highlighting and contouring is a key technique. Since these are two-dimensional mediums, the job of the makeup artist is to make the face appear three-dimensional or rounded. You must create the depth in the face so that the lighting doesn't make the person appear flat, like a cartoon character. This is achieved by properly placing highlights and shading onto the face.

This technique rests on the basic premise that white or light colors make things appear closer, and that dark shades appear to be farther away or receding. This can be done with other makeup such as shades of blush and eye shadow and even on the lips, but is most importantly done with the foundation. Contouring/shading can also be added to or totally done in the powdering stage too, so we will revisit this technique later.

Your concealer is considered a highlighter, or you can use a foundation a couple of shades lighter than your foundation. You'll want a third color that is a couple of shades darker than your foundation for shading.

The general rule of thumb is that anything that is coming forward should be highlighted and anything that is receding should be shaded or contoured.

- Areas that need to be highlighted include the bridge of the nose, the cheekbones, the peak of the forehead area right above the nose, the bone right under the eyebrows, the eyelids (although not necessarily for a "smoky-eye" look), and the tip of the chin.

- Shading should be applied to the sides of the nose, near the hairline and on the temples, under the cheekbone and in the creases of the eyes.

- The foundation that matches the skin is applied everywhere else.

All of these areas then need to be blended together to create gradual transitions from one feature to the next. You may need to add more of one color to blend down another one. As long as you have not yet set your foundations with powder, you will be able to easily blend colors on the face to create the desired result.

Be careful not to move your highlight or contouring beyond the area that it is supposed to be in. Also, you should not see any harsh transitions between highlighted areas or contoured areas. Use short strokes with your sponge and blend areas together.

Highlighting and contouring can be used not only to build dimension back into the face but also to correctively reshape features altogether. For instance, to downplay round cheeks you would use the darker foundation under the cheekbones. For a prominent nose; if the nose is wide, put the darker foundation in long vertical strips on either side of the nose. If the nose is long, dab the darker foundation on and beneath the tip, and blend it in.

To make a round face more elongated, shade the sides more and make contouring and blush to the cheek area more vertical than horizontal. For chins, noses, or cheekbones, you can also brush the area with a dusting of white eye shadow or lighter-colored powder, blending it in gently.

For more visual examples and information on how and why to highlight and contour, the books listed at the end of this guide in the resource section will help you out, particularly *Making Faces* by Kevyn Aucoin, *Fine Beauty* by Sam Fine, and *Stage Makeup* by Richard Corson.

## Setting Powder

After you have applied your concealer and foundations where you want them, they must be set with powder, unless they are powder foundations. You may choose to use loose or pressed.

You want to set the area under the eyes first, as it will crease quickly. If it has already creased, have the client to look up and gently rub away the creases with a sponge. Do not use a powder brush around a client's eyes, as powder will inevitably get in them.

While they continue to look up, use a clean sponge or an under-eye brush (it is larger than an eye shadow brush, with slightly rounded soft bristles) to gently press the powder into the foundation under the eyes. For the rest of the face a large powder brush can be used.

For more control of application a "blush-sized" brush can be used to apply powder. Do not use powder to set the foundation over the eyes, for reasons we will explain in the "eye shadow" section to come.

## 2.2.4  Eye Makeup

Because eyes are the focal point of the face, eye makeup is your greatest opportunity to add drama to the look. There are no hard and fast rules when it comes to the colors you choose, other than complementing the cool or warm undertones as explained earlier.

The colors can match or flatter the client's eye color, or will go well with the color of the outfit. The client may voice a preference for a certain range of colors, or you may choose colors yourself to achieve a certain effect. Using something like a frosted eye shadow will highlight the area if that's what you want to achieve.

## Eye Shadow

To ensure that eye makeup lasts, prepare the eyelids with a thin layer of foundation. Eye shadow is just like face powder in that it acts as a setting agent to concealers and foundations. Applying eye shadow on top of a creamy base not only helps the eye shadow adhere to the eye, but also ensures that you get the richest possible look from the pigment in the shadow. Shadows used over foundations are truer to the colors that you see in the container.

Remember that the tissue around the eyes is very sensitive, so be sure to use a gentle touch. Use a sponge to blend the foundation or concealer from the top lash line upwards to the brow. You may apply the shadows while the cream is still moist for a more concentrated, bolder application, or allow the foundation to dry for a few seconds with the client's eyes closed. Be careful to put the eye shadow in the area where you want it, because especially with dark shades, the first color you put on will be blendable but not movable.

The basic eye technique described below works with the natural curves of the eye, and uses two or three eye shadow colors. Because the lid comes forward it requires a light-to-medium shade. The crease recedes so you use a deeper shade, and the bone right under the brow that comes forward would take a light-colored shade. This technique helps to give the eye the illusion of lift. You may use the same color on the lid and the highlight under the brow, so you'll want a neutral base shade, plus at least two and possibly three colors of eye shadow.

- Use a medium-sized makeup brush for the lid color of the eye makeup being used (the light or medium shade). Starting at the inner corner of the eye and moving outwards to the outer corner, sweep this color over the eyelid from the lash line up to the crease of the eye. For a more dramatic look make sure not to get any of this color where you plan to place your contour color, as this will set the foundation and your dark color won't appear as strong. For a softer look include this area, and then put your contour color over it.

- Use a clean shadow brush to apply the lightest shade of shadow onto the client's eye area just below the eyebrow, taking care to keep the shadow off their eyebrows.

- Use a small crease or detail brush for the darkest shade. Brush it in a thin line along the socket line, working from the inner corner of the eyelid to the outside corner. If you want it to look dramatic, leave this color as a line. If you want it to look softer, you can blend it in with a large eye shadow brush.

- You may use a small angle or eyeliner brush to make a thin line of the darkest color underneath the lower lash line, beginning at the center of the eye (under the colored part of the client's eyeball) and working to the outside edge. Moistening the brush will create a creamier, stronger line. A dry application will give a more smudged look.

Sometimes when you apply shadows, they can fall onto the cheek area and stick. To combat this you can place extra loose powder under the eye. Make sure that it is lighter in color than the face powder—it should be a highlighter. Any shadows that fall can then be easily dusted away with a brush.

Another effective remedy is to rest your hand on a tissue that you place on the cheek of the client. Both of these techniques also help to keep the oils from your hands from damaging your application.

## Eyeliner

Eyeliner comes in liquid and cake forms for a dramatic, lasting effect or in pencil form for a softer, smoky look, and can be applied before or after the eye shadow. Some cosmetic companies such as Stila also make gel eyeliners that give you the crisp line of a liquid or cake, but unlike cake liner, you don't have to wet it. If you apply it before, you can disguise any imperfections in your application with the shadow. If you apply it after, it will create a bolder look.

- If you are using a liner that is applied with a brush (i.e. cake or a gel), an extremely thin angle brush or an eyeliner brush will be needed. For cake liners, spray the brush or the liner with water and mix with the brush until it's able to be applied in a nice, rich, clean line. Don't get it too wet or it will run.

- Hold the skin of the client's eyelid taut by gently pressing outward just between her eyelid and temple. Beginning at the inner corner of the eye and working toward the outer corner, draw a clean line on the eyelid as close to the lash line as you can get it. For a heavier line, build from the lash line out. To paint the inner corners of the eye without the liner skipping, have the client shift their gaze to the extreme right or left, depending on the eye you are working on.

- If you want to line the lower lid, it is better to use pencil eyeliner for this, as liquid looks too harsh in this area. With the client looking up, and beginning at the outer corner of the eye, draw a thin line as close to the lower lash line as possible. Some makeup artists choose to draw this line along the inner rim of the eye, while others choose to draw it on the outside, beneath the eyelashes.

- To correct wide-set eyes, emphasize the inner corners of the eyes with eyeliner. For close-set eyes, emphasize the outer corners, keeping the inner corners highlighted. For drooping eyes, turn the outer end of the line in an upward direction.

TIP:     White eyeliner on the inner lower rim of the eyes is a trick used to make the whites of the eyes (and therefore the entire eye) appear larger.

## Eyebrow Color

Eyebrow color is used to fill out any thin spots in the eyebrows and to create a more perfect arch. You can fill in the brows after applying your shadows and liners.

- Using an eyebrow brush, sweep the eyebrows upward and outward.

- With an eyebrow pencil that matches the color of the client's eyebrows (usually brown or brownish black), make light strokes directly onto the skin of the eyebrows, moving in the same direction as the brow hairs. Emphasize the natural curve of the eyebrow. To create a softer look, use a brownish eye shadow instead of the eyebrow pencil.

- To blend in the pencil lines, brush the eyebrows with the eyebrow brush again.

TIP:     For a different look, you can use facial bleach on the eyebrows before beginning your makeup application. Downplaying the brows by lightening them brings the emphasis back to the eyes. Make sure your client is in approval first, though.

## Eyelashes

You may want to curl eyelashes that are naturally straight, or that hide the eyes (common in people of Asian descent). It's better to curl eyelashes before applying mascara. Place the eyelash curler so that the eyelashes protrude between the blade and the pressing edge. Using care, gently close the handles, hold for a moment, and release.

False eyelashes can give a glamorous, exciting lift to a client's look for a special occasion, and can accent the eyes for any live event. False eyelashes should be applied after the eyeliner and eye shadow. They are available in strips you trim to fit, or in clusters that must be glued on individually, but which offer more flexibility in terms of where they are placed—you can even cut a strip eyelash into clusters using scissors.

The glue for strip lashes is different from the adhesive used for cluster lashes. The strip adhesive usually comes in a tube, and can be found in a black that dries darker for a more dramatic look, or in white, which dries clear. The adhesive for cluster lashes come in a small bottle, is clear, and dries clear.

- Holding the false eyelashes (grip the lashes, not on the base) with a pair of tweezers, apply a thin line of eyelash glue along the base of the strip or a dab on the base of a cluster. Carefully press the base of the eyelashes to the client's closed eyelid, as close to the roots of the natural eyelashes as possible. Make sure both ends of the strip are firmly attached. If you are using cluster eyelashes, repeat as needed until all the lashes are attached.

- Ask the client to keep her eyes closed for about 30 seconds while the glue dries. You may choose to run a strip of liquid or cream eyeliner along the glue line to disguise it. Then you're ready to apply mascara as usual.

- To remove strip lashes, peel them off gently, starting at the outside edge of the lid. The glue is soft and rubbery and peels up easily. The glue used for individual eyelashes is stronger, and requires a solvent to dissolve it. The client may want to wait for them to fall off after a few days, as to try to pull them off can be painful and damaging to the client's own natural lashes.

## Mascara

Mascara is the finishing touch for eye makeup, and it is applied to the eyelashes. Choose black for a dramatic look, or blackish-brown or brown for a softer look. You may want to emphasize the client's eye color or eye makeup color with a fashion shade of mascara such as blue or purple, if it suits the look. Lengthening mascaras tend to be thinner while thickening mascaras tend to be thicker. Experiment with different brands of mascara to find out which you prefer.

For stage, television, and location work, waterproof mascara works well because it's long-lasting and will stand up to sweating and tears. For everyday use, you can ask your client what they prefer. For events like weddings, recommend the waterproof product even if the bride doesn't usually wear it. She'll thank you later! Some makeup artists prefer to always use the client's own mascara to reduce the possibility of introducing bacteria into the eye. To apply mascara:

- Dip the brush into the mascara tube, or rub it over the cake mascara, which has been dampened with a few drops of water.

- For the upper lashes, wiggle the mascara wand back and forth at the base of the lashes to deposit color before rolling the brush through the lashes. Coat lashes from the very base to the tips with full strokes.

- Turn the wand vertically and apply mascara to lower lashes, moving from side to side. Be careful to avoid smudging the under-eye area. When applying more than one coat, combing through lashes between coats (using a clean mascara brush or an eyelash comb) will help prevent clumping.

## 2.2.5 Blush

Blush adds warmth and color to the face, and it is applied to the cheeks to give an attractive glow. Generally speaking, pink blush looks best on blondes, and rose or brownish blush looks best on dark-haired clients. Red-haired clients should use peach-toned blush. You may also use a lighter-colored blush on the top of the cheek area and a deeper color below it, working along with your contoured area.

- If you are using cream or gel blush, do this before you apply powder. Dab small spots of it along and below the cheekbone. Blend it in with your fingertips into a teardrop shape, ensuring there are no sharp edges.

- If you are using powder blush, you'll want to apply it after you've applied powder. Brush a wide blush brush over the blush color, and sweep it upward over the client's cheekbones, from the roundest part of the cheeks (if you can't find it, ask them to smile, and look for the most prominent part of their cheek) upward along the cheekbone toward the top of the ear. Again, aim for a teardrop shape.

- With both types of blush, be sure to blend the blush thoroughly at the edges so that there are no sharp lines. If you've used too much blush, you can tone it down with a dusting of powder.

## 2.2.6  Lip Color

Lip color is used to emphasize the client's lips and to lend drama to a look. You may want to use lip liner as well as lipstick or lip gloss, or lipstick or lip gloss on their own. For a natural look, choose a color that matches the client's natural lip tone, complements the colors of her makeup, or goes with the color of her outfit. If you have given her an especially dramatic eye treatment, you may want to opt for a more neutral or pale lip color to let the eyes do their thing. If her eyes are done in neutral tones, you can offer a more dramatic or darker lip color.

TIP:  Holding your pencil at an angle instead of straight on will help you draw a line that is less likely to skip (this holds true for eyeliner pencils as well!) Using a nice sharp lip liner pencil will give a clean edge to the lips that is less likely to bleed than lipstick or gloss alone.

## To apply lip color:

- Go over the edges of the lip line with your sponge that you used for foundation, making sure that the edge of the lip line is covered. Then dust a little powder around the lip line. This will help ensure that the lip color that you use won't bleed. Getting foundation on the actual lips can alter the shade of your lipstick, although it can help some lip colors to adhere better.

- If you are using a lip liner pencil, gently outline the shape you want the lips to be by drawing the tip of the liner around the lips, top first, then bottom. Some makeup artists skip this step as it provides a sharp-looking line, but sometimes you'll want that definition. Don't just put a thin line of color around the outside edge of the lip line. You will help yourself to blend with the lip color if you continue penciling small vertical lines from the outer edge onto the lips as well, avoiding the center of the lips.

- Chip off or scoop out a small amount of lipstick onto your makeup palette, and apply it to the lips with a lip brush. Use your palette to mix lipsticks, if needed. The color that you choose should match the lip liner or be slightly lighter.

- Have the client hold her mouth taut or slightly open. Beginning at the outer corner of the client's top lip, brush the lip color on, stroking towards the center of the mouth and blending in your lip liner. Repeat with the bottom lip, working from the corners in toward the center. Blend the liner and lipstick together until you see a gradual transition between the two, or no difference at all.

You may also use lip gloss instead of lipstick, letting the gloss and lip liner determine the color of the lips. Or you may brush on a small amount of clear or shimmering lip gloss over the lip color. For a more matte effect, dust on a small amount of translucent powder.

TIP: For lips with more dimension and fullness, they should be lighter on the inside than they are on the outside. A "pouty look" can be created by putting a lighter or shimmery color of lipstick or lip gloss on the inside of the bottom lip.

## 2.2.7  Complete the Look

You may choose to finish your makeup job by setting the makeup with finishing powder brushed lightly over the entire face. While powder is available in colors to match many foundations, many makeup artists choose translucent powder, which is a multi-purpose powder as it works to set the makeup and prevent shine while not changing the color of the makeup beneath it. Be aware that some powders, while they claim to be translucent, may tend to make darker complexions appear ashen.

You can always use your main powder color at the end to smooth out any areas that need it. Be careful not to get any powder over your eye or lip area, or on the lashes or brows. This can dull the brilliance of the colors that you have worked so meticulously to apply. You may also need to reapply cheek color. This is the time for any last-minute finishing touches before your client heads off to their destination, be it the set or a New Year's Eve gala.

## Removing Makeup

If you accidentally get a dab of makeup where you don't want it—a smudge of mascara under the eyes, for example—you can remove it easily by dipping a cotton swab into makeup removal cream and using the tip to gently wipe away the smudge.

You may not always be on hand to help your clients remove their makeup, but you might find yourself helping actors remove makeup between scenes, for example. Depending on the situation and the type of makeup used, you may have to help remove the work you've done.

To remove most types of makeup, help the client massage cold cream or makeup removal cream over his or her entire face, using the fingertips and working in small circles, moving outward from the center of the face and from top to bottom, out and down.

Wipe off the cream and smeared makeup with facial tissues, and then wash the face with a cleansing product and water. Finish with skin toner or freshener and a good quality moisturizer.

# 2.2.8 Airbrushing

Airbrushing is a makeup trend that is catching on fast. Makeup, particularly foundation, is sprayed onto the client in a fine mist using a small compressor, a hose attachment, and a pen-like tool.

The result is a more natural-looking makeup that lets the client's natural skin tone and glow shine through. It also allows the client to go through a makeup application without their skin suffering the tugging that goes into the makeup application, which can be damaging over time.

Industry rumor has it that airbrushing is now being used on top TV shows such as *Will and Grace* and *48 Hours*, and that it was introduced on the set of *Friends* before the cast took its final bow.

## What It Can Do

Airbrushing technology for makeup has been around for years, but now with the advent of high-definition TV and digital photography, picture quality is improving and the fine application of makeup becomes more crucial. Airbrushed makeup looks flawless and sheer even close up, but offers the fullness of coverage makeup artists used to turn to pancake foundation for. The airbrush is also attractive for hygiene reasons—the makeup sits in a jar attachment, and no contamination can occur between clients.

There are single-action brushes, which have one button to release the compressed air and another button to control the amount of color being released, and double-action brushes, which use the same button to control both processes. The double-action ones can be used with one hand while single action ones require two hands to operate.

If you choose to invest in an airbrush, you will be able to use it for all kinds of applications, from live and glamour makeup to fantastic theatrical and film makeup. You'll also be able to create temporary tattoos that last up to a week by using special long-lasting inks instead of cosmetics.

There are also airbrush tanning cosmetics available, which allow you to give your clients a natural-looking suntan by spraying them with sugar-based concoction that reacts with amino acids in the skin to produce a tanned look. Airbrushing is also a good alternative for people with physical needs for makeup coverage, such as psoriasis, scars, or vitiligo.

## Equipment and Cost

An airbrush is not terribly expensive—you can expect to spend a few hundred dollars on the different components. You might also choose to invest in more than one brush attachment, as like manual makeup application, big and small brushes are better for different types of application. Airbrushes can also be operated with cans of compressed air as opposed to a compressor, but if you plan to use it regularly, a compressor is a more economical and environmentally friendly choice.

Airbrush cosmetics, which are specially formulated to spread evenly and not clog your airbrush cost between $15 and $30 per 1.5- to 2.5-ounce bottle, although they are good for a number of applications. You'll need to purchase at least one bottle of each color to begin with. You may find that there are some colors you'll use up more quickly than others, but to start with, count on buying a range of skin tones (from very pale to very dark) and the full spectrum of colors (red, orange, yellow, green, blue, indigo, violet) plus black and white.

## Buying One and Learning More

The real challenge with an airbrush is learning how to use it. It comes with instructions and you can practice on your own, although most professionals opt to take a class in using the airbrush. You can learn more about the uses of airbrushes, watch short videos of them being used, and look for classes in airbrushing makeup at the following websites of airbrush manufacturers. Many of the workshops listed in section 3.3.3 have classes in airbrushing as well.

- *KopyKake Airbrushes*
  **www.kopykake.com/ac_airbrushes.html**

- *Temptu Body Art*
  **www.temptu.com**

- *Kett Cosmetics*
  **www.kettcosmetics.com**

- *Air Craft Cosmetics*
  **www.aircraftcosmetics.com**

Dinair Airbrush Makeup Systems offers workshops in Hollywood, Miami, New York, and Montreal, Vancouver and Toronto to learn to use their product. At the time of publication this class cost $695 in the US or $550 in Canada, and included a 15 percent discount on product purchase.

- *Dinair Airbrush Makeup Systems*
  **www.dinair.com**

- *Dinair Workshops*
  **www.dinair.com/dinair_workshops_2.htm**

- *Dinair Classes in Canada*
  **www.dinair.com/workshop_canadaschedules.htm**

# 2.3 Specialty Makeup

Not all makeup will use the types of makeup and techniques exactly as explained above. You may need to use additional products and different ways of applying them when it comes to anything beyond beauty makeup. Here are some types of specialty makeup and applications you might encounter on the job.

## 2.3.1 Makeup for TV, Film and Video

TV, film and video projects are often intense, and a day's filming can be as long as 18 hours. You'll need to be on the set at all times, and on hand for whatever makeup touch-ups are required. This type of work is intense but rewarding, both financially and professionally.

### TV Makeup

When you do makeup for television, you'll need to consult with the director or the artistic director of the program in order to ensure your work fits with their vision for the show. Some questions to ask are:

- What the project is

- The date(s) of the project

- Who will be responsible for the cost of the makeup

- How many people will you be working on

- Details about the set or location

- Services available at the location; electricity, running water, a room designated for makeup

- Pictures or sketches of costumes

- Pictures of the models or actors you'll be working with

- What type of lighting will be used

The main makeup concern with television is keeping shine away. No performer or news reporter wants a big greasy spot on his or her forehead. If someone has particularly oily skin, professional stores and suppliers like Alcone sell "mattifiers" that are great for television so that shine is controlled without powder build-up. Sometimes the best thing to do is provide the actor with a rice paper blotter to hit "hot spots" during breaks, because it may not always be convenient for you to hop on set between takes.

Airbrushing foundation is becoming a popular technique with television makeup artists because of the sheer, but complete coverage it offers. It's a technique that looks good if it's done correctly. It is advised that you take a seminar or watch an instructional video before using airbrushing on a paid booking.

On the set, always look at the actor on the monitor before shooting begins. If you see something that looks odd, fix it immediately. A blush that worked in-person may be too dingy or too bright on camera. As long as you are quick, no one will hassle you for getting in there and changing something.

Also, any skin that shows should be made up with body makeup in tones that match or are slightly darker than the actor's natural skin tone. This will give the person a healthy glow and will prevent the natural skin tones from looking mottled on camera.

If you'd like to take a one or two-day class on makeup technique for television as well as script breakdown, The Makeup Shop in New York City has a workshop specifically designed for television and film. Check out their website for details at **www.themakeupshop.com**.

# Film Makeup

When you are hired to do makeup for a film project, you'll need to do some preliminary work before the actual shooting begins, including visiting the location, preparing "schematics" or sketches of your makeup ideas for the artistic director to approve, and scheduling your day. If you are assisting, this work will be done for you, but if you are the Department Head, this work will be yours to do.

When you are on the job, your responsibilities include ensuring everyone is made up properly and on time. You may be asked to make changes, and you will be responsible for maintaining the makeup. There is usually a room set aside for makeup application and then you will move to the set or location to be available for touch-up work.

> **TIP:** For film, men usually require hardly any makeup. Film will reveal much more clearly than television if a man has too much makeup on, so use a light hand and check how your work looks on camera before you decide on a look.

## Read the Script

When you sign on for a feature-length film, you will be given a copy of the script. Make sure to read it thoroughly, and make notes to yourself about the characters. It will help you to understand the story and the actors you are responsible for making up.

Once you've read the script, you'll know a lot about how the characters should look. For instance, if a character is a down-on-his luck drifter, he'll need to look scruffy and perhaps dirty and somewhat battered;

quite different from the makeup you would use for a successful businessman.

## Research the Time Period

Just like clothing, makeup styles change from decade to decade, sometimes even from year to year. For example, in the 60s, heavy eye makeup and false eyelashes with pale lipstick were just as important to the look as mini-skirts and go-go boots. If the movie is set in 1962, you want to find pictures from that period and be true to them.

You can search for period pictures online, go the library and look for books on period makeup, and try to find magazines from the era. One great resource for period makeup is Rosemarie Swinfield's *Period Makeup for the Stage*. Although the makeup shown is designed for stage work, the book provides valuable information on looks from the 1700s on up to the present.

## Visit the Location

If a project is going to take place somewhere you've never been before, you should try to visit the location. Take Polaroids or digital pictures that you can add to a project folder to help you prepare.

Check to see how much light is in the room you'll be using for makeup and see if there is a lot of light or shadow.

Also, find out if shots are being planned for the outdoors so you can prepare for the weather. Heat and humidity cause sweating and can "melt" makeup. If a scene is being shot in the pouring rain, then waterproof makeup needs to be used, unless the scene requires the actor look drenched and disheveled.

Look for areas out of the direct sun for between shots, and bring plenty of powder and brushes for frequent touch-ups. If the day is cloudy, the shooter will need to use more lighting, so makeup will need to be heavier. It's your job to adjust to the conditions. Check the weather forecast in advance, and come prepared for last-minute changes.

## Prepare Schematics

If you are doing complicated character makeup, you will need to create a schematic for each makeup look that you'll be doing. These are line drawings of faces that you will use to document what kind of makeup you put where on the performer's face. When a makeup artist can draw the design on paper for the creative director of a film in advance, it allows for experimentation, input and changes in advance, and saves time and money in the long run.

Below are sample schematics which are included on the CD-ROM with this book. You can use these schematics or create your own.

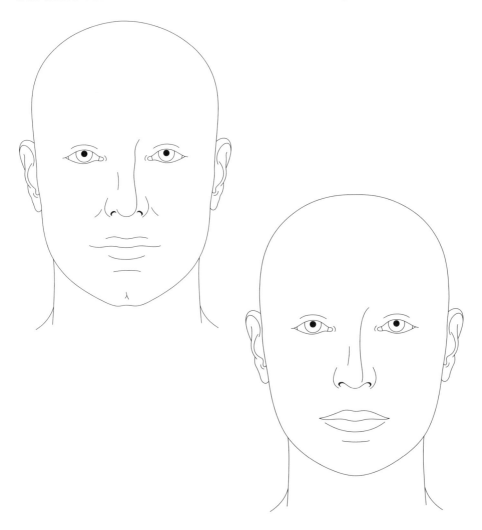

Script content is very important in film and video. Much of your direction will come from what the effect is supposed to be. There may be an overall mood or feeling that the director is going for, such as the urban, gritty look in the classic *Taxi Driver*, or the more recent *21 Grams*. Once you have developed sketches for the makeup you will apply, you should meet with the director to get approval of your designs.

To do a schematic, draw a life-sized outline of a generic face that has no hair obscuring it. You can do one male and one female, if you like. You can trace the outline and major features from a photograph.

Document the makeup on your schematic by drawing it on the paper just as you did on the performer's face, using colored pencils or strokes of the makeup itself. If you use colored pencils, try to match as closely as possible the colors of the makeup used, or write down the color names on the schematic to ensure you remember.

Label each schematic with the performer or character name, plus any pertinent details such as the production name, scene, and date, and note any body makeup required.

## Set a Daily Schedule

Once you have gotten your makeup plans or sketches approved, you will have a good sense of how much time each look will take to apply. Using the "shot sheet" (the director's list of what shots or scenes will be filmed on a given day) or timeline for the project, you can now establish the order in which to make up each person.

If one actor's makeup is complicated and he appears in earlier scenes, you'll want to get started on him first. Follow the simple rule of thumb that the makeup for each actor should be done in the order in which she is needed on the set.

Pack your makeup kit well in advance so you are sure you have everything you need. Bring your makeup sketches and plans and a carry kit. If you have to leave the area for any reason, make sure that someone knows where you are in case you're needed. To give you an idea of pace and timing, a sample schedule for a project day appears on the facing page.

## Sample Daily Schedule

| | |
|---|---|
| 7:00 a.m. | Call time |
| 7:00 to 7:30 a.m. | Set up makeup |
| 7:30 to 8:00 a.m. | Make up Actor A, who is in first setup, or scene |
| 8:00 to 8:30 a.m. | Make up Actor B, also in first setup |
| 8:30 a.m. | First Setup Scheduled |
| 8:30 to 8:40 a.m. | Get makeup approval for Actors A and B |
| 8:40 to 9:15 a.m. | Make up Actor C (who is in second setup) |
| 9:30 a.m. | Get makeup approval for Actor C Second Setup |
| 9:30 a.m. to 12:00 noon | Stay on set for touch-ups |
| 12:00 noon | Lunch |
| 12:30 to 12:45 p.m. | Touch up actors |
| 1:00 p.m. | Third Setup |
| 1:00 to 5:30 p.m. | Stay on set for touch-ups |
| 5:30 p.m. | Day Wraps; Clean area and pack supplies, check on call time for the next day |

## Video

Music videos are almost extensions of the fashion world, with their hip clothes and sexy makeup trends. Most makeup artists working on videos are very aware of what's current before the rest of the world knows. Sometimes they are the ones dictating the direction of the trends. Many of the artists working on music videos are the same folks creating the trendy looks for the fashion pages of magazines like *Harper's Bazaar* and *Cosmopolitan*.

A key difference in music videos is that the song will be driving the concept of the shoot. Therefore you need to listen to the song and read the lyrics. In the same way that a script tells you what is happening in a movie, the lyrics and music are the keys to the mood of a music video. You need to hear the song and discuss what the artist wants to convey so you can match that feeling in the makeup. Is it a country song, a rap piece or a sultry blues creation? Determining the mood and message of the song will help you to prepare your makeup looks for the artists involved in the production.

Video is also a format that relies on movement, as opposed to a static image. Doing makeup for this type of work requires constant attention to how the work is holding up while the actor or model is performing. This is a job where tissues, towels and extra hands are in high demand. Plan to use extra powder to ensure the makeup is set.

"I worked as an assistant on Lauren Hill's video for 'That Thing', and it was the longest day in my life," says makeup artist and contributing author Todra Payne. "We were in New York in 80 degree weather with sweltering sidewalks, and about 70 extras/dancers who were going from modern makeup to period makeup. I heard the song, which initially I liked a lot, about 875 times before my 14-hour day was over."

## 2.3.2  Makeup for Fashion and Live Shows

Fashion work is unpredictable. One season, the idea is to create drama, so outlandish clothes and makeup will dominate the shows. The next season the models will look like they just woke up and walked down the runway.

A few seasons ago a very famous designer sent the models down the runway naked with mesh bags over their heads—not the greatest situation for a makeup artist! Styles and color trends are constantly changing in the fashion business. If you choose to work in this field, stay on top by reading both mainstream and trade magazines.

For live event shows, you might choose to go with a more dramatic application of makeup, as your client will also be viewed by an audience during these occasions, and as such, will be further away from many of those looking at them. That means you can use brighter, bolder colors and should emphasize the subject's features more than you would for everyday makeup.

Keep in mind, though, that the media will be in the audience and back-stage taking pictures of the models or contestants, or the event may be filmed up close. They should not look clownish or exaggerated. Some-times the makeup is striking (or for fashion, odd), but it's rarely larger than life.

## Fashion Shows

Behind the scenes of any major fashion show there is a flurry of activ-ity. There are hairstylists, makeup artists, and seamstresses, all mov-ing at "warp speed" to get the models ready to step out onto the cat-walk. It's an exciting scene and one you can be a part of as a makeup artist.

When you're hired for a fashion show you will meet with the clothing designer and with the producer or director of the show to find out what the overall look and theme is for the show. You'll see sketches of the clothing and get pictures of the models you'll be assigned to on the day of the show.

Using the theme of the show and the clothes as your guide you'll cre-ate makeup sketches for each model in each outfit he or she will be wearing, and get approval from the producer and designer for your looks. The idea here is to be flexible, creative and really good at edito-rial makeup—the makeup you create for magazines will come in handy here because unlike theater, the catwalk is not hundreds of feet away. Most of the audience will have a pretty good view of the model and the clothes.

Just like any stage production, fashion shows will have rehearsals be-fore the actual event. You will need to attend these to take notes on the model's makeup and get the producer, designer or director's input as to any changes that need to be made. There will then be a final dress rehearsal with lights, music and everything done just as it will be on show day. (Ask permission to take pictures of your work at dress re-hearsal.)

Whatever makeup you normally stock in your kit plus anything special you may need (think large, blue false eyelashes) will work for the shows. Remember to stock enough of the special products to hand out to your assistants as well.

On the day of the show expect to work fast and furiously. Stay calm and don't let unexpected problems fluster you, because they will inevitably crop up. Have the models ready as quickly as you can and be available at all times in case a model needs touching up or a quick repair on her makeup.

## Beauty Pageants

From hometown events to national pageants, young women who compete in this arena need professional makeup consultations and application in order to look their best. To do this type of work you need to familiarize yourself with the different types of pageants, and what looks they favor. Some pageants prefer a more wholesome appearance, while others are all about glamour.

Consider subscribing to Pageantry Magazine (**www.pageantry magazine.com**) or one of the other leading trade publications for the latest information on the pageant world. For links and subscription information on pageant publications, go to **www.PageantPage.com**. Then you can add this specialty to your resume or website, and apply directly to pageant organizers to be listed as a resource for their competitors.

## 2.3.3   Makeup for Print Photography

When you see pictures of models, whether it's in a newspaper or in *Vogue* magazine, you're seeing a makeup artist's work. Editorial jobs are abundant and are a great way to gain experience, although they often pay less than other types of work.

The clothes are an important component, and in the case of a fashion spread, the real stars of the shoot. Before an editorial or fashion shoot you will meet with the photographer and client. Copy or storyboards should be provided that describes the action of the shoot and the feeling that is to be created.

You will be asked to create makeup that brings out the mood and feeling of the clothes, whether they are sporty, elegant or casual. Shots of the clothes or the clothing itself should be available for viewing at pre-production meetings. Pictures of the models involved should be provided so that you can see how many people you are working on and what they look like. You will work closely with the stylist, who determines which model is wearing each outfit.

Because many photos are taken under bright studio lights, the makeup colors you choose for this purpose should be stronger than normal but not necessarily brighter. Film can pick up on bright, sharp tones, which will look unnatural when the photographs are developed. If a lipstick is too dark, simply add a lighter tone over top. Make sure lip liners and eyeliners are applied perfectly so the eye will not be distracted by them.

In addition, the various tones in human skin are often emphasized by the camera, and it's important to have a good foundation to even out those tones and make the client look natural. Blending is the name of the game. This is accomplished with the help of excellent quality natural hair makeup brushes—some great brands are Bobbi Brown and Trish McEvoy. If you're strapped for cash, you can even browse art stores and buy small natural bristle paintbrushes to start out.

## The Environment

Photographs that are taken outdoors in natural light require softer colors of makeup, whereas strong studio lighting requires darker, more vibrant colors. A general rule of thumb is that photographic makeup should be brighter than street makeup and less dramatic than stage makeup.

If the photos are to be taken outdoors, you'll want to use rosy or peach tones to counteract the bluish effect of natural daylight. If the photos are to be taken in the studio, you'll want to aim for cool colors or peach tones to counter the yellowish effect of tungsten studio lights.

## Black and White Photography

While makeup you apply will remain pretty basic in color photography, black and white film has a tendency to produce sharp contrasts and flatten colors, so you'll need to accommodate that with the colors you choose.

If you can visualize tones of gray in your head it will help. For example, deep tones will look almost black, no matter what the color is—burgundy, forest green or chocolate brown. Use the difference in tones to create the picture you want. If both color and black and white shots are being done, you will need to adjust the makeup for the different types of film.

When you apply makeup for black and white pictures, you need to apply good contouring on the face. Eye makeup looks best in lighter shades than you would use for color film. Avoid red for lips and cheeks, as it will look black when photographed. Also, if lines are crooked it's much easier to pick up in black and white photography than color. Use peach or pale pink blush, which will end up looking more natural on film, or brownish-toned blush for dark skin. Powder thoroughly, and be sure to brush off any excess powder with your powder brush.

## 2.3.4  Makeup for Stage and Shows

The facial expressions of actors on stage would be completely blank to the audience if it were not for makeup techniques that accentuate the natural light and shadow of their features.

As a makeup artist for a stage production, you'll need to be on hand to do makeup for the performers once or twice, at the dress rehearsal, in particular. You will also need to teach the actors to do their own makeup, as most productions don't keep a makeup artist in house for the entire run of a show, unless the makeup is particularly complicated or impossible to do alone.

## Design a Look

Before you design the makeup for a stage production, you'll meet with the director or artistic director for the show. This person will tell you about the show and about their vision for it, and will probably ask you to create some schematics of each character's makeup. You should make a copy of the schematic for the actor, who will likely be doing his own makeup for the duration of the show. At this meeting, be sure to ask questions, such as:

- What is the plan for the stage lighting?

- What gels (light colors) will be used?

- Will there be any special effects?

- Are any rapid or drastic costume or makeup changes needed?

- What costumes will be worn?

The answers to these questions will help you determine what kind of situations you'll face when it comes to making the actors look the way they should. If a yellow light gel will be used, for example, you may need to compensate when applying the actors' foundation.

Sometimes the best way to learn is to work on high school plays and local church productions to see how the application looks on stage under the lights. Keep detailed notes of each production you work on and schematics for them so you can refer back to them later. If you are doing theater work, schematics also make a handy tool in your portfolio, as they demonstrate your ability to document and record your work, and indicate that you are able to provide consistent results.

Stage makeup must be visible to all members of the audience, and it must be brighter colored to withstand the bright lights of the stage, which is very bright and washes out facial features, making the actor's faces appear flattened. Because the eyes and mouth are where feelings are expressed, making up these areas helps the actor convey emotions to the audience. The size of the theater will determine the extent to which you will need to exaggerate each character's features for them to be seen by every member of the audience.

## Special Stage Supplies

Pancake foundation is used as a foundation for stage makeup, as it provides thorough coverage, is quick and easy to apply, and sets itself without need for powder. As with all foundations, the face should be thoroughly cleaned before applying pancake, as it does not stick well to an oily or sticky face. To apply pancake foundation:

- Wet a sponge with enough water so that it is saturated but not soggy. Wipe the sponge over the surface of the makeup cake and quickly spread wide strokes of the makeup over the broadest areas of the face (forehead, cheeks, nose, and chin). Do this lightly, as it will look unnatural if it is spread on too thickly.

- Next, squeeze any extra water from the sponge, and use it to blend the makeup over the client's face, working from the center outward and from hairline to chin. Avoid the hair, as pancake can stick.

- Once you have smoothed the makeup over the entire face and blended it down to fade out below the jaw line and over the fronts of the ears, check to see if there are any areas you missed. Work quickly, as it is difficult to correct blotchiness after the makeup dries.

For quick touchups, it is possible to stroke a sponge directly over the surface of dry pancake foundation and stroke it onto the parts of the face that require it. For the stage, follow the same steps you would use to shape and affect face shape for any other makeup application. A foundation base that matches the skin or is slightly darker is applied all over, even on the lips and then lighter foundation is applied in areas where the light hits the face such as tops of cheekbones and chin.

Darker foundation is applied in the cavernous spaces of the face, like under the cheekbone. If an actor is being aged to play a character, it's important that the texture of the skin is not as smooth as it would be normally. For a bolder look, make broader strokes of darks and lights, and apply the makeup in larger blocks of color, but still blend the edges, of course.

If an actor or performer will be wearing a costume that reveals arms, legs, or other areas of skin, you may want to apply body makeup to even out or improve the skin tone. Body makeup is similar to pancake makeup and is used in much the same way, although the sponge you use should be slightly less damp. Choose the same color you used for the client's face. Work quickly, and use the sponge to wipe and blend the makeup over exposed skin areas except the palms of the hands and soles of the feet. Cover the backs of the hands, the tops of the feet and the ears if they will be seen.

Greasepaint comes in sticks (like crayons), tubes, and small containers and is a thick, pigmented oil-based makeup. The colors are very vivid, and the makeup spreads easily on the skin. Its thick covering properties and vivid colors still make it a favorite among professional clowns, and it may be appropriate for certain live events.

## 2.3.5  Corrective Makeup

Corrective makeup is any makeup that is applied to conceal elements of the face or body rather than highlight or enhance them. It can be simple, like concealer on a pimple or freckles, or covering tattoos, wrinkles, under-eye circles, large pores, beard stubble, acne or similar blemishes. However, corrective makeup can also be used to minimize larger problems like birthmarks, spider veins, age spots, scars, burns, and skin conditions like rosacea, vitiligo or psoriasis.

In addition to covering up the undesirable elements of the appearance, corrective techniques also include contouring and shading to move attention away from the area, or airbrushing for more complete and even coverage of the problem.

Corrective makeup can be an entire specialty of work for some makeup artists who partner with plastic surgeons, dermatologists, or medical centers. It can be used to conceal temporary post-surgical bruising and redness, or some of the physical effects of long-term illness.

Corrective makeup is usually done with special products that are heavier in pigment, thicker and meant to be applied more heavily than traditional makeup. For more serious skin conditions it is also referred to as "camouflage makeup". They need to be set with powder or spray so that they don't smudge or wash off over the course of a day's wear. Two well-known brands are DermaBlend (**www.dermablend.com**) and Covermark (**www.covermark.com/pages/home_en.html**).

Colortration (another corrective makeup company) has techniques detailed on their website for use of their products with various skin markings or conditions. You can visit their webpage for makeup application directions for specific conditions at **www.colortration.com/application_ tips_new1.htm**.

Look Good, Feel Better (**www.lookgoodfeelbetter.org**) offers makeup training and techniques for women who are being treated for cancer. You can apply online to volunteer to help out at a branch in your area and get some experience in this specialized field.

## 2.3.6 Makeup for Men

While men don't typically wear cosmetics in their daily lives, men who work as models, actors and news anchors, or who are in the public eye do need makeup to enhance their looks. Their needs might be as simple as a dusting of powder to control shine, or could get more involved, as explained below.

The trick with makeup for men is to apply makeup in the subtlest of ways, and use it to enhance natural intensity and definition in the face. Here are a few points to note:

- If the man is not clean-shaven, he should shave immediately before his makeup is done, as this will allow for the most successful foundation application. Choose a color that matches or is one shade darker than the skin at his neck. Use concealer on any visible razor nicks.

- You can groom unruly eyebrows and sideburns with a special brush or disposable mascara brush, and use a bit of gel to hold them in place. Trim down any wild hairs if the client approves.

- If the client's lips are dry, use lip moisturizer.

- Gaps or uneven coverage in facial hair (sideburns, beard or moustache, and eyebrows) can be filled in, with a similar technique to enhancing women's eyebrows. You can use this method to define a cleaner edge to goatees. You can alternately use a bit of eye shadow and a stiff brush to fill these gaps.

- Foundation can be used on men if there is a big difference in skin coloration where the beard grows. If there are blemishes on the rest of the face you may choose to cover the entire face as well—don't forget to dust the face with powder to set. On television sets, which are heavily lit, you may add a little bronzer and blush to lighter complexions so that they don't look washed out.

- For everyday or "straight" makeup, men do not need eye shadow. Eyeliner and eyebrow pencils can serve to enhance the intensity of a gaze. Opt for shades of eyeliner that match the client's hair color—brown or brownish black will be your favorite choices, and will be used very sparingly very close to the bottom lash line, applied with a very thin brush. It's very easy to overdo it on a man and make him "too pretty."

You can look at some makeup products especially for men, and order an instructional CD-ROM on applying masculine cosmetics from the Studio5ive Cosmetics Company at **www.studio5ive.com**.

---

## Makeup for Drag

Some men enjoy dressing as women, either recreationally, as a lifestyle, or as performers. This is usually referred to as "drag" or "going in drag." If drag is done recreationally or as a lifestyle choice, cosmetics for daily use are more likely to be used. If it is for performance, stage makeup is usually a better option. The film *Priscilla, Queen of the Desert* offers stunning examples of drag performance makeup.

Most men who wear drag do their own makeup. However, if you find yourself with a client who wants you to apply their makeup, keep the following in mind:

- Be open-minded. Ask questions about the makeup he'd like, and the look he'd like to achieve. Try to avoid stereotyped looks, unless that is what they want.

- You'll be helping transform not only the person's looks, but also his gender appearance. Offer suggestions for makeup that provides good coverage and effective contouring, for example, and suggest other ways he can make himself look more feminine, such as hairstyles, accessories, and clothing.

- If you're doing makeup for a drag performance, the client may want to model himself after a particular celebrity, in which case you'll need a picture to work from. If the client doesn't have a celebrity in mind, then over-the-top glamour is not only acceptable but desired. Break out the false eyelashes and glitter eye shadow, and have fun!

GGreg.com offers plenty of makeup tips for men who want to transform their gendered appearance, but the tips are useful for makeup artists as well. Visit **www.ggreg.com/bm/dragqueen101.asp**

---

# 2.4 Special Effects (SFX)

Special effects makeup is a very broad category because there are so many different effects that can be done. This kind of makeup includes everything from small scars and bruising to prosthetic noses, chins or even full-face masks. It can be done for Halloween haunted houses, theater, television or films. There are even large special effects studios or production houses devoted entirely to this aspect of the makeup business.

While makeup artists who do character work are asked to do "special effects" from time to time, a different career is possible as a full-time special effects artist, building rubber masks, prosthetics, etc. This branch of film work is quite different from glamour or fashion makeup, and is beyond the scope of this career guide, as it is specialized and highly technical.

If you decide you want to specialize in SFX makeup, traditional beauty school training is not going to be much help, so choose a course of training or education with this specialty in mind. Many special effects makeup artists learn their techniques hands-on, either apprenticing or building skills working on smaller projects.

The work environment for someone who specializes exclusively in special effects is often offsite in a "lab" or "shop", working with a team of other special effects professionals. The majority of this kind of work is found in Los Angeles and Vancouver, although you may be able to find work in other major centers where filming takes place.

Even if you don't want to do special effects full-time, it is good for all makeup artists to have a general talent in basic effects, as you will need to produce the occasional cut or bruise. This section will introduce you to some basic supplies and techniques.

## 2.4.1 SFX Supplies

Creating special effects often requires specialty products. Here are a few of the most important ones you should have on hand if you will be doing character makeup for TV, stage or film, in addition to the traditional makeup and stage supplies mentioned earlier.

## Cream Makeup

Available in sticks and small containers in a variety of colors, cream makeup is a staple of special effects. Applied with sponges for wide coverage and with brushes for more precise effects, cream makeup can be blended easily and must be set with powder.

## Crepe Hair

This is artificial hair used to create beards, moustaches, and even werewolf effects. It comes in a variety of colors to match natural hair colors, and is sold in long skeins that can be cut and separated to meet your needs.

## Rigid Collodion

This is a liquid that is brushed onto the skin to create realistic-looking scars and wrinkles. When it dries, it pulls the skin tight and sets hard. It can be removed by peeling it off. Avoid using it around the eyes.

## Liquid Latex

Liquid latex is painted onto the skin to create special effects such as wrinkles, wounds, and other skin effects. It looks white when it is wet, but dries clear. Because it looks slightly shiny, it is used under foundation. You can also buy liquid latex in a range of colors for body painting and creating special effects on skin.

## Liquid Blood

Yes, once in a while you'll need liquid blood, especially when you're doing stage work. You can buy it from the same supplier you get your other theatrical makeup from, or you can make it yourself. Just color a small amount of corn syrup with red food coloring and a dash of chocolate syrup to create gory effects. Add more chocolate syrup to make the blood look older or more dried and less chocolate syrup to make it look fresher. You can also reconstitute freeze-dried powdered beets to create a large quantity of liquid blood.

Jeremy Gordaneer, a Canadian theatrical props designer, suggests mixing two teaspoons of Coffee Mate coffee whitener into your supply of liquid blood. "It makes it easily wash out of anything," he explains.

# Putty or Derma Wax

This Plasticine-type material is used to build up areas of the face to create bumpy noses and other deformities. It can be attached to the skin with spirit gum and shaped in place. It should be covered with foundation after being applied.

# Prosthetics

Prosthetics are three-dimensional pieces, usually molded to fit an actor's face. They are then applied and removed for each scene during filming. Prosthetics pieces are used for everything from changing the shape of Nicole Kidman's nose for *The Hours* to full face masks used in fantasy movies such as *The Lord of the Rings* or *Star Wars* series. Studios or production houses that specialize in these effects employ sculptors, painters, designers, and other trained craftsmen to create their amazing results.

As a makeup artist you might work in a studio or be trained to apply and remove the masks or prosthetic devices for characters on the set. Because of its unnatural appearance, latex or rubber masks are usually covered with grease mask paint and then blended in to match the actor's skin.

Unlike putty or wax, prosthetics are more durable and are reusable and are therefore good for long-running productions. Prosthetics are attached with an adhesive such as spirit gum or double-sided tape before the foundation and other makeup is applied. To give you an idea of what you'll be dealing with, some excellent photographs of various facial prosthetics can be found at the Malabar Online Retail Store at: **http://store.malabar.net/index.php?cPath=1_2_3**.

# Adhesives and Removers

Adhesives and adhesive removers are critical for special effects work. They allow you to attach facial hair and other transformative material.

Spirit gum is a type of adhesive. A small amount of spirit gum is brushed onto the skin wherever you need to attach something like a beard, for example. It is allowed to dry slightly, and then the material to be attached is pressed onto it.

Spirit gum remover is a liquid that dissolves spirit gum in order to remove the material from the skin. Soak a cotton ball with remover, press to the area where the spirit gum is dried, and let it soak in for a moment. After pulling off the material, you can dab at the area with the cotton ball to ensure all the gum is removed from the skin.

## Other SFX Supplies

### Stipple Sponges

Use these for creating stubble and bruising effects. These are natural ocean sponges with various-sized holes, as opposed to the more uniform manufactured sponges.

### Hair Whitener

This is a spray-on paint that washes out easily; you can also keep a small amount of cornstarch on hand to put a dusting of whiteness into an actor's hair.

### Glitter Gel

This is sparkly glitter suspended in a clear gel that dries quickly. Glitter gel is smeared or dabbed on the skin to create fantasy and special effects.

### Bindis

Used for exotic glamour or fantasy looks, these attractive spots worn by women in India are gaining in popularity in other parts of the world. They are likely to be stickers or small patches of fabric, plastic, or rhinestones that can be applied with spirit gum.

### Temporary Tattoos

These can be airbrushed, but you can apply the type of temporary tattoos that come as transfers on plastic backings. While holding it firmly in place, wet it thoroughly with water, wait a minute or two and then carefully peel the backing away from the skin. You can set the tattoo with loose powder, and they'll last three to seven days.

## 2.4.2 How to Achieve SFX Looks

Many makeup artists who do character work for actors are called upon to perform basic special effects, such as aging, bruises and cuts. Here is a primer on how to achieve various special effects looks.

## Age a Young Face

Before applying foundation, stipple a thin layer of clear liquid latex over areas of skin with a sponge or small brush, paying attention to the cheeks, lips, and the area around the eyes. You will need to stretch the skin taut with one hand while stippling the latex with the other. Work from top to bottom, beginning with the forehead.

Work from area to area, as the skin in each area must stay stretched while the latex dries. You can use a blow drier on a cool setting to speed this process. When the latex dries, it will pull the skin into realistic-looking wrinkles. To create an extreme old-age effect, you can lowlight the largest of the wrinkles.

> **TIP:** If you need the mouth to look especially lined, have the client fill their mouth with air so the lips are puffed out while you apply the latex.

Comb a small amount of white cream makeup through the eyebrows. To complete the effect, brush reddish brown lipstick thinly on the lips, and powder to finish.

This frequently used look can be created using basic items from your regular kit as well. Use a brown or very dark pencil in the creases of the face—even subtle ones. If there are very few, imagine where lines might appear someday and accentuate them. Have the person raise their eyebrows and trace the lines in the forehead. Make crow's feet at the eyes, and draw in the smile lines and in the lines at the corners of the lips. Darken the under-eyes with a deeper foundation than their normal color, or create deep bags by highlighting the puffy part and drawing a shaded line below the puff.

To make wrinkles appear more visible, use a very light or even white-colored pencil or foundation over the areas where you have created lines. This will give the illusion of a puffy area along with the dark line that appears to be carved deeper into the face. This look is created by using highlight and shadow very close to one another. You may also use a blue or pinkish pencil on fair skin to make a veiny look. White powder on the face creates an unhealthy and sickly complexion.

## Make a Face Look Younger

Using a lighter shade of foundation or cream makeup than the base color, brush highlights onto the hollows of the cheeks, the forehead, and between the eyes and eyebrows. You can emphasize these high-lights by brushing them with a touch of pale pink or white shimmering eye shadow. You can create the illusion of wide-set eyes by applying a small highlight to the sides of the nose, next to the eyes.

Have the client smile broadly, and apply pink or peach cream or pow-der blush to the roundest part of the cheeks. Blend it in a circle, and powder to finish.

## Scars

False scars are easily created using rigid collodion and colored cream makeup. You'll want to do this after the first layer of foundation has been applied. Using the brush that comes with the rigid collodion, paint along the area where you want the scar to appear. Let it dry, and add a second coat if you want the scar to appear larger.

Using a small brush, paint highlights of pale-colored cream makeup around the edges of the scar. Paint the interior of the scar with thin layers of first yellow, then red and brown cream makeup, and powder to finish. To remove, peel up an edge of the application, then gently but firmly peel it away from the skin.

## Cuts and Wounds

For a small cut, powder the area first, and then using a finger, smear a tiny amount of dark red cream makeup thinly over where the cut should appear. Using a narrow makeup brush, paint a line of the dark red makeup along where you want the cut to be. Paint it on thickly in the middle, and make the line thinner at each end, and powder to finish. You can make the skin look swollen by smearing a small amount of the darker red along either side of the cut.

After the initial application of foundation, you can also create a gorier cut or wound on the body. Apply a thin layer of pale concealer or foundation or a well-blended, thin layer of grayish-green cream makeup. Powder the area, and then paint on a thin coating of rigid collodion where you want the cut to appear. Allow the collodion to dry, then apply another layer and allow that to dry.

Paint the line of collodion with a dark reddish-brown cream makeup. To make the cut look deeper, smear a small amount of the reddish brown along either side of the cut, a few millimeters away from the edges of the cut. Then powder the area. You can make the cut look fresh by adding a few drops of fake blood at the center of the cut and letting them drip naturally from it.

To create a scrape that doesn't have a cut, you can begin as for a cut, with the grayish-green foundation, and stipple the dark reddish-brown cream makeup onto the area. Build up layers gradually until the desired depth and size of the scrape is achieved, and powder to finish.

After the foundation and powder layer is finished, you can also create a deep cut. Roll a small amount of derma wax into a tube and then flatten it. Apply the wax to the area where you want the cut by pressing it into place. If you want it to stay on for a long time, paint a small amount of spirit gum on the area first, and apply a small tuft of cotton wool to the spirit gum before covering the whole area with the wax. Smooth the edges of the wax to blend with the skin.

Using a small, sharp knife, carefully cut a gash into the wax. Watch out for the skin underneath! Use a fingertip or a makeup sponge to carefully stipple the same deep reddish brown around the outer, pressed edges of the wax, avoiding the edges of the gash. Using a small brush, paint the inside of the gash with the same deep red you used for the simple cut.

You can mix in a small amount of petroleum jelly to make it look wet. To make it look as though the cut has been repaired with stitches, tie small knots into short pieces of black thread, and glue them onto the cut with eyelash adhesive. And if you apply cuts to parts of the face and body that aren't likely to move, it will help them last as long as possible.

## Bruises

Stipple or brush on cream makeup in various colors, depending on whether the bruise is supposed to be new (reds and purples) or older (greens and yellows). Apply the lighter color of the bruise first, and blend it around the edges of the bruise. Apply the darker color of the bruise on top of the lighter one, leaving the edges of the lighter color visible around the darker color. Aim for an asymmetrical shape, and build up layers to enhance the color, then powder to finish.

## Beards and Moustaches

On a clean face, brush a horizontal line of spirit gum where you want the facial hair to be. If you are creating a full beard, work in sections, beginning with the bottom of the face first, and build up vertical layers until you reach the cheeks, or wherever you want the beard to stop.

Cut a small amount of crepe hair to the length you want it to be. Spread it out so that it is in a thin layer. Press this to the spirit gum, and hold it there for a moment with your fingers to ensure it's stuck. Apply another layer of spirit gum just above the first, then apply more hair in the same manner. Continue until the beard or moustache is as full as you want it to be.

To remove a false beard or other material affixed with spirit gum, dab the area with a cotton ball soaked in spirit gum remover, and then pull the material off the skin. Use the cotton ball to remove any extra bits of spirit gum, and then apply regular makeup removal cream.

## Noses

Roll some derma wax between your fingers until it softens and is pliable enough to mold into the shape you want. A pyramid shape is a good beginning for a pointed nose. A bean-shape is good to add a bump or ridge to a nose.

Brush a dab of spirit gum onto the client's clean, makeup-free nose, where the wax is to be applied, and let it dry for a moment or two. Press the wax directly onto the client's nose, and blend the edges of the wax to make it seamless. Shape the wax to the desired look. To enhance the effect, you can highlight the tip of a pointed nose, or the ridge of a bumpy nose, with light-colored cream makeup.

Apply foundation to the nose and wax, taking care not to let it get under the edges of the wax, and powder to finish. Remove the wax by pulling it off gently.

## Fantasy Looks

You can create any number of looks such as animals, aliens, and fairies by using your imagination and a good supply of colored cream makeup. You will combine makeup highlighting and lowlighting techniques, plus the use of colored cream makeup and false hair wherever needed.

- For aliens, emphasize the eyes and lowlight (or even erase) the mouth. Use silvers, grays, greens, or pale blues for the base color.

- For fairies, emphasize the eyes and cheeks, and provide a magical sparkle with glitter gel on the highlighted parts of the face, such as cheekbones, eyebrows, and nose.

- For trolls, use false noses (roll derma wax into false warts and moles and stick them on with spirit gum) and use dark or greenish foundation for the skin.

- For clowns, use white foundation or greasepaint, and then brush on the outlines of exaggerated eyes and mouth using black cream makeup. Color inside the lines with bright red for the mouth, and blue or green for the eyes, or leave them with just black lines. Finish with bright red circles on the cheeks.

If you're not sure what the character or creature should look like, sketch it out first using a face schematic, as explained in section 2.3.1. You can study animals in photographs to get an idea of how they should look. Break down their faces into major sections such as eyes, whiskers, and teeth.

# 3. Getting Ready

Chances are you've had a passion for makeup for a long time. Maybe you were always begging your siblings and friends to let you give them "makeovers." Or maybe you have always been a "people" person and love helping others feel good about themselves. You've got the basics down, but before you start applying for jobs or looking for clients, it's a good idea to take some preliminary steps to prepare yourself for a career as a makeup artist.

The information you'll find in this chapter will help you learn which skills are important for makeup artists, and help you evaluate yours. If you find you need to round out your talent with training, the chapter concludes with a look at getting both formal education and informal experience in professional makeup application.

# 3.1 Developing Your Skills

Every career demands certain things from its professionals. Surgeons need steady hands, firefighters need to be able to carry people out of buildings, and baseball players need to be able to catch a ball. Some key traits that are common to successful makeup artists are a natural talent for designing and applying makeup, an ability to speak and listen well, a good manner with people, as well a flexible nature and an eye for detail. Let's take a look at each of these.

## 3.1.1 Visual/Aesthetic Sense

There's a reason the job is called makeup "artist" and not makeup "technician". It takes an artist to transform a person's face or body into something completely different. You will need an eye for what works in terms of color, lighting and design, even before you begin the technique of application. Some people have a natural flair for visualizing makeup design and applying it well. Quite possibly you already have some raw talent if any (or many!) of the following are true for you:

- You notice when other people wear makeup poorly, and make mental notes of what you would do to correct it.

- You can draw straight lines, consistent shapes, and have good hand-eye coordination.

- Your friends ask you to do their makeup for special occasions.

- If you are a woman, you have a large collection of personal makeup, and use it differently for different occasions.

- You are artistic or creative.

- You appreciate beauty—in art, in people, in nature, or in things.

- You receive compliments on your own makeup or the makeup work you do for friends and family.

As you will read later in this chapter, all the skills you need to succeed as a makeup artist can be learned. However, if you are a "born makeup artist" with a natural talent for makeup application, entering this career will be even easier for you. If you still think your makeup skills could use some work, take a look at section 3.3 on getting some formal training at a beauty or makeup school.

## 3.1.2 Communication Skills

Makeup artists need to be able to express themselves well, and interpret what other people are saying or feeling accurately. This skill will allow you to communicate your vision to their your effectively, and really hear what your clients are looking for. Effective two-way communication can mean the difference between a happy client, and an unhappy one who demands you redo the job.

### Speaking

Makeup artists need to be able to tell clients what they can do and how they will do it—all in a professional, educated manner. As mentioned earlier, first impressions can last forever, and strong communication skills can make that first encounter stand out for clients. After they agree to give you a chance, you can let your talent with cosmetics do the talking for you. Remember that your speaking skill set also includes your telephone manners and presentation.

Does your speaking ability need some work? To answer this question, think about how often you are asked by friends to repeat yourself, or to explain a task to a coworker a second time. If you want, you can ask friends and family for feedback on how you could communicate more effectively. Your friends or family can point out speech issues you may not have noticed, including using slang terms, incorrect grammar, and voice quality and tone.

If no one wants to volunteer for this task, try videotaping or audio-taping yourself and listening to what you sound like to others—just about everyone could improve in one way or another.

### Listening

Listening is a key communication skill for makeup artists as well. You may have a vision for a client that you think would look fantastic, and the client has something else in mind. Of course, makeup artists are the professionals, and they should feel confident making suggestions and backing them up. However, a good listener can interpret the client's original plan, and create a happy medium between the two visions.

To become a better listener, don't interrupt the other person, and don't assume you know what the other person is thinking or saying. Let them speak their mind, just to be sure. Also, you should focus your attention on the speaker. This may be challenging on a busy film set or hotel room full of bridesmaids, but if you are distracted, you are not going to fully absorb what they are telling you.

Another helpful technique is to summarize what you understand the client has told you: "So you want something dramatic in pinks, with an emphasis on your eyes, correct?" Spelling out the request will help you and the client ensure you are thinking the same thing.

## Nonverbal Communication

Reading a person's body language and facial expressions can help you determine if you are on the mark with the design, or if they will be going to the bathroom to wash their face as soon as you leave. This technique is generally more important with private than professional clients.

A television producer will tell you in no uncertain terms when he or she doesn't like what you have done with an actor's makeup, and a fashion photographer will let you know if the model's makeup is wrong. However, when you're working with private clients, the individual may not feel comfortable saying that he or she is not happy with part or all of the application, so be in tune with them.

Makeup artists also need to project their own appropriate nonverbal cues. A makeup artist with an assertive voice and a confident posture suggests to clients that they know what they are doing, and are certain the client will be thrilled with the finished product.

However, if you are wincing or looking nervous as you apply the makeup, your client will sense your apprehension, and question your work. According to a UCLA study, if there is conflict between the words being said ("You look great!") and the message communicated by the body

(Wow, did I ever make a mess of this!), the body is more likely to be believed.

Ask a close friend to watch you when you do a makeup application and give you feedback. You might be giving off negative or nervous signals you are unaware of. Ask them to watch for things like:

- crossing your arms

- sucking air in through your teeth

- wincing or squinting

- rarely smiling

- pulling down a corner of your mouth

- furrowing your brows

- wringing your hands

- clenching your fists

- avoiding eye contact

- bouncing one knee as you sit

- any repeated gesture you are unaware of

An excellent book on this topic of nonverbal communication is *Reading People* by Jo-Ellan Dimitrius and Mark Mazzarella. Dimitrius draws on her experience in choosing jurors for criminal cases to explain how people are quite often speaking volumes with their non-verbal cues.

## 3.1.3  Working with People

*"Be a very personable individual, and caring, because… we're in a very caring business."*
— Marvin Westmore, Westmore Academy of Cosmetic Arts, Hollywood, CA

Do you like making people feel good about themselves? Many successful makeup artists will tell you one of the greatest rewards of the job is the enjoyment of making people happy, confident, and excited. Doing this isn't entirely based on your talent for makeup application; it's about building likeability and trustworthiness in your character.

Applying makeup is very intimate. You'll often meet someone for the first time when they sit down in your makeup chair. They may be worried about the event they're preparing for; they may be unused to wearing makeup or feel uncertain that you can make them look their best. It is very important for you to stay relaxed, to be warm and friendly and reassure them and let them feel confident about their makeup. Building relationships is critical. If you can do that well, you will become trusted and generate repeat clients.

> **TIP:** Part of how you interact with a client is also physical. You should be well-groomed and wash daily, and use deodorant. You should not use any perfume or cologne, or if you feel you must, use it sparingly. Also, makeup artists who smoke risk losing work because of their smoky odor—if this is a habit of yours, now might be the time to break it.

There are many ways to work on building relationships with people. One resource is Dale Carnegie's well-known book, *How to Win Friends and Influence People*. Carnegie offers advice you can practice socially (for example with the clerk in the grocery store or your hairdresser) and then translate these skills into working with clients.

## Three Keys to Success

Here are three of the major keys to successfully interacting with people as a professional makeup artist. Use them to charm employers and clients alike—these can be your "strengths" in an interview setting!

### Be Friendly

As discussed earlier, a makeup artist has to be a "people" person. This means he or she needs to have strong interpersonal skills and build great working relationships with clients and employers.

Look at it this way: if there are two equally qualified makeup artists up for the same job, the one who is better liked will most often get the position. To be that person, an artist needs to be more than competent. She or he needs to be friendly, sincere, and honest as well. Being pleasant to be around on top of being good at the job is a great way for makeup artists to build relationships and attract business.

It's natural to gravitate toward positive people and want to develop relationships with individuals you enjoy being around. A cheerful and capable makeup artist will find more work than a sour and capable one—and much more than a sour and inept one.

## Be Confident

When you apply makeup, it is your job to be reassuring, calm and confident. Your professional approach will help your clients feel as though they are in capable, competent hands and will allow them to relax and enjoy having their makeup done.

Makeup artists need to be able to converse with their clients and put them at ease. They may need to persuade a client or artistic director to embrace an outlandish or unusual look, or just a break from the traditional. As a makeup artist, that is how you will distinguish yourself from the others in the business. There is an art to persuading people to thinking the way you do, and a large part of it is confidence in yourself.

## Keep Your Cool

An even temper is important in this industry as well. In many cases, the job is done racing against the clock. Staying calm under pressure and being able to perform well in a hectic environment are useful traits.

## 3.1.4  Other Important Skills

The following traits will help a makeup artist find work and be successful. They can all be developed with awareness and practice. You can start preparing for your new career now with these characteristics and skills in mind in your everyday life.

# Flexibility

The ability to "go with the flow" is an important skill for makeup artists. One day you might be preparing a client for a wedding and the next you might be applying off-the-wall makeup to models at a photo shoot. You may have to find ways to overcome humidity at one shoot, or repair the sudden results of unexpected tears before a wedding.

Although some makeup artists who work in stores or salons keep regular hours, this career is not always a position that starts at 9 a.m. and ends at 5 p.m. A shoot may require an artist to be on set at 6 a.m., or after midnight. Hours can be long, and a lot of time is spent waiting, just in case a model or actor needs a touch-up. Not every makeup artist will work these kinds of hours, but if you are looking at film, TV, or theater, you will want to keep it in mind.

Start thinking now about how you can adapt your current responsibilities and commitments to this career. Discuss with your significant other, if you have one, about how working long days or odd hours would affect your relationship. If you have young kids, make sure your daycare or school allows for early drop-off and late pick-up.

## Should You Do Hair?

Many makeup artists also work with hair and wigs. Having that ability will definitely get you more jobs, as many productions cannot afford to pay for both a makeup artist and a hair stylist. In major markets like New York and California there are usually two people to handle those jobs, but smaller markets often rely on a makeup artist/hairstylist.

If you have attended a beauty school or worked in a salon and are a licensed stylist, you can bring those skills to your makeup artist career. If you are hired to do both hair and makeup, remember that just like the makeup, the hairstyles must match the wardrobe, the mood of the project and the characters portrayed (if actors are involved). Even if you aren't an expert hairstylist (yet), being able to do simple styles and keep hair sprayed and maintained can be a big asset to your career.

## Attention to Detail

As a makeup artist, you will be working on a relatively small area where details matter: the human face. You will need to pay attention to little things that might make or break a particular look. Was that mole on the left or the right last time? Is the blush even, or does the left cheek need a bit more work?

In television and film, shooting scenes out of sequence can pose a challenge for makeup artists, who have to make sure that the actors' makeup looks consistent from one scene to the next, even if they are shot days apart. Photos can help jog the memory about what a character looked like from one day to the next, as can detailed notes.

When applying makeup for television and film studios, makeup artists may be called upon to recreate a certain era for a project. Makeup artists need to be able to transport a model or actor to the 1920s or 1970s—or even the future—in a way that is authentic and believable for the audience. These transformations require historical research and an artist's touch as well as an eye for small details, from the colors that were popular at a given time to the way they were used.

## A Steady Hand

A key to the success of a makeup artist is his or her ability to do the same movements consistently and steadily. Like fine artists who are asked to practice drawing a "perfect circle" until they can do it in their sleep, so should a makeup artist be able to apply lip color or eyeliner. You need to create a specific look with one eye, and then duplicate it on the other.

The way you learn this is to practice over and over, on any models who are willing, or your own face. Observe your consistency of pressure as you apply, your coverage, and your color balance… and then do it again until it is perfect.

# 3.2  Ways to Learn the Job

Especially if you are not planning to study makeup in a school setting, getting experience in applying makeup is the best way to train yourself.

Self-training still requires training of a sort—it is just done without an institute or formal instruction.

Some of the world's most famous and talented makeup artists were self-taught, including makeup legend Kevyn Aucoin, who worked with such stars as Elizabeth Taylor, Madonna, and Cindy Crawford throughout his career. Aucoin attended beauty school for a short time but dropped out, opting to learn the trade on his own by working.

Another icon in the business, Sam Fine, worked as an illustrator before starting in makeup artistry. Now he teaches master classes, writes books, and has launched a cosmetics line. It takes hard work and patience, but a self-taught makeup artist can truly be successful.

Self-taught artists study makeup techniques and styles from magazines, runways, and movies, and they often practice applications on anyone who will sit still for them. They put in hours of time at studios, salons, and film sets interning and "testing" to learn all they can from professionals.

This section will look at the following ways to "learn as you go":

- Study Makeup on Your Own

- Find Makeup-Related Work

- Volunteer Your Services

- Apprentice or Find a Mentor

- Become an Intern

# 3.2.1 Study Makeup on Your Own

If you want to work with makeup, you should learn as much about it as possible. There are a wide variety of products on the market, and technology is constantly changing. You will want to match the product to the client's needs, the lighting, and the event, so you'll need to know what's out there.

A professional makeup artist will always be reading and learning about:

- New types of products

- New uses for products

- Application techniques and style

There is a list of cosmetics companies and their websites at the end of this guide for you to bookmark on your computer and check often, as well as other resources listed there designed to help you self-study.

Contributing author and makeup artist Eva Jane Bunkley makes the following recommendations:

*Stage Makeup* by Richard Corson is a wonderful manual to learn the theory behind makeup artistry. It includes in-depth study of highlighting and shading and includes the bone and muscle structure of the face and neck. It is the textbook used by many theatrical makeup classes. It also includes how to create different illusions on the face.

When it comes to beauty makeup, three books that can be enormously helpful are *The Art of Makeup* and *Making Faces* by Kevyn Aucoin, and *Fine Beauty* by Sam Fine. The last two mentioned have wonderful illustrations on the placement of highlight and contouring.

*Allure* (**www.allure.com**) can be a good monthly publication that can keep you up to date on the latest products put out by the major cosmetic lines, and they even offer an industry discount.

Even more specific to just the makeup industry, *Makeup Artist Magazine* includes not just the basics in beauty makeup, but what is used in the film industry including special effects and sci-fi. This magazine is published once every two months, and can be ordered online for about $25 for a year's subscription. Visit **www.makeupmag.com**.

## Keep Up With Trends

Just as with clothing styles, makeup fashions change from season to season. Colors that are hot one year are passé the next. You will need to know who is bronzing, who is shimmering, and who is looking natural in celebrity circles. Is eye makeup smoldering or sharp? What colors are coming and going? Again, use the resources listed at the end of this guide to immerse yourself in the goings-on of this industry so you know how your clients will want to look.

If you continue to learn, your makeup will never look like "paint by numbers". One editorial makeup artist interviewed for this guide warned that "you can get in a rut, doing the same style of makeup on everyone. I go out and look at new brands that come on the market. I play with application techniques just to see what I can do differently. I have every brand imaginable in my kit and I use a little bit of everything to keep my work fresh and exciting."

If you decide to launch a cosmetics company, or are working with high-end trend-setting clients like runway models or celebrities, you may find you want more in-depth information on trend forecasts. The Infomat website has compiled a listing of 25 fashion forecasting websites for you to browse at **www.infomat.com/publications/infpu0001576.html**. Many of them are for companies that offer paid consultation, but in some cases it can be information worth paying for.

Robert Jones, a makeup artist and trend consultant to Mary Kay Cosmetics, advises that while following trends is important, not every trend will be right for you to follow. When the "grunge look" was prevalent in fashion magazines during the 1990s, Jones didn't like it, and chose not to do that look of makeup.

"I think you have to make certain choices and have your own style," he explains. "You don't have to follow every trend that comes along if it's not something you believe in. Having your own style is what will provide a niche for you, and makes people ask for you."

## Keep a Makeup File

Makeup professionals need to keep makeup information on hand for easy access. Some artists use file folders to collect and separate information about different looks. Files for the techniques used to achieve these styles for the different parts of the face—such as lips, eyes, and cheeks—are helpful too.

You can work out a system that suits you, whether it's making different scrapbooks of articles, pictures and ideas that inspire you, or tearing pages from magazines and popping them into file folders for a filing system.

Experts interviewed for this guide also said that you don't need to stop at fashion photos, either. If you are planning on doing movie or TV work, or even costume and theater makeup, you can collect and file magazines or pictures from different eras. You will use these files as references when you are asked to create an era-specific look.

Makeup artist Davida Simon, who is profiled at the end of this guide, keeps a massive research library. For example, along with fashion magazines from the 1930s, she has a 1930 high school yearbook. "Sometimes it is not what glamorous people look like that you need to know," she says, "but what the real people of that time period looked like."

Garage sales are a great way to build up your library, according to Simon. "I have old Time-Life Books from the 50s, 60s, and 70s," she says. "National Geographic is a great magazine to hold on to."

Simon also collects makeup books that feature topics ranging from Kabuki (Japanese) style and Latina beauty to theatrical makeup. She even has some paramedic books on file.

"You have to be observant," she says. "If they say, 'Dirty them up,' what does that mean? If you have to create a gunshot wound, you need to know what one looks like. You want to be as real as they will let you be."

# 3.2.2 Find Makeup-Related Work

One of the best ways to learn about makeup is to use it as often as possible. If you can land a part-time or full-time job that allows you to work with makeup one way or another, you will be taking a step towards becoming a makeup artist with every day you work, until you are ready to look for full-time paid work as a makeup artist.

## Makeup Home Sales

The people who sell Mary Kay, Avon, and BeautiControl, etc. quite often do in-home demonstrations for clients, and will get a discount on the products they buy.

Doing this benefits a future makeup artist in a number of ways: meeting future clients, building up your makeup supply cheaply, free education on the product line and upcoming products, and of course, the all-important experience putting makeup on a variety of faces. Plus you get some extra cash!

You should be aware that some or all of these "multi-level marketing" companies will expect you to "recruit" new salespeople for them, and you will be not just applying makeup, but pushing to sell their products. You will be expected to learn about and probably use their line as well.

If any of these concepts bother you, you can try partnering with a sales agent as their makeup artist/expert. They can handle the sales work and recruiting, and you can handle the makeup application. If you bring a few business cards and hand them out, chances are you may drum up some future business for yourself from people who like the application job you do—even if they don't buy the products.

- *Amway*
  **www.amway.com/en/default.aspx**

- *Avon*
  **www.avon.com**

- *BeautiControl*
  **www.beauticontrol.com**

- *Mary Kay Cosmetics*
  **www.marykay.com**

- *Oriflame*
  **www.oriflame.com/en/home.html**

## Makeup Supply House

Depending on where you live, there may be a place nearby that sells makeup wholesale to other makeup artists. Of course for a business like this to thrive, there needs to be a good-sized local film, TV, fashion or theater industry, so you're more likely to have this option if you live in entertainment and fashion cities like Los Angeles and New York, or Vancouver and Toronto in Canada.

You can ask local makeup artists where they shop, look in your Yellow Pages under "Cosmetic and Beauty Supplies" or "Theatrical Supplies", or consult film production directories under "Suppliers".

You can see that working in a place where established makeup artists purchase their supplies gives you an opportunity to make contact with people in the industry. You need to be willing not only to promote yourself but also to ask—literally—for the opportunity you want:

"Wow! Working with Will Smith? I know I'd love that. Didn't you say you were busy? I bet you could use some good help. Have I shown you my portfolio?"

If you can develop a rapport with a working makeup artist, you may get on a fast track to the big leagues. This section also has more information coming up on assisting other makeup artists.

## Modeling or Acting

If you are lucky enough to be good-looking and talented, a great way to work with makeup is to have it applied to you by a professional while you get paid to model or act.

You will meet all the right people, including the ones like directors and fashion designers who can hire you once you are ready to break in as a pro. You will also be able to network with professional makeup artists, and ask questions to learn their secrets and techniques.

Of course, breaking into the world of modeling or acting is no small feat in itself, but if you already have an interest, the right look, and talent, you are off to a good start.

If you are interested in pursuing one of these careers, you can pick up the *FabJob Guide to Become a Model* or the *FabJob Guide to Become an Actor*, which, like this guide, give you step-by-step practical advice for entering these fields of work.

## Work in a Salon or Spa

Even if you work in a salon or spa as a part-time receptionist, you're better off than slaving away in an office for similar pay. You will be able to ask licensed cosmeticians and estheticians for advice, and possibly get the company to help train you towards a career in makeup.

Especially if you are looking to build a business around serving private clients, this is also a great way to meet future clients, who are people willing to spend considerable money on their appearance. Think about this: while you are chatting up a client as she pays her bill, you find out that she is getting married in three months, and still hasn't found anyone to do her and the bridesmaids' makeup. Who would you recommend?

> **TIP:** Working in a salon or spa, you may also acquire "bonus skills" such as hairstyling, massage, or aromatherapy that will give you leverage in finding private clients down the road, by offering them added value to your makeup service.

### 3.2.3 Volunteer Your Services

In order to get experience and build a portfolio of your early work, you can volunteer your help applying makeup to anyone who will sit still. If you plan to build a business working with private clients, make sure you take before-and-after photos of your work to add to your website and portfolio. You'll also want to leave a few business cards with anyone you volunteer with, so they can refer you to future paying clients.

> **TIP:** Before-and-after photos, while suitable for private client work, are not appropriate for the professional makeup artist industry. At that point, your portfolio should consist of tear sheets from magazines or professional-quality photographs of published or public work, which you will get by assisting established artists and "testing", explained later in this guide.

Rather than work for free, some experts feel you should charge a stipend for any work you do, even if it is minimal, or exchange-based. For example, if you do makeup for the mayor's daughter, she gives you two free passes to the zoo. If you do makeup for the coffee shop owner, you get three months of free coffee at her shop. The rationale behind this is that once you work for free, it is difficult to decide who to charge and who not to.

You don't want to hear this too often:

> "My friend Bonnie told me you do makeup for free! Can you do mine and my girlfriend Kelly's makeup too?"

While you can spend time thinking of tons of creative ways to showcase your makeup work in your community, some of the most common routes for volunteering will be:

- Makeup for friends and family

- Amateur theater and film, or public access TV

- Public makeup events (women's shelters, kids groups, proms)

# Friends and Family

After your own face, doing makeup for friends and family is the logical place to start. They are the most likely to give you honest feedback on whether you poked them in the eye, or made them look silly or strange. You should be the go-to person in your circle of friends for Christmas parties, Halloween, etc.

For example, when makeup artist Marie Augustine of the Alex Roldan Salon in West Hollywood, CA was just starting out, she did complimentary makeup jobs for people who she knew would tell their friends, and whose friends would tell their friends. "Maybe they would buy one lipstick or whatever their needs were," Augustine explains. "But I could build a foundation. When they come in, you develop a rapport with them, [which may help you go] further in your career."

A good skill to practice is imitation, where you'll look at a picture of a professional makeup job, and then trying to recreate it on a friend. There are websites listed in the resource section of this guide that give breakdowns of celebrity looks and how they were created, and most fashion magazines will list the products they used on the model to create her look.

After you have made up your friends and family, take a picture for your records, and give them some business cards to pass around to other people they know. Chances are you won't have to look far before you find paying clients coming back to you from these referrals.

# Amateur Theater, Film and TV

Just about every community has one or more amateur theater groups who are desperate for volunteers backstage—everyone wants to be a star! The same goes for public access TV and indie filmmakers. Even someone with a little experience in makeup is better than no one at all. Other community volunteer opportunities could include school plays and charity fashion shows, or whatever is going on in your area.

You will get used to the terminology and pace of these industries, and get experience working with the correct makeup for them, which is not always your everyday makeup. Best of all, you will get to work in different lighting situations, and will learn how to adjust your makeup accordingly. Even if you can't work on makeup right away, offer to work in another area if you can watch or assist the makeup person from time to time. Soon enough, an opportunity will open up for you if you are persistent.

To find local theater groups, see if your town or city has an arts section of the paper, or an entertainment weekly paper. You could also run a classified ad in either of these, advertising your makeup services to independent filmmakers. You will know if you have local public access TV, and can contact the station to ask about volunteering.

## Public Makeup Events

To get experience with a variety of faces, as well as good publicity if you plan to start up a business, consider putting on a makeup event for a local group. You can approach the local high school, the local woman's shelter, or working woman's networking group. Set up an event where you do a 15-minute consultation with each woman about her makeup. You can find more information about publicizing and putting on public events in section 5.3.7.

## 3.2.4 Find a Mentor

Some of the best resources for learning makeup artistry are other makeup artists. They know firsthand what the job entails, and they can help you get on the right track to finding steady work in the field. Many of these people will have experienced the same things you are going through and have picked up tricks and tips to make things easier. Keep in mind, however, that while some makeup artists might be quite willing to talk, others may be too busy. You will have to do a bit of calling around to find the right mentor for you.

You can go one of two routes with a mentor: you can simply ask them questions about the work, or you can assist them when they work. Quite often the first one will lead to the second if your approach is right. Section 6.1.3 has information on assisting other makeup artists, while doing information interviews is covered below.

## Find a Makeup Artist

To find makeup artists who might be willing to help you learn about doing the job, you can try searching the Internet. Many makeup artists have websites that include their email addresses and phone numbers. This enables you to locate makeup artists across the country as well as in your immediate area. Search the term "makeup" or "make-up" along with any specialties you have in mind.

If you are in a city with a large entertainment scene, you might also find makeup artists listed in the classifieds of an entertainment magazine or a trade magazine for the industry you want to target (TV production, brides, etc.). You can also use the makeup artist message boards listed at the end of this guide, or even try the Yellow Pages.

## Set Up a Meeting

You will attempt to set up an informational meeting, either by phone or in person, with the makeup artist who may be able to offer you advice. Keep your approach professional, as shown in the sample approach letter on the next page.

Don't worry if you have to send out a few of these query letters to get a response; some people may simply be too busy to respond.

One way to speed up the process is to offer to pay the makeup artist for their time and advice. Money opens many doors! For a list of makeup artists willing to "tutor" you for pay, you can visit **www.makeup lessons.com**. Note that these artists do not want to be contacted to mentor you; they are available on a paying basis only.

## What to Ask

Once you have someone who is willing to speak with you, set up a date and a time, as well as a time limit, so they don't feel barraged with questions. If you don't get a chance to ask everything you want, and the interview goes well, you can always request a second interview at another time.

---

## Sample Approach Letter

Dear Marla Makeup-Artist,

My name is Brenda Beginner. I am doing research online about makeup artistry because I am planning on pursuing this career here in New Orleans. I found your website while doing a quick search of professional makeup artists, and was extremely impressed with your online portfolio. In particular, the unique spread you did for the J.J. Riggs catalog really caught my eye.

I am looking for an expert makeup artist who wouldn't mind answering a couple of questions I have about the profession. From the look of your website and a glance at your portfolio, I would be lucky to get a chance to speak with you.

If you would be willing to answer a couple of questions for me, I would truly appreciate it. I can call you, or if you prefer, I can correspond with you by email or whatever works for you. Please let me know if you would be willing to speak with me. Thank you in advance for your time.

Sincerely,
Brenda Beginner
Phone: (555) 555-1234
BrendaB@email.com

---

Here are a few questions that you may want to ask a makeup artist during your informational meeting:

- How did you learn to apply makeup?

- How did you get your first paying job?

- What is the best way to approach potential clients or employers?

- What is the biggest challenge in your job?

- What are some of the most exciting projects you've worked on?

- Based on my experience, what should be my next three steps in my career?

- Is there anyone else you know I can contact to learn more or assist?

Answers to these questions will give you a better idea of what makeup artists do, and can offer guidance as you move into their ranks. Keep in mind that every makeup artist is different, and each person's experiences will be unique. You can't expect to be successful just by following another person's path. However, general advice from someone who has been there can save you time and energy down the road.

## Keep in Touch

After your conversation, be sure to send a note to thank them for taking the time to speak with you, and for sharing their insight into the business. This gesture is not only polite, but it may also create a valuable contact for you in the business. Keep in touch with makeup artists who are helpful and friendly with you. If they are too busy to take on a job down the road and need to refer a client to someone else, they may offer your name as a suitable replacement.

## 3.2.5 Intern with a Cosmetics Company

Some makeup artists-to-be become interns with cosmetic companies to learn more about the product, build a good-looking resume, and possibly find work with the company. A few of the major cosmetics companies also employ on-staff makeup artists, as you'll learn in section 4.1.

Interning is always a good way to get your foot in the door, though it's unlikely you'll be applying makeup in this position, except maybe your own. At the very least, you should finish the summer with a bunch of free products to fill your makeup kit, and a better knowledge of the products you'll work with in your future career.

If you are currently enrolled in a college program or have experience that might translate well to the cosmetics industry (e.g. business, marketing, promotions, or science and engineering) you can use the information below to find out more about how and when to apply.

Most of these internships are unpaid, or pay only a small amount, and you will have to go to where they have their corporate offices. Additionally, many of the internships are only available to college students, so be sure to check details before you apply.

**TIP:** If you are not a college student and don't have many marketable business or science skills, you can still work with that company's products by applying directly to the cosmetics counter at the retail centers that sell their products.

In addition to the companies listed below, you can also visit the website of your preferred cosmetics company to see if they have internship opportunities. Click on "careers" or "career opportunities"—it's usually at the very bottom of the page.

The website WetFeet.com specializes in internship information, and lists Estée Lauder among their profiled companies. The page to visit is **www.wetfeet.com/advice/internships.asp**.

## Avon

Avon's U.S.-based internships are paid (or earn you educational credits) and generally last between 9 and 12 weeks. The majority of the internships are available in the summer at their New York City offices in departments such as marketing, communications, public relations, creative agency, human resources, and website. They have Information Technology and Research & Development internships in different parts of New York State as well. The program is open to college students currently enrolled in a degree program. Interviews are held from early February to late April. For information visit **www.avoncareers.com**.

No internships were listed as available in Canada at publication, but you can still send a resume to their Point-Claire (Montreal) office, as positions may be available now. Visit **www.avon.ca/discover_avon/avon_careers.html**.

## L'Oreal

L'Oreal USA is headquartered in New York City, but has satellite offices across the country. L'Oreal Canada's office is in Montreal. Internships are offered throughout the year in a variety of areas, including marketing, sales, communications, international logistics, information systems, engineering and research. They last anywhere from three months to a year. To participate, you must be a student enrolled in your last or next-to-last year of study.

To see what's available and apply for a L'Oreal internship, visit them online at **www.lorealusa.com**. L'Oreal's Canadian website is **www. en.loreal.ca**.

### Estée Lauder

The Estée Lauder Companies (MAC, Bobbi Brown, Aveda, etc.) offer internships designed to suit any applicant they find intriguing. Rumor has it you get free makeup, too! You can send your resume to: The Estée Lauder Companies, Human Resources Department, 767 Fifth Avenue, New York, NY 10153.

### Neutrogena

Johnson and Johnson, which owns Neutrogena, has internships available to students. They are typically hired for a three-month full-time assignment during May or June through August. Part-time internships are available if you have a busy class schedule and want to work during the year. For information visit **www.jnj.com/careers/intcoop.html**.

## 3.3  Educational Programs

There are many educational programs out there teaching people to apply makeup, which range from a few days to more than four years in length, depending on the type of school and program. Here's some information to help you decide if school is right for you, where you can find them, and what they should offer, as well as a listing of makeup schools in North America, the UK and Australia for you to choose from.

### 3.3.1  Alternatives to Formal Education

In years past, cosmetology schools with strong reputations had salons and spas on waiting lists for their graduates. These days, most employers are likely to be concerned strictly with whether you know your stuff—how you got there is irrelevant.

In the world of makeup artistry, your work is what counts. Self-trained makeup artists build their portfolios and practice their art, just as those with formal educations do after graduating. Clients all want to see proof of an artist's ability—examples of what he or she has done in the past. Ability shines through, and if your work is exceptional, all the education you may require is a high school diploma.

Whether or not you need to pursue a classroom education, then, depends on your current level of skill in the area of makeup artistry that interests you. Some areas of specialization require more technical knowledge than others. For example, in a highly specialized industry such as special effects makeup you will have to learn how to build prostheses, make someone look like a burn victim, etc. While it's not impossible to learn these things on your own, some hands-on formalized training will speed up the process, in a classroom or with one-on-one mentoring.

Anthony Pepe, owner of DPFX, a makeup effects company in New York City says, "I went to a makeup trade school called Joe Blasco Makeup Center East in Orlando. The makeup techniques I learned there combined with my years of experience working hands on in the business basically gave me a well-rounded education."

Also, if you want to specialize in something like live theater makeup, you might consider an entire theater studies program that teaches you industry-specific information such as wig making, rather than a course in everyday makeup design.

Some work as a makeup artist that combines with cosmetology or esthetician work requires certification, which may have a requisite of a certain number of hours of training. Makeup artists who want to work in cinema, film, TV and live theater may also benefit from some specialized training in the area they choose to specialize in, but these are also the kinds of makeup artistry that lend themselves well to learning through apprenticing, as we'll explain in Chapter 6.

Freelance makeup artists who work with private clients don't need formal training to work. If you want to make up brides, models, etc. you just need to start doing it. If you are unsure of your technique or design abilities, or want to be the best you can be, you can consider going to a beauty school. The added benefit of learning hairstyling and nails will make your business easier to market in the long run.

If you have yet to develop any makeup application skills, or if you want to pursue a specialization but don't want to or can't get an apprenticeship or internship, then a formal education is likely the best option for you, especially if you are young and can afford it.

TIP:   If you are currently in high school or college and are considering a career as a makeup artist, you should look at taking fine art, theater studies, film studies, chemistry, and photography. These classes will teach you more about the products you will use, the theory of design, and the environments you may be working in.

## 3.3.2  What a School Should Offer

If you want to look for a school, make sure you shop around. While it may seem like a lot of work, it will be worth it. So what kinds of things should you be looking for? Here are a few to keep in mind while you look at schools and talk to teachers and admissions staff.

- Are the teachers working professionals, or have they been teaching forever? If they are the latter, you run the risk of someone teaching you skills, styles and techniques that are out of touch with today's industry. Also, if your teacher is working as a makeup artist and likes your work, there is a chance he or she will refer work to you later, or might take you on as an assistant. When you talk to admissions, make sure that the "founder" of the program is actually the one doing the teaching, or you could be in for a surprise there, too.

- Make sure the curriculum is up to date, and also advanced enough for your level of skill. Will you be taught the latest techniques for High Definition TV and airbrushing, or will you be applying looks that went out with *Flashdance*? Ask questions about what the most recent changes or additions have been to the curriculum, and ask if there are both beginner and advanced levels, or if everyone is lumped in the same group.

- If the class or program is a longer one, does it offer on-the-job training, co-op programs, or job shadowing so you can learn the "etiquette" of your future job environment? Does the school have any kind of published placement rate of its graduates?

- Will the class teach you about looking for work in a specialized industry? At the very least, it might say that it will give you photos for your portfolio—ask to take a look at some from past graduates to ensure they are not amateurish and unusable for a professional portfolio.

- How big is the average class? The pace of information can move quickly in a three-week course, and if there are 40 students, there's little time for individual questions.

- How much time is spent applying makeup? One school's promotional material stated that many makeup schools expect students to take turns applying makeup to each other. This means that half of your time is spent sitting quietly being a model. You can ask if the school supplies outside models, in a variety of face shapes and colors.

- If the school has a stated specialty, make sure that is the area of makeup application you are interested in. You can ask what percentage of course material is devoted to each topic for an idea.

- If you are applying for a longer program (six weeks or more) it is realistic to ask if you can sit in and "audit" a class for a short time to see what the teacher and material are like. If the school says no, this should send up a red flag that they are cranking out graduates and don't really care about helping you.

- Make sure the program has a cancellation policy in place, and find out what it is. If they don't get enough students for a session and cancel it, you will want your money back right away to reapply elsewhere. Make sure you don't have to wait until the next session is scheduled in three or six months.

- Find out if there are past graduates you can talk to. If the school won't help, that's another red flag. If they do supply a list, ask any of them you talk to for a referral to someone else they graduated with. One degree of separation is more likely to get you an honest review. You can also try posting for information on some of the makeup artist message boards that exist, to see what the general consensus is, but take these opinions as what they are: anonymous, sometimes spiteful or melodramatic, and sometimes financially motivated ("No, come to MY new school!")

### 3.3.3 Makeup Courses and Schools

Here is a list of makeup schools in North America. These are not cosmetology schools, but places that specialize in teaching makeup application for different purposes or media. These are not all that exist, as there may also be other smaller or more specialized classes or courses closer to where you live, possibly in conjunction with a local trade school or college.

Please note, these schools have been researched for the most recent information at publication, but things change, so ask questions to confirm, especially about cost. This is also not an endorsement of any of these establishments, but simply an alphabetical list of what's out there. Only you can decide what school, if any, is right for you, based on your personal situation and the answers to the questions above.

**Artists Within**

| | |
|---|---|
| Location: | Calgary, AB |
| Phone: | (403) 208-0034 |
| Website: | **www.artistswithin.com** |
| Duration: | 182 hours |
| Includes: | Workbook to use for future reference |
| Specialties: | Hands-on practical work; on-site photo studio; post graduate support |
| Cost: | Tuition plus kit fee; call for current prices |

**Award Studio**

| | |
|---|---|
| Location: | Los Angeles, CA |
| Phone: | (310) 395-2779 |
| Website: | **www.mediamakeupartists.com** |
| Duration: | 12 weeks |
| Includes: | A kit of brushes and cosmetics |
| Specialties: | Lots of time spent applying makeup; classes offered days, nights, and weekends. Bonus 2-day program to learn fashion shoot makeup for an additional $695. |
| Cost: | Approximately $2,700 |

## Blanche Macdonald Centre for Applied Design

Location:       Vancouver, BC, Canada

Phone:          (604) 685-0347

Website:        **www.blanchemacdonald.com**

Email:          info@blanchemacdonald.com

Duration:       670 hour day program; 524 hour evening program

Specialties:    Fashion/photographic, Stage TV and Film; Special Effects, Airbrushing, Prosthetics

Cost:           Approximately $10,000 CDN for the day program; call for evening program pricing

## Cinema Makeup School

Location:       Los Angeles, CA

Phone:          (213) 368-1234

Website:        **www.cinemamakeup.com**

Email:          info@cinemamakeup.com

Duration:       Ranges from 35 to 630 hours

Specialties:    All types of application; includes access to a fully equipped photographic studio

Cost:           Tuition varies from $750 to $8,900, plus lab fees, materials fees and registration fees

## Complections International

Location:       Toronto, ON, Canada

Phone:          (416) 968-6739

Website:        **www.complectionsmake-up.com**

Email:          info@complectionsmake-up.com

Duration:       Ranges from 2 weeks – 8 months

Includes:       Registration fee, tuition, and student kit

Specialties:    Animatronics, Fashion Makeup, Film and Television Makeup

Cost:           Ranges from $2,225 - $19,739

## Dawn til Dusk

| | |
|---|---|
| Location: | Nutley, NJ, multiple locations across the US for classes |
| Phone: | (973) 662-0111 or Toll-Free 1 (877) 329-6845 |
| Website: | **www.makeupclasses.com** |
| Email: | makeupclasses@mail.com |
| Duration: | Ranges from 40 to 100 hours |
| Specialties: | Advanced Makeup Techniques, Media Makeup Training |
| Cost: | $1,450 - $2,299 |

## Elegance Academy

| | |
|---|---|
| Location: | Hollywood, CA |
| Phone: | (323) 871-8318 |
| Website: | **www.ei.edu** |
| Email: | admission@ei.edu |
| Duration: | 12 months |
| Includes: | Registration fee, Tuition, Materials, and Textbooks |
| Specialties: | Film & Television Makeup, High Fashion Photography Makeup |
| Cost: | $10,900 |

## Empire Academy of Makeup

| | |
|---|---|
| Location: | Costa Mesa, CA |
| Phone: | (714) 438-2437 |
| Website: | **www.makeupempire.com** |
| Email: | mee4makeup@aol.com |
| Duration: | 60 hour (intro); 80 hour (glamour) or 100 hour (expert) |
| Specialties: | TV, film, print, beauty, bridal, SFX |
| Includes: | Certificates or diplomas |
| Cost: | Call or email for current pricing |

## Joe Blasco Makeup Schools

| | |
|---|---|
| Location: | Hollywood, CA |
| Phone: | (323) 467-4949 or toll free (800) 634-0008 |
| Website: | **www.joeblasco.com/blascoschools/hollywood** |
| Email: | hollywood@joeblasco.com |
| Duration: | Varies from 4 ½ to 11 weeks |
| Specialties: | Professional makeup artistry, Beauty makeup artistry, Advanced Prosthetics |
| Cost: | $2,100 - $7,100 plus material costs |

## LIBS Film and TV Makeup Program

| | |
|---|---|
| Location: | Manhattan, Brooklyn, Queens, NY |
| | Boston and Malden, MA |
| Phone: | (800) 319-8542 |
| Website: | **www.libsbeautyschool.com** |
| Email: | Visit website and choose the 'Contact Us' link |
| Duration: | Four courses ranging from 75-110 hours each |
| Specialties: | Film and Makeup Technology |
| Cost: | Call or email for current pricing |

## Makeup Designory (MUD)

| | |
|---|---|
| Location: | Burbank, CA |
| Phone: | (818) 729-9420 |
| Website: | **www.makeupschool.com** |
| Email: | information@makeupschool.com |
| Duration: | Varies from 8 weeks to 19 weeks |
| Specialties: | Courses in beauty makeup, character makeup and SFX makeup; bonus classes in hair styling and wardrobe styling |
| Cost: | Varies from $2,400 to $11,400, plus lab and kit fees |

## MKC Beauty Academy

| | |
|---|---|
| Location: | Los Angeles, CA |
| Phone: | (877) 798-1785 or (323) 661-8425 |
| Website: | **www.mkcbeautyacademy.com** |
| Email: | admin@mkcbeautyacademy.com |
| Duration: | 322 hours (masters) or 70 hours (advanced) |
| Includes: | Certificate |
| Specialties: | Beauty, fashion and print or photography makeup; hands-on instruction; basic and advanced level of instruction; shorter specialized programs also available |
| Cost: | $9,000 plus kit fees (masters), $3,500 (advanced) |

## School of Makeup Art

| | |
|---|---|
| Location: | Toronto, ON, Canada |
| Phone: | (416) 340-1300 |
| Website: | **www.schoolofmakeupart.com** |
| Email: | info@schoolofmakeupart.com |
| Duration: | Varies from 4-18 weeks |
| Specialties: | Extensive Makeup Design; Makeup & Fashion Image |
| Cost: | $1,865 - $7,900 (CDN) plus lab and kit fees |

## School of Pro Makeup

| | |
|---|---|
| Location: | Toronto, ON, Canada |
| Phone: | (416) 603-3332 |
| Website: | **www.promakeupart.com** |
| Email: | info@promakeupart.com |
| Duration: | Varies from 6 weeks to 6 months |
| Specialties: | Creative & Corrective Makeup Design, Special Effects & Prosthetics - Advanced Makeup Techniques for Television & Motion Pictures |
| Cost: | $2,600 - $8,000 (CDN) plus kit & lab fees |

## Studio Makeup Academy

Location:      Hollywood, CA, in a film and TV studio

Phone:        (323) 465-4002

Website:      **www.studiomakeupacademy.com**

Email:        studiomakeup@msn.com

Duration:     3 week day/5 week night (beauty), or 6 week day/10 week night (master)

Specialties:  Entertainment and Fashion; will teach you "set etiquette" and train you to work on one, master program includes some SFX training

Cost:         $2,175 (beauty) or $3,950 (master)

## The Skin and Makeup Institute of Arizona

Location:      Scottsdale, AZ

Phone:        (480) 949-6643

Website:      **www.skinandmakeupinstitute.com**

Email:        correctskincare@earthlink.net

Duration:     6 weekends, 100 hours

Specialties:  Camouflaging and Special Effects

Cost:         Call or email for current pricing

## VFS: Makeup Design for Film and Television

Location:      Vancouver, BC, Canada

Phone:        (800) 661-4101

Website:      **www.vfs.com**

Email:        info@vfs.com

Duration:     24 weeks

Includes:     2 professional-grade makeup kits, access to the studio and its products, portfolio and resume tips, and a diploma

Specialties:  Focuses on Makeup Design for Film and Television, includes some character and some SFX, also teaches basics of makeup for other media

Cost:         $9,000 CDN, includes materials, supplies, and books

## Westmore Academy of Cosmetic Arts

Location:     Burbank, CA

Phone:        (818) 562-6808 or toll free (877) 978-6673

Website:      **www.westmoreacademy.com**

Email:        info@westmoreacademy.com

Duration:     Varies from 3 to 12 weeks

Includes:     Makeup kit, Lab fees, Art supplies

Specialties:  5 Courses available: Spa and Salon, Photography and High Fashion, Motion Picture and Television, Medical Makeup, and Special Effects Makeup

Cost:         Approx. $5,000 - $10,000

# Short Classes or Workshops

You should stay open to learning new things throughout your career. Makeup artists never stop exploring new territories and products. Even artists with years of experience in the industry take workshops and courses like costume history and airbrushing to become more marketable and knowledgeable in their craft. Here are a few workshops and short classes you might consider now and during your makeup career.

## Debra Macki Makeup Class

Location:     Classes in Boston, Los Angeles, Las Vegas, Miami, and Chicago

Phone:        (800) 463-3272

Website:      **www.nvo.com/debramacki/makeupclasses**

Email:        info@debramaki.com

## Elan Makeup Studio

Location:     Dallas, TX

Phone:        (214) 370-3333

Website:      **www.elanmakeup.com**

Email:        info@elanmakeup.com

## Fred Segal Beauty

Location:    Santa Monica, CA
Phone:    (310) 451-7260
Website:    **http://shop.fredsegalbeauty.com** (click on Workshops)
Email:    jstaser@fredsegalbeauty.com

## JLS Makeup Artist Courses

Location:    Los Angeles, CA
Phone:    (800) 433-8545
Website:    **www.jlsmakeup.com**
Email:    info@jlsmakeup.com

## The Makeup Shop

Location:    New York, NY
Phone:    (212) 807-0447
Website:    **www.themakeupshop.com**
Email:    tobibritton@aol.com

## The Makeup University

Location:    New York, NY
Phone:    (212) 533-5900 or toll free (800) 711-7182
Website:    **www.makeupmania.com/artists_only/class_schedule.htm**
Email:    classes@makeupmania.com

## The Powder Group

Location:    New York, NY
Phone:    (212) 627-7447 or toll free (866) 876-9337
Website:    **www.thepowdergroup.com/events.html**
Email:    info@thepowdergroup.com

## Tina Earnshaw

| | |
|---|---|
| Location: | Marina Del Ray, CA |
| Phone: | (310) 827-4493 |
| Website: | **www.tinaearnshaw.com** |
| Email: | staff@tinaearnshaw.com |

## Tom Savini's Special Effects Program

| | |
|---|---|
| Location: | Monessen, PA |
| Phone: | (724) 684-DOUG (3684) or toll free (800) 413-6013 |
| Website: | **www.douglas-school.com/pages/savini.html** |
| Email: | dec@douglas-school.com |

## Vanessa Mills Makeup Artistry

| | |
|---|---|
| Location: | Classes in Florida, Los Angeles, New York, Seattle, Vancouver, Toronto |
| Phone: | (888) 828-8480 |
| Website: | **www.vanessamills.com/classes.htm** |
| Email: | classes@vanessamills.com |

# UK Makeup Schools

- *Brushstroke*
  **www.brushstroke.co.uk**

- *Delamar Academy*
  **www.themake-upcentre.co.uk**

- *Greasepaint*
  **www.greasepaint.co.uk**

# Australian Makeup Schools

- *Artistry of Make Up Academy*
  **www.makeupschool.com.au**

- *Australian College of Make-up and Special Effects*
  **www.makeupcollege.com.au**

- *Cameron Jane*
  **www.cameronjane.com.au**

- *Makeup Glamour Technicians*
  **www.makeupglamour.com.au**

- *Mask and Make-up Beauty*
  **www.maskmakeup.com.au**

- *The Make-up Biz*
  **www.themake-upbiz.com.au**

# BFA/MFA Programs

The universities in this section are schools that offer undergraduate and graduate programs leading to a bachelor's and master's degree in fine arts, specializing in makeup and wig design. The undergraduate programs are the standard four years in length, and the graduate programs require another two to three years' commitment.

### North Carolina School of Design and Production

Location:     Winston-Salem, NC

Phone:        (336) 770-3399

Website:      **www.ncarts.edu/ncsaprod/designandproduction/**

Program:      Offers a program in wig and makeup design. Classes give comprehensive training that prepares graduates for careers as makeup artists, wig-makers and period hair specialists in theater, dance, opera, television and film. Courses include Millinery/Masks, Makeup I and II, Advanced Wig and Makeup.

Cost:         *Undergraduate*:    $2,755 (in-state)

              $14,035 (out-of-state)

              *Graduate*:         $3,167 (in-state)

              $14,601 (out-of-state)

**University of Cincinnati CCM Theater Design and Production**

Location:   Cincinnati, OH

Phone:   (513) 556-6638

Website:   **www.ccm.uc.edu/tdp/makeupwigdesign.html**

Program:   Students in this highly selective program are exposed to all aspects of the theater along with a focus on makeup, makeup application, and wig making and designing. The four-year undergraduate program includes an emphasis on makeup and wig design. Graduate students spend 2-3 years expanding their art skills in areas such as painting, drawing and sculpture. Some of the courses include Makeup I, II, and III, and Costume Technology I, II, and III.

Cost:   *Undergraduate*:   $8,380 (in-state)

$21,350 (out-of-state)

*Graduate*:   $9,975 (in-state)

$18,400 (out-of-state)

# 3.3.4   Cosmetology and Beauty Schools

If you want to learn about makeup along with other beauty training, or if you want to work in a salon or spa, you will want to go to a cosmetology or beauty school. Many programs at cosmetology schools incorporate both hair and makeup in their training. Some include elements of spa training as well.

Be forewarned: some graduates of cosmetology or beauty schools who go in wanting to study makeup are disappointed with how little makeup is covered. Check over your curriculum and make sure you are getting what you want. Although hair and skin training is a terrific foundation for makeup artists, you will be disappointed if you expect to learn everything you need to become a makeup artist for film or TV.

The National Accrediting Commission of Cosmetology Arts and Sciences (NACCAS) is an excellent source for finding out information about the many schools and programs available.

A program is said to be "accredited" when it meets national standards of educational performance that have been determined by an impartial agency. For information visit **www.naccas.org/schools/new/ accredForm.html** or phone (703) 600-7600.

For a directory of beauty schools and colleges by state or province, as well as the cosmetology regulations for your geographic region, visit the Beauty Schools Directory at **www.beautyschool.com**.

You can also phone your state cosmetology board for more information. Phone numbers for each state's board are listed at: **www. experienceispa.com/ISPA/Education/Resources/Cosmetology +Boards.htm**

Peterson's Educational Portal (**www.petersons.com**) is another source for finding out about educational programs in cosmetology and related subjects.

## 3.3.5 Online or Correspondence Courses

Another option is to take an online course in makeup artistry. While you won't get face-to-face instruction, it provides theory-based learning as well as some home-based projects for you to work on, and feedback on what you submit. Here are a few for you to look at. As with any program, learn about what you are buying before you purchase.

### Cosmetics on the Go Makeup Artist Course

Cosmetics on the Go Makeup Artist course is an instructor-assisted course that combines Internet resources with "snail mail" correspondence. Students are given feedback through grades as well as an online meeting with the instructor, and send video footage of themselves completing assignments for instructor evaluation.

Courses include such areas as color analysis and usage, skin care, bridal makeup, and corrective makeup, and cost between $99 and $279. For information visit **http://groups.msn.com/WorldwideAllianceof MakeupArtists/onlineclasses.msnw**.

## Dick Smith Courses

In response to the popularity of Dick Smith's advanced makeup course (see below), this icon of TV and film makeup who created the makeup in *The Exorcist*, among other projects, has now begun to offer beginner level training in special effects makeup. *The Basic 3-D Makeup Course*, costs $350 and is available to anyone who wants to evaluate their SFX makeup talent. You follow instructions to work on a mask-building project at home, and then the photos you submit of it will be evaluated in terms of strengths and weaknesses. Information about the Dick Smith Beginner Course is at **www.dicksmithmake-up.com/newcourse.htm**.

Dick Smith's advanced course offers a certificate and 700 pages of illustrated text to keep and learn from, as well as professional advice and follow-up for as long as you need it. You apply with samples of makeup work, sketches or sculpture work you have done. If Mr. Smith feels you are qualified, you will be admitted to the program, which costs $1,995. You will need to purchase some equipment and supplies, listed on the website. Visit **www.dicksmithmake-up.com/mainmenu.htm** for information about the advanced course.

## Professional Beauty Network and Learning Center

The Professional Beauty Network and Learning Center teaches professional makeup artistry, including color theory, skin care, how to properly apply makeup to the lips, eyes, and face, and the essentials that should be in any makeup kit. Students also learn how to hide or downplay flaws in a person's appearance. The makeup and skin care classes cost about $270 each, and the airbrushing class is offered for $600. For information visit **www.pbnelearning.com**.

# 4. Getting Hired

Some makeup artists choose to seek part-time or full-time employment in the field, as opposed to being self-employed or freelancing. If you enjoy making a person look her best in everyday situations or for special occasions, a job in salons or spas, image improvement or portrait photography may be right for you.

Small towns might not have much in the way of professional clients (fashion photographers, filmmakers, etc.), and so this is also a good route if you live in a smaller-sized town and don't want to relocate. If (or when) you decide that you are ready to start your own business or freelance, Chapters 5 and 6 will help you get started.

## 4.1 Types of Employers

Types of employers for makeup artists include:

- Salons and Spas

- Retail Stores and Boutiques

- Cosmetics Companies

- Portrait Photographers

## 4.1.1  Salons and Spas

If you plan to obtain your cosmetology or esthetician license, you can approach salons and spas about becoming their resident makeup artist or expert. Even if a makeup position does not exist, with the right persuasion you can convince them to offer their clients this added value, possibly on a part-time basis.

There is no standard protocol for finding work at these places; each company will have its own way of looking for prospective employees. For example, if a spa is attached to a hotel, you may have to work through the hotel's human resources department to get the ball rolling.

One of the best ways to get hired by a salon or spa to do makeup is to have related marketable skills. If you have hair or skin care experience, you are more likely to be considered for a makeup job. That way your employer knows that if there are no makeup clients that day, you can pick up the slack doing pedicures or styling hair. Other considerations that will make you more attractive to salon and spa employers are an existing client base, and customer service and sales experience.

If you want to work exclusively with makeup, be prepared to just work part-time, or you can explore the idea of being a contractor who is self-employed, but works out of a salon. Chapter 5 will explain more about locations for setting up your own business.

### Salons

Makeup artists who work in salons tend to deal mostly with brides, their families and their wedding parties, party-goers, special event attendees, young women going to the prom, and occasionally people looking for an everyday new look or improvement.

To find salon work, make it your business to check out the salons in your community, eliminating from your prospect list any that do not wish to offer makeup services to clients. Start the ball rolling by contacting your salon of choice through a telephone call, a letter, or a visit. If they don't have a makeup artist on staff, a quick chat with the manager will determine if they would ever consider such a thing.

Remember that not all salons are going to have an opening for a makeup artist in the way that they might have a spot for a hairstylist. You'll want to target neighborhoods where people have plenty of discretionary income and can afford the extra service. Finer hotels that have a salon on the premises are one example of such a facility.

Opinion is divided on whether it's acceptable to just show up at a salon asking for a job. Marvin Westmore believes that it's best to visit the fancier salons in person and bring along your resume and pictures of past work. Before you show up, though, it's best to identify whom you need to speak with, and be prepared to wait if they are busy.

If you get an interview, come with your kit, prepared to do a makeup demonstration. Also be prepared to fill out a typical job application, which can be used to check your references and verify information on your resume. If you're just starting out, you might be hired on a trial basis, or as an assistant to the salon's established makeup artist.

# Spas

Beauty spas tend to cater to a higher-end clientele than salons, and spas often market themselves to stress the fact that in addition to hair, they work with the rest of the body. The common procedure is for the client to arrive relatively early in the day and go through a series of beautifying procedures—exfoliation, a facial, etc.—and end up having her makeup done toward the end of the day.

The two most common types of spas are the day spa and the destination spa. The day spa offers clients a series of treatments for various body parts over the course of a day. It may be attached to brand-name cosmetics, and is generally located in a somewhat urban area. Some spas are associated with image improvement facilities such as plastic surgery centers.

The destination spa may be near a fancy hotel or weight-loss facility. Some spas take advantage of the mineral waters spouting from natural hot springs and locate the facility nearby. Some resort hotels are organized around health and fitness, and other resort hotels have spa services as an adjunct to hotel services. Spa services are also available on various cruise vacations and may be organized around either fitness regimens or client-pampering activities.

You may be able to find employment leads in the newspaper, but also look at spa magazines. Trade publications are also a great source of actual names of people who are working and hiring. Pay attention to who is being quoted and to which company the person is working for, especially when it comes to information about what the companies need in the way of employees.

## 4.1.2 Retail Stores or Boutiques

Working at a cosmetics counter or cosmetics retail store like The Body Shop is another employment option for makeup artists. Finer department stores, such as Saks, Bloomingdale's, Macy's, Marshall Fields, and Neiman Marcus, have one or more counters devoted to single-brand sales of makeup, such as those by Clinique, Estée Lauder, Lancôme, and others.

Getting a position at a department store cosmetic counter will give you hands-on experience that will serve you well when called upon to do any type of beauty makeup. One reason counters are great is the variety of ages and skin tones that you work on in any given day.

When you're looking for a counter job at a retail store, pay a visit to the venue to see which companies are represented there. You can drop off a resume or fill out an application at your local retail makeup vendor. Make sure you let them know that you are interested in working with makeup. These types of jobs don't pay much more than minimum wage and sometimes commission, but can be a good experience for the budding makeup artist.

Once you are on the job in a retail store, the focus will be largely on making product sales. Your job will be giving advice to consumers for the most part, not being a hands-on artist. If there's some wiggle room, you could suggest doing in-store makeovers or 15-minute Saturday morning classes for young people in which you provide makeup tips. If these promotions pay off in increased sales, you may have an opportunity for advancement.

> **TIP:** You will probably get discounts on your purchases of makeup, and you will be aware of the newest products on the market. For non-commercial work, this is a great way to build up your makeup kit cheaply!

Always keep your eye open for additional professional opportunities, both in the store and with the makeup company you may represent. Mary Augustine, who went on to lead her own cosmetics firm, began at the retail level and was recruited by Vidal Sassoon to become the company's national spokesperson.

## 4.1.3  Cosmetics Companies

There are two ways you can work applying makeup for a cosmetics company: you can work as a "resident artist" at a single counter or retail location, or you can become a part of the company's promotional team.

If you want a job that keeps you in one place and offers a steady income, working in a department store selling a makeup line is a great option. You'll attend training sessions to learn about your products and then have the chance to practice your skills with in store demonstrations and makeovers on customers.

The second is a bit trickier, and requires more knowledge and experience, as you will represent the company to a broader range of people. You are basically being hired as an ambassador for their products, to help teach people about them and convince them to buy them. The bonus is that you will be trained by and work with top-level artists.

In many cases, the top cosmetics companies work with celebrities and events by invitation, which would be a great way to grow your resume. They also go to makeup trade shows where buyers from different stores look for new and exciting products for their stores. For example, in 2004 MAC makeup artists provided the makeup services for the opening and closing ceremonies of the Athens Olympics.

To find resident job openings with cosmetics companies, visit the job posting websites listed in section 4.2.1, or send a resume to the "careers" email address of the company you are interested in. For example, the Smashbox Cosmetics Company, started by the great-grandsons of makeup legend Max Factor, has postings for counter help right on their website at **www.smashbox.com**. Other companies, such as the MAC cosmetics company, suggests that to work for them at a retail level, you apply directly to the retail establishment.

Realize that above and beyond makeup artist talent, these companies will be looking for employees who are knowledgeable about makeup, comfortable with encouraging people to purchase certain products, and who have an easy and friendly manner with people. You will probably be expected to do a demo application in your interview, so keep these traits in mind.

If you can't find an opportunity with a cosmetics company, you might get an inside track on their next hiring by working for a retail store that sells their products. The cosmetics companies have relationships with these stores through their account managers, account executives, and beauty advisors. They work with retailers to provide training to their counter consultants, and this is a great way to network with someone who could tip you off to a corporate opening.

Some cosmetics companies also hire a promotional team of senior makeup artists who do makeup applications at regional promotional events. These are not entry-level positions, and require you to have a portfolio of professional work to show them. For example, the MAC Cosmetics company has this posted on their website:

"MAC Senior Artists are individuals whose knowledge and expertise meet the highest standards of professionalism at MAC. Our Senior Artists are based in several major markets around the world, and their job requires them to travel and work on events worldwide. Hiring for these individuals takes place within the market where the posting is open. Interviews for the position would include demonstration of makeup and communication abilities as well as examples of personal portfolios and a video reel. Resume submissions can be forwarded to the offices in New York."

Once you have assembled a strong portfolio of your work, as explained in sections 4.3.3 and 6.2.1, you can use the list of cosmetics companies in section 4.2.1 to send your resume to. In as many cases as possible, the links go directly to an employment page. If not, they list a mailing address for your resume.

## 4.1.4 Portrait Photography

Mass-market retailers such as Sears, Wal-Mart and Kmart offer portrait photography to customers, as do some small-market or independent photographers and the Glamour Shots upscale portrait studio. With their knowledge of lighting, a makeup artist can make sure that the facial features of the customers don't fade into the background against the glare of bright lights.

Because customer traffic for family or personal portraits may be light on a day-to-day basis, the need for makeup services may be only part-time, unless you can find a busy studio that caters mostly to women or brides. For example, Glamour Shots franchises advertise frequently for full-time makeup artists. Your services would include consultation and application on a steady stream of clients.

Just as department stores have a need for makeup artists to improve the results of their portrait photography, so do amusement parks. Novelty photography, in which customers put on antique clothing and pose for "antique" or fantasy pictures, has been a staple of the amusement business for some time. If you live in an area where there is a big amusement park and the novelty photo concession is busy, you might get a full-time position there, or at least for the park's season of operation.

## 4.2 Finding Job Openings

Makeup artist positions can be found in the classifieds of your local newspaper, but it's also a good idea to expand your search to trade publications and websites, online job boards, and company websites, in order to find a position faster. If you don't find what you are looking for posted, send a resume and cover letter anyway—this section also explains the "cold-call approach" at the end.

# 4.2.1 Advertised Positions

While you are not likely to find film or TV work advertised, salon, spa, cosmetic counter and portrait photography work is frequently advertised in print and online. Here are some places to start your search.

## Classified Ads

Keep an eye on the classified ads in your local newspaper for openings, under such headings as:

- Aesthetician
- Esthetician
- Cosmetician
- Beauty Advisor
- Makeup
- Resorts or Retreats
- Salons
- Spas

If you have a location in mind, you can find a list of U.S. and Canadian daily newspapers and their websites at NewsDirectory.com.

- *NewsDirectory*
  **http://newsdirectory.com**

## General Job Sites

General job sites have jobs posted for makeup artists who want to work with the general public. Use the search terms identified above at:

- *Monster.com*
  **www.monster.com**

- *CareerBuilder.com*
  **www.careerbuilder.com**

- *HotJobs.com*
  **www.hotjobs.com**

# Spas and Salons

Some spa and salon job websites include:

- *Salon Channel*
  **http://salonchannel.com**
  Click on "job & career center"

- *Spajobs.com*
  **www.spajobs.com**

- *International Spa Association*
  **www.experienceispa.com/ISPA/Jobs**

Trade publications and career-specific websites for salons and spas are:

- *DaySpa Magazine*
  **www.dayspamag.com/index.htm**

- *Skin Inc.*
  **www.skininc.com**

- *Spa Magazine*
  **www.spamagazine.com**

- *Salon Magazine and Beautynet.com*
  **www.beautynet.com/index.html**

- *Les Nouvelles Esthetiques (LNE)*
  **www.lneonline.com/index.php**

- *About.com Careers in Cosmetology*
  **http://careerplanning.about.com/cs/occupations/p/cosmetology.htm**

Name brand spas and salons with career opportunities on their websites include:

- *Elizabeth Arden*
  **www.reddoorsalons.com/currentopportunities.aspx**

- *Estée Lauder*
  **www.esteelauder.com/home.tmpl**

# Portrait Photography

Some portrait photography studio websites are:

- *Glamour Shots Store Locator*
  **www.glamourshots.com/storelocator.htm**

- *Wedding and Portrait Photographers International (WPPI)*
  **www.wppinow.com/index2.tml**

- *Wedding and Event Videographers Association International*
  **www.weva.com**

- *Antique and Amusement Photographers International*
  **www.oldtimephotos.org**

# Cosmetics Manufacturers

Most companies advertise job openings on their websites, or at least tell you where to send a resume for future consideration. If there is no link for "jobs" or "careers" on the home page, click on the link for information about the company. That will usually take you to a page that includes a link to job postings.

Many of these companies also list store locations at their websites, so you could apply directly to the store or stores where you are interested in working.

In as many cases as possible, the links go directly to an employment page. As websites are frequently reorganized, you can also use the resources listed at the end of this guide to locate the company's home page.

- *Bobbi Brown Cosmetics*
  **www.bobbibrowncosmetics.com**
  Send resume and cover letter to: Human Resources, 41st Floor, 767 Fifth Avenue, New York, NY 10153

- *Clinique*
  **www.clinique.com/customerservice/employment.tmpl**

- *Cover Girl (Procter and Gamble)*
  **www.pg.com/jobs/sectionmain.jhtml**

- *Estée Lauder*
  **www.esteelauder.com/home.tmpl**
  Send cover letter and resume to: Estée Lauder, Inc. Attn: Human Resources, 767 Fifth Avenue, New York, NY 10153

- *Lancôme*
  **www.lancome-usa.com**

- *Laura Mercier*
  **www.lauramercier.com/site/careers.htm**

- *L'Oreal USA & Maybelline*
  **www.lorealusa.com/Career/working.aspx**

- *MAC*
  **www.maccosmetics.com**
  Phone: (800) 588-0070
  Send cover letter and resume to: Attn: Irene Waxman, Director of Human Resources, 130 Prince St., 4th Floor, New York, NY 10012. If you want to work for MAC at a retail store, you apply directly to the store. To locate a store near you visit **www.maccosmetics. com/templates/door/finder.tmpl**

- *Revlon & Almay*
  **www.revlon.com/corporate/corp_jobs.asp**

- *Sephora (NARS)*
  **www.sephora.com/help/about_sephora.jhtml?location=jobs**

- *Shu Uemura*
  **www.shuuemura.com/Content/Salons.aspx**

- *Smashbox*
  **www.smashbox.com/employment.asp**

- *Stila*
  **www.stilacosmetics.com/templates/door/finder.tmpl**
  According to the website: "If you are a Makeup Artist with proven talents, please stop by your nearest Stila store and drop off your resume or see the Human Resources Manager in your nearest department store. You can find a complete list of store locations and phone numbers on the Stores and Events page."

- *Ulta*
  **www.ulta.com/control/storelocator**

## 4.2.2  Unadvertised Positions

So you've searched the want ads and had no luck. In competitive industries, many times the best way to get a job at a place you really want to work is by contacting the organization directly. Sometimes a manager will have just decided that he or she needs a new person. Most employers would rather find someone this way than invest all the time and effort in advertising the job, screening resumes, and interviewing numerous candidates. Plus you look like a go-getter.

You can make contact by telephone, email, or mail. Tailor your resume, and prepare personalized cover letters explaining why you want to work with that particular company. A form letter and standard resume isn't as likely to get looked at.

If possible, identify the name of the person who does the hiring, such as the owner or a senior artist on site. One way to do this is by requesting from the company's receptionist the name of the person who holds the position you are hoping to connect with.

Whether you make contact with a live person or get forwarded to voice mail, explain that you are looking for employment as a makeup artist and would appreciate an interview. Some people at that point will ask you more about your background and training, and others will just tell you to mail or fax your resume. Still others may give you the brush-off. Don't worry about rejection; it's par for the course and happens to everyone. Just move on to the next company on your list.

It's always best to have a referral of some kind, such as through a friend or former instructor. Since this is a people-to-people business, a personal touch can really make a difference. When a small-business owner needs a new employee, she will typically ask friends, business associates, and current staff members if they know anyone who might be suitable for the job. In many cases, this is how she finds the right person.

As you prepare for your career in makeup artistry, whether it's at a beauty school, workshops, or apprenticing, keep your future full-time employment goals in mind, and make it your business to get business cards and keep in touch after.

Be especially aware of any names of salon owners or established makeup artists the instructors at a training course mention, and if the name is linked to an area of employment that you're interested in, write it down and make a note of why it's relevant. You might even ask the instructor if you can use his or her name when you go to ask for work. If you make it your business to think ahead toward employment from the moment you choose a career, your chances of employment are likely to increase.

# 4.3 Job Hunting Materials

Companies you contact for the first time will want to see your resume, which should be accompanied by a persuasive cover letter. Their purpose is to get the person who reads them to contact you, by making yourself look talented and intriguing. You will also have a portfolio of previous work and some references or letters ready should you get called in for an interview.

# 4.3.1 Your Resume

Employers want to know if you have the specific skills required to fulfill the duties and responsibilities of the position. This is what your resume will communicate. Once you have professional work to highlight, your resume will focus on naming the publications, movies, shows, etc. you have worked on, separated into categories such as print, film, etc., and in order of how impressive they are. In the meantime, a traditional resume of skills and experience is the way to go.

The employer will be looking at your past experience in applying makeup. If you're just getting started and don't have a lot of experience, you can highlight any volunteer work you've done. You don't have to call attention to the fact that you worked for free—it doesn't mean the work you did didn't have the same value as if you were paid.

Another tip for those with limited experience is to find a way to relate other things you've done to the job at hand. Previous sales experience is often an asset, as well as any fine arts training. Were you doing people's taxes five years ago? That involves a degree of consulting skills. Were you the runner-up in the Miss Anytown pageant? Well then, you know backstage etiquette and all the fine elements of beauty. Draw conclusions between your past and the future you want for yourself.

Our experts interviewed for this guide had some serious advice about resumes: don't fake experience. You will be caught, and you'll ruin your chances at finding good work. If you don't have experience in a particular area be honest, but express a willingness to learn. You don't want to be busted on the job not knowing what to do.

Try to keep your resume to a single page unless you have extensive relevant experience. Also, you don't need to go back further than 10 years on your resume, since some employers may judge anything you learned before then to be outdated. You can also use a skills-based resume, which focuses more on what you can do than where (or how long ago) you applied it.

Something else to keep in mind is that you are applying for a job where appearance matters. Choose an attractive paper stock, lay it out nicely on the page, and make sure there are no typos. Ask someone else to look it over before you send it out.

# Sample Resume

**Kay Forrest**
**123 Evergreen Ave.**
**Gardenfield, MO 12344**
**(816) 555-5555**
**kforrest@emaildomain.com**

## OBJECTIVE

To work in a beauty spa as a full-time makeup artist.

## EXPERIENCE

| | |
|---|---|
| 2004-2005 | Burfield's Department Store, Gardenfield, MO<br>Cosmetics consultant, Primavera Cosmetics<br>Began as part-time assistant clerk. Promoted to full-time within 2 months. Increased sales with Saturday morning makeup tips and demos. Attended Primavera Institute, received certification. |
| 2003 | Mary Kay Cosmetics, Gardenfield, MO<br>Sales Associate<br>Conducted makeup demonstrations for prospective cosmetics buyers. Brought in sales of $12,000 on part-time basis while attending school. |
| 2002 | *The Railroad Flowers*<br>(American Plains and Prairie Preservation Society film)<br>Did all makeup for 90-minute documentary for journalist host and nonprofessional interviewees. |
| 2002 | Central Missouri Bluegrass Festival<br>Backstage crew, assisted with makeup, lighting. |

## EDUCATION

| | |
|---|---|
| 2003-2004 | Nonpareil Academy of Aesthetics, Gardenfield, MO<br>Honors certificate completed |

## VOLUNTEER

Jaycees' Children's Halloween Party (face painting)
Handley Home for Women (makeup consultation)

## 4.3.2  Your Cover Letter

Employers want to know what value you will bring to them, which is why you write a cover letter. Your cover letter should be personalized and explain why you are a good candidate for the job.

It's important to mention the company you are applying to by name. If you have any connections who referred you, be sure to drop their name in the first paragraph so the employer will be "hooked" by the referral.

It's also important that you read the job description carefully and speak to the specific concerns the employer conveys. Don't simply rehash what's printed in the description, but you can use similar language to match your skills to their requests.

Proofread carefully before you send your cover letter. You'll never hear a compliment on an error-free resume or cover letter; they're supposed to be perfect. While there's no correlation between good spelling and intelligence, nothing turns off a prospective employer more than a sloppy resume. The attitude is that a sloppy resume equals an employee that doesn't pay attention to details.

Furthermore, don't rely too heavily on your word processor's spell check since it won't catch mistakes such as using "two" instead of "too." Ask a friend to read the letter for you—the most difficult part of proofreading anything is catching your own mistakes.

If you have a choice between sending your resume online or via regular mail, you may get a better presentation if you use regular mail. A submission on good paper stock is more likely to get noticed than just another email, if you can get it there on time. Once you send your resume and cover letter, you need to follow up by phone to set up the appointment.

# Sample Cover Letter

Kay Forrest
123 Evergreen Ave.
Gardenfield, MO 12344
(816) 555-5555
kforrest@emaildomain.com

February 9, 2006

Mrs. Christy Berg
Millamont Salon
425 Westfield Plaza Centre
Kansas City, MO 12345

Dear Ms. Berg:

Patrick and Jane Kerchner at the Merle Norman shop downtown very kindly suggested that I contact you in my quest for full-time work as a makeup artist. Having completed the licensing program at the Sheldon Academy and earned my aesthetician's license, I am eager to go to work full time as a makeup artist.

You will see from my resume that I have done a good deal of makeup work for a variety of clients, from novelty projects for children at the Jaycee Fair to demonstration makeover projects for the ladies at the Handley Home. Last summer I also worked with Diane James, helping her make up the bridesmaids for several makeup wedding parties done by Wondrous Weddings at the Hyatt.

I would appreciate an opportunity to show you my portfolio, which I can bring in at your convenience. I'll be calling next week in hopes of speaking further. Meanwhile, please feel free to contact me: 816-555-5555.

I look forward to hearing from you.

Sincerely,

Kay Forrest

## 4.3.3  Your Portfolio

A portfolio is a collection of photographed samples of your previous work with clients. You can use your portfolio to show both employers and clients what you can do for them.

Most professional portfolios are bound in 11x14 display binders, which you can buy online or at an art store, but depending on your market, even a "scrapbook look" can be effective.

The majority of portfolios for work with private clients use before-and-after photos to showcase the makeup artist's talent. You've probably seen these many times. You take a quick photo of your subject before they are made up, and then snap a fabulous photo of the after-effects of a great makeup job. In your book, you might want to identify specific images with a brief label (for example, "Bridal Party, Benavidez Wedding, June 2005, Los Angeles Biltmore").

For a more dramatic contrast in before-and-after photos, take the "before" photo in less flattering light, without hair or wardrobe or even a smile, if possible. You can even take this photo during your initial consultation with the client, and then snap your "after" photo just before the event or once they are looking their best.

Your portfolio should contain only your best work. It's better to have fewer photos than some that are just "average". Make sure that whatever presentation format you use, you can later add to or remove pages from it. This will keep you from having to replace the entire book as looks become outdated, or your skill improves.

Some makeup artists also have different portfolios for different kinds of work. A bride-to-be is really most interested in previous bridal work you've done, so if you have a "bridal only" portfolio, she won't be distracted by your corrective work… and vice-versa.

If you are running your own makeup business (and you'll learn how in Chapter 5!), your portfolio could include additional elements such as:

- Your brochure

- Copies of letters or email messages from satisfied customers

- Copies of press coverage of your business

- Photographs of you working one-on-one with makeover clients

And finally, if you decide to pursue work in film, fashion, etc., you will need a totally different kind of portfolio, which is detailed in section 6.2.1.

Your portfolio is a very important possession. If you lose it, you have no proof that you can do beautiful or amazing work. Therefore, safeguard your portfolio by keeping a backup copy. You can either scan the photos and store them digitally, or get two copies of every photo made and physically create a second portfolio to store in a firebox or other safe place.

You might also consider insuring your portfolio against fire, theft, and other mishaps. Include your own ID information in the front of the book so that if your portfolio gets lost or misplaced, it can make its way back to you.

Here are some sources for high-quality portfolio binders in a range of prices:

- *Get Smart Products*
  **www.pfile.com/products/index.html**

- *Light Impressions*
  **www.lightimpressionsdirect.com**

- *Fast Portfolio*
  **www.fastportfolio.com**

- *Dick Blick Art Materials*
  **www.dickblick.com/categories/portfolios**

- *The House of Portfolios*
  **www.houseofportfolios.com**

If you are sending your resume and cover letter out via email, explain in your cover letter that your portfolio is available and that you'd be happy to present it at a meeting. If you feel that sending your portfolio along will give you a competitive edge (and it often does) consider scanning your photos and creating a digital portfolio you can burn onto a CD and send out with each application.

If you have a laptop computer, another option is to develop a PowerPoint presentation, which you can carry around on a laptop computer. You can scan all of the visual aids that would normally be included in your portfolio for easy viewing.

## 4.3.4 Letters of Recommendation

Letters of recommendation can go a long way toward helping you get a job as a makeup artist. A letter of recommendation from a professional in the industry means that someone has vouched for your skills. You can also include letters of recommendation from past employers if the letters say good things about your abilities in areas that are relevant to the position. Recent school graduates can also ask for letters from instructors. You can also include any appropriate thank-you notes you have received from brides or other clients.

When you ask someone to write a letter for you, keep in mind that many people are busy, so they are more likely to do what you ask if you can make it as easy as possible. To help get the kind of recommendation letter you want, and to make the job easier on the person writing the letter, you could supply a list of points they might mention. For example:

- The specific work you performed for them (write it out—chances are you remember what you did more clearly than they do)

- Your exceptional knowledge of products or trends

- That you were on time, professional, and worked efficiently

- You came up with many creative ideas

- Occasions when you listened and delivered exactly what your client wanted

- Cases when people have commented on how beautiful your client's makeup was

Of course, all these things don't have to be included in a single letter. The specifics will depend on the particular job you did. But even a few glowing sentences can help you look good to employers.

# 4.4 Interviews

Interviews for makeup artist positions are generally similar to interviews for other jobs. You will show up looking great, preparing to sell yourself. You are often expected to do a makeup application, sometimes in a certain time limit, and have proof of your licensing or qualifications on hand. If you are expected to do an application they should tell you in advance, and might ask you to bring a model as well.

One key thing to remember through the interviewing process is that the company seeking a new employee has a need. Interviewers are truly hoping that the perfect candidate is out there somewhere, and that the company needs will quickly and relatively painlessly be filled by you— the applicant.

If you were not qualified for the position (at least on paper), you wouldn't have been called in for an interview. From what the company has seen so far, you fit their needs. Accept that, and then go on to show the interviewer that you possess all the qualities that make up their definition of a fabulous employee. Here is how to prepare to win them over with your charm and skill.

## 4.4.1 How to Prepare

If you are invited for an interview, do yourself a favor and prepare in advance with these tips for success.

- If you are applying to a cosmetics company, familiarize yourself with their line of products so you are not fumbling around during the application part of your interview. You want to reach for products with confidence, and be able to explain to your model why you are choosing that product, and why it is so great.

- Use the Internet to research the company, their place in the industry (i.e., their niche), and their major competitors. Have something intelligent to say about all of these.

- Re-read the job posting you applied to, or find out the skills needed for the job. Think about how you are qualified, as well as what you liked and disliked about your past jobs so you can determine if this job will be a fit for you. Interviewing is a two-way street.

- Determine your personal key career achievements and be ready to describe them. Know your resume and letters of recommendation inside out (or they'll sound made up).

- Conduct mock interviews prior to your appointment. Enlist the help of a trusted friend to act out the part of the interviewer. Give your friend a list of possible interview questions, and go through the whole interview—from the first smile and handshake to the last thank you. Sample questions and answers are included later in this chapter.

- Make sure you know the exact address of the facility and what the parking arrangements are. If you're unprepared with regard to what door or which floor to go to, where to park, or how long it takes you to get from home to the location, you may arrive flustered and upset.

## 4.4.2 What to Wear

Your entire personal presentation—including your own makeup, if you are a woman—should be perfect for your interview. You're a walking advertisement for the job you do. And make no mistake: in this business, in the first five seconds there will be an instant judgment on whether you've got what it takes to work in the finer salons or high-end department stores, or to represent a cosmetics company.

Black is always appropriate and fashionable, and is a uniform-look that emphasizes that you are a professional. Industry rumor has it that black is "the" color to wear to a cosmetics company interview (MAC in particular). You want to look trendy, but professional. You can liven up your black with a purse, shoes, or other accessory in whatever shade is in this year.

You don't have to be ultra-conservative here. The key is to show that you know what is in style, and that you have the discretion to choose the components that put your look together. One of the reasons people get their makeup done by a pro is because they want someone who is tapped into the market and trends—otherwise, they might as well do it themselves. Your clients need to feel you are more fashionable than they are, or they will doubt your judgment.

If you are totally stumped on what to wear, see if you can arrange to visit the place ahead of time and see what the current employees are wearing. If you dress like an employee, that's how you will position yourself in the decision-maker's mind. That doesn't mean a smock or company uniform, but there should be a general "look" to the environment that you can try to mimic. Maybe all the women wear black, or everyone is in a skirt with knee-high boots. Be observant, and then do your best to fit in.

Here are a few more appearance tips from our experts who work in the industry:

- You want your clothes to allow you to move freely, especially if it is an interview where you are required to do a face.

- It almost goes without saying, but smell pleasant and don't wear overbearing perfumes.

- Make sure that you have mints for your breath and possibly for the person you may be working on. You will be well within the range of what constitutes the other person's "personal space" and lots of people are glad if you tactfully offer them a mint after you have taken one yourself.

- Don't schlep a lot of different cumbersome packages. Take only what is necessary. Try to consolidate what you must carry, such as your portfolio, purse, makeup kit etc. if possible.

- Your hair should be neat and not distracting, not something that you will have to sweep out of your face every few minutes. That can get annoying, and no one wants someone working on their face who is constantly digging in their hair.

If you are a woman, your own makeup application will be scrutinized—don't doubt it. Be up on current trends in makeup (see the industry resources at the end of this guide) and have your makeup reflect the latest and greatest, even if it's not your normal look. Apply it well, and blend it perfectly. Your makeup should demonstrate your skills but don't overdo it. You can scare away a potential client by having on too much makeup. They may get the impression that all you know how to do is pile it on!

Make sure that your makeup application is even and symmetric. You don't want a crooked line over your eyes or on your lips and you don't want the right side of your eye shadow to be more intense than the left. Take your time and don't do your face in the car on the way there. Do a pit stop before the interview, and check to make sure it is still perfect before you walk in the door or up to the counter.

## 4.4.3  How to Make a Great Impression

From the moment you are called into the room, be as confident as possible. Be the first one to make eye contact, smile, extend your hand, and introduce yourself. Speak clearly, neither too loudly nor too softly.

Be outgoing and enthusiastic, but don't over-do it. This isn't always easy because interviews can make people nervous, and nervous people tend to smile less and act more stiff than they normally would, or blurt out inappropriately. The employer wants to see that you are comfortable even in a potentially uncomfortable situation such as an interview.

If you have done your research on the position, the company and the industry, you will be eager to ask questions. Don't derail the tempo of the interview, but if the moment seems appropriate, be sure to jump in with a question. To the interviewer, this will show that you care enough to have done some thinking about the position and that you would be an asset to the team.

Talk about the job at hand. All too often, experts say, prospective employees spend too much time asking about promotions and supervisor positions when they should be discussing the job they're being considered for. Focus on what value you would bring to the company as an employee, and not on what you want to get from the job. For example, don't discuss how much vacation time you want or bring up salary until the employer does.

Be assertive, but not obnoxious. The company probably has more than its share of people who just coast along. If the opportunity avails itself, don't hesitate to express your opinion (respectfully) on a work-related issue or concern. Taking the initiative to broach a subject with confidence will show your leadership potential and will underscore your confidence and ease with others.

Be positive. Avoid saying anything negative, especially about former employers.

Before the interview, remind yourself how much you have to offer, and that there are many opportunities out there for you. Believe that if this particular job doesn't work out, you will find something else. Exude confidence, poise, leadership, and capability, and chances are you'll get that call that says you are the newest makeup expert on the block.

## 4.4.4 Interview Questions

You can expect to be asked standard interview questions such as the ones that follow. It's a good idea to prepare some answers before the interview. Some suggestions are listed here as well.

### Why Do You Want to Work For Our Company?

Prospective employers do not want a "cookie-cutter" answer to this question, so be specific. Maybe you are a former client, and found their atmosphere and staff warm and caring, which is in line with your own attitude towards personal image care. Maybe you strongly support the product line they produce.

### What Drew You to a Career in Makeup Artistry?

"For the money" is not a good answer to this question, but, "I'm creative and I like working with people," would serve you well. Try to be honest: What excites you about being a makeup artist? Who are some of the people you admire in the field? This is a chance to share your enthusiasm for your profession.

## What Are You Doing Now?

Here, the employer wants to know if you're currently in the business and, if so, whether your current duties and responsibilities match those of the position you're applying for. Explain how your current role relates to the job you are applying for. Also remember to mention any current volunteer experience that relates to the job.

## What Kind of Position Are You Looking For?

With this question, the employer is trying to get a feel for whether you are a good match for the position he or she is hiring for. Stay positive and focused on the job description. "A position that offers growth possibilities and a different challenge every day," is a good option.

## What Experience Do You Have With _____?

Depending on the company, the interviewer may want to know about your experience with a certain aspect of makeup artistry, customer service, working in teams, supervising, juggling many projects at once, and other things. Give specific examples from your experience. This is your opportunity to show that you know your stuff.

## What Are Your Strengths and Weaknesses?

Focus first on naming your strengths—that's usually easier. Think about the duties and responsibilities of the job, and answer accordingly. For instance, "My ability to figure out what people want, even when they don't know themselves. I'm fairly intuitive."

Avoid talking in terms of weaknesses. Instead, turn the statement into a positive one, by pointing out a personal goal you'd like to meet or an achievement you'd like to earn.

For example, instead of saying you have trouble managing your time, you could state that one of your goals is to take a time management seminar to make sure you are maximizing your potential. That answer tells the interviewer two things. First, you have the strength of character to recognize a weakness; and second, you have the will to do something positive about it.

## Where Do You See Yourself in Five Years?

Sometimes employers ask this because they want to know whether you are looking at their company for long-term employment or simply a short-term job until something "better" comes along. Other employers want to judge your ability to plan for the future. Most employers do not want to hear that in five years you hope to be retired or plan to start your own business. "In five years, I'd like to hold a position with responsibility and respect in this company," is a good answer.

## How Do You Feel About Overtime?

Depending on the type of makeup work you are applying for, overtime and odd hours may be a requirement. As the prospective employee, you need to know how much overtime the company would be asking for and decide whether you're willing to make that kind of time commitment. This is a personal question, but obviously the right answer is unbridled enthusiasm for extra work.

## Behavioral Questions

Also be prepared to answer behavioral questions. These are questions that ask you about an experience you had in the past and require you to answer with a specific real life example. The interviewer might say "Tell me about a time you experienced conflict with a coworker. What happened, and how was it resolved?" The interviewer won't be satisfied with a hypothetical answer about what you "would" do in such a situation.

They want to hear about an actual time you experienced conflict. The purpose is not to see if you have ever had a conflict (they expect you have); the purpose is to see how well you resolve difficult situations and, if something didn't work out in the past, what you learned from it. You can expect to hear behavioral questions such as:

- Describe your most successful makeup project so far. What did you do to make it a success?

- Describe a project where something went wrong. How did you solve it?

## Do You Have Any Questions For Us?

"Yes!" is the appropriate answer here. Take your time and do some research so you can ask very pointed questions. Interviewers want an interview to be interactive, not just with them sitting behind a desk talking about how great the company is. Some standard questions you might ask are:

- Will the work consist of consultation, application, or both?

- Am I expected to sell certain products?

- Will I be provided with all the tools I need to do the job?

- How many clients would I generally see in an hour?

- What are you looking for in an employee?

- What opportunities are there for growth or continuing education here?

- What is it about your company that differentiates you from your competition?

# 4.4.5  Discussing Salary

One of the touchiest questions that may come up in an interview situation involves salary expectations. Employers will often want to know right from the start what kind of pay you are looking for to rule out anyone who is completely out of their price range. If you are the first one to mention a specific salary figure, and it's lower than the one the employer had in mind, you risk getting hired for less than they might have been willing to pay you.

If at all possible, avoid discussing salary during a first interview. If the potential employer asks you about salary expectations, it is perfectly acceptable to be polite but vague. Saying "I'd rather wait to discuss salary until we both have a better idea of how I would fit this position," or something similar can help you get out of a sticky spot.

The second interview is a better time to discuss salary. Ideally you will receive a formal job offer, and you can use that as your negotiating point. If there is a certain range of compensation that you feel you must receive, be up front with the hiring manager without being demanding.

According to the Bureau of Labor Statistics, the median annual earnings in 2002 for salaried cosmetologists, hairdressers and hairstylists, including tips and commission from products you recommend, ranged from about $13,000 to about $35,000.

The median annual earnings in 2002 for salaried skin care specialists, including tips and commission from products you recommend, was about $22,000. With a specialty in makeup application, you could potentially charge a premium on top of these amounts, and take tips and commissions into consideration.

## 4.4.6  Following Up

It is imperative for you to write an immediate follow-up letter thanking the person or people you interviewed with for the chance to be considered for a position.

Send the note even if the answer was no. Consider the experience a chance to have made a contact in the trade. Even in large metro areas, the beauty business is small and personal. Also keep in mind that a kind note is evidence of a positive attitude—the kind of thing that is remembered when someone does have a job opening.

Your note should do three things:

- Thank the interviewer for their time

- State whether you do or do not wish to continue the interview process

- Make one final pitch as to why you're the right person for the position

---

## Sample Follow-Up Note

Kay Forrest
123 Evergreen Ave.
Gardenfield, MO 12344
(816) 555-5555
kforrest@emaildomain.com

February 19, 2005

Mrs. Christy Berg
Millamont Salon
425 Westfield Plaza Centre
Kansas City, MO 12345

Dear Christy,

It was a pleasure to meet with you yesterday and talk about employment as a makeup artist at Millamont Salon. I appreciate your taking the time to explain the routine at the salon. As we discussed, I'd be willing to begin as an assistant and work my way up.

If your salon's needs change and you find that you do have an opening, even in the future, I hope you'll keep me in mind and contact me: 816-555-5555.

Meanwhile, many thanks for the opportunity to meet with you.

All good wishes,

Kay Forrest

---

# 4.5 Success on the Job

Suppose you ace the interview and get the job. What do you do now? Your best, of course! Don't get discouraged if you have to start as a part-time assistant and prove yourself. Approach an assistant's job with a positive attitude and a long-term outlook.

As Marvin Westmore explains: "Be handy, and willing to go beyond your basic job. If your job is makeup and the trash basket is full, take it out."

Also, when you are new, don't broadcast your inexperience, advises makeup artist Florence Johnson. You've got to hit the ground running as a pro, whether you are stacking makeup or applying it. "Nobody wants to have somebody there who might not know their business. At a beauty-school demonstration if something goes wrong, the instructor can straighten it out. But not in the real world," says Johnson.

If you are working as a representative of a particular cosmetics line, say, at a cosmetics counter in a department store, not only will you know your products and their attributes, but you'll also be able to suggest which ones will work best for your client.

Pay attention to the client's comments, and explain how your products will help them solve their beauty problems. If she complains of dry skin, for example, tell them about the benefits of your cosmetic line's moisturizing products. If she wants a long-lasting lip color, explain which lip products can meet her needs. The more you experiment with your own products, and the more makeovers you do, the more comfortable and familiar you will feel recommending specific products for specific needs.

Remember, a makeover at a cosmetics counter is meant to familiarize a client with your cosmetics line, so be sure to share your knowledge freely. If a client ends her makeover with a big purchase, so much the better. But keep in mind that some clients like to think this kind of thing over for a while, so if they don't appear ready to purchase anything at the time, don't push. Simply give them your business card and invite them to call on you anytime should they have questions. Chances are they will, and they will think of you when they're ready to invest in new cosmetics.

Here are some more tips for excelling in the workplace:

- Speak up. If you want management to be watchful of career opportunities where you are working, you must make them aware that you want to advance. Don't be shy about your accomplishments, but don't brag about them either.

- Be highly visible. Make sure the management team knows who you are.

- Find someone with more experience than you and learn from them. If they're good at what they do, there are reasons for it.

- Don't settle for the status quo. Being creative will get you noticed.

- Take on more responsibilities. Become the expert on at least one aspect of your job.

- Always present the highest quality work ethic. Be early, stay late, and solve problems.

- Start or continue to take classes that keep your skills up to date, and let your supervisor know you're doing so.

# 5. Starting Your Own Business

As a self-employed makeup artist, you can work with private clients and enjoy freedom and the potential to make a higher income than you might earn as an employee in a salon, spa or portrait studio. The information in this chapter will give you resources and information to get started.

## 5.1 Getting Started

Starting your own business is a thrilling thing to do. Your enthusiasm should carry you through to doing your own research as well as reading this guide, as the topic is a complex one. You want to be sure that you are ready to take this big step. Here are some articles and checklists that you might find helpful to help you figure out if running a business is right for you.

- *Start-up Basics: Are You Ready?*
  **www.sba.gov/starting_business/startup/areyouready.html**

- *Business Start-Up Assistant (Canadian)*
  **http://bsa.cbsc.org**

On a practical level, your business plan will help you decide the right time to start your business. It will help you determine if you have enough funds set aside to support yourself while you get the business up and running. No matter how skilled you are as a makeup artist, you can't count on having lucrative, quick-paying, repeat clients the very first week!

You may find over the course of your research that your thoughts change about how you will set up your business. For example, you may have been planning to just do makeup for weddings and other events, but you find that most of the customers who come into the store are looking for both makeup and hairstyling services. This may lead you to hire staff to do hair so that you can provide both services. Be open and flexible in your planning and allow for shifts in thinking.

## 5.1.1 Creating a Business Plan

Creating a business plan involves putting on paper all the plans you have for your business. Basically, the main body of your business plan will be divided into these four sections:

- a description of your business

- your marketing plan

- your financial plan

- your management plan

In addition to those parts, your plan should include the following appendices:

- an executive summary

- supporting documents

- financial projections

- a cover sheet

- a statement of purpose

- a table of contents

If the idea of writing a business plan sounds overwhelming or confusing to you, hang in there. We'll take a closer look at each of these parts.

## Description of Your Business

A description of your business is just that—a description of the business you plan to start and operate. The trick is to include the unique and special things about your business so that everyone who reads your business plan will know you're on to something really unique and exciting.

You'll need to state in this section that, as a makeup artist, you'll be operating a service business. Don't be afraid to get specific about the types of services you'll be providing. If you're going to specialize in makeovers, for example, state that in your description. If you're going to focus on makeup for weddings and other events, include a little information about what those areas involve, and don't hesitate to point out why your services are important. The idea is to paint a picture of the business you plan to start.

You should also explain what the legal structure of your business will be. Will you have a sole proprietorship, for instance, or perhaps a partnership? You'll learn more about legal structures a little later in this chapter.

Also in this section, you'll need to explain why your business will be profitable and how your makeup artistry business will be different and better than any others in the area. What do you plan to offer that will have clients beating down your doors, begging you to be their personal makeup artist? What is the current need for the service you want to provide?

Describe your business hours. As a makeup artist, you may need to have flexible hours to accommodate the schedules of your clients, but if you plan only to work from 10 a.m. until 2 p.m., three days a week, you should make that clear. You should also identify the planned location of your business, the type of space you'll have, and why it's conducive to your business.

Conclude the description of your business by clearly identifying your goals and objectives, and supporting them with information and knowledge you've acquired about being a makeup artist. This is important, because it's here that you're explaining exactly why you're starting this business, and what you hope to accomplish with it.

# Your Marketing Plan

Your marketing plan must address the following areas:

## Your Clients

The most important elements of a good marketing plan are defining your market and knowing your customers. Knowing your customers is important because it allows you to identify their likes and dislikes and tailor your services to accommodate them.

You don't want to limit yourself to a market that is too narrow—that can limit the scope of your business once it's underway. For example, if you're going to specialize in makeovers, your market should probably be all women over the age of 13, not just one age group, unless that is your "angle" that makes your business stand out from the rest. Your marketing plan should paint a picture of a wide and ready market that is just waiting for you to do your makeup artistry magic.

## Competition

All businesses compete for customers, market share, and publicity. So it's smart to know who your competitors are and exactly what they're doing. To provide services that are different from and better than those of your rivals, you need to evaluate your competitors' products and services, how they're promoting them, who's buying them, and other information.

## Pricing

You'll learn more about setting fees later in this chapter, but know that you should address this issue, at least briefly, in your business plan. This section should consider factors such as competitive pricing, costs of labor and materials, and overhead.

## Your Market Strategy

You'll need to think about how you'll advertise your business, making sure that whatever means of advertising you choose accurately portrays the image you want to convey. Have a budget in mind, or at least set percentages of your income that you'll invest back into marketing the business.

## Your Financial Plan

Your financial plan should describe both your start-up costs and your operating costs, and then show how you are going to make a profit. The start-up budget includes all the costs necessary to get your business up and running. Operating costs are ongoing expenses, such as advertising, utilities, and rent.

Remember to include the following items in your budgets. Notice that some expenses on the start-up and operating budgets overlap.

### Start-up budget

- Legal and professional fees

- Licenses and permits

- Equipment

- Insurance

- Supplies

- Advertising and promotions

- Accounting expenses

- Utilities

- Training expenses

## Operating budget (First 3 to 6 months)

- Salaries

- Insurance

- Rent

- Loan payments

- Advertising and promotions

- Legal and accounting fees

- Supplies

- Utilities

- Dues and subscriptions

- Taxes

Experts suggest that it takes at least a year for a new business to begin to make a profit, which means that if you're just starting out, you should plan to live on your savings or other income (not from the business) for at least six months while your business is getting off the ground.

# Your Management Plan

No matter how big or small your business is, managing it requires organization and discipline. Your management plan should be carefully thought out and written and should address issues such as:

- Your background and business experience and how they'll be beneficial to your makeup artistry business

- Assistance you expect to receive (financial help, advice you receive, or other forms of aid)

- The members of your team (even if you'll be the only member)

- The duties for which you and any employee or employees will be responsible

- Plans for hiring employees, either now or in the future

- A general overview of how your business will be run

# Appendices

As mentioned earlier, your business plan should also include:

- **A cover sheet**. This identifies your business and explains the purpose of the business plan. Be sure to include your name, the name of the business, and the name of any partners, if applicable. Also include your address, phone number, email address, and other relevant information.

- **Table of contents**. This goes just under your cover sheet and tells what's included in your business plan. Use major headings and subheadings to identify the contents.

- **Statement of purpose**. This is important because it summarizes your goals and objectives. A statement of purpose should sum up your current and future plans for the business.

- **Executive summary**. Basically, this is a thumbnail sketch of your business plan. It should summarize everything you've included in the main body of the plan.

- **Financial projections**. This should give readers just an idea of how much money you'll need to start your business and how much you expect to earn. Remember to back up your projections with explanations.

- **Supporting documents**. Include your personal (and business, if applicable) tax returns for the past three years, a personal financial statement (get a form from your bank), and a copy of a lease or purchase agreement if you're going to be buying or renting space.

## Resources for Further Study

A good business plan will require some time and work on your part, but it's really essential to getting your business off on the right track. If you make the effort to draw up a good plan now, you can be confident that it will pay off in the future.

A business plan doesn't have to be overly complicated, and there are some good models available that you can use as guides. Many entrepreneurs use the Small Business Administration's business plan outline as a model. The Canada Business Service Centres (CBSC) also provides a sample business plan.

- *SBA: Business Plan Basics*
  **www.sbaonline.sba.gov/starting_business/planning/ basic.html**

- *CBSC: Sample Business Plan*
  (enter the site then look under "Session 4")
  **www.cbsc.org/osbw**

- *Creating an Effective Business Plan*
  **www133.americanexpress.com/osbn/Tool/biz_plan/**

## 5.1.2 Start-Up Funding

If you begin your business as a makeup artist in your own home, your start-up costs can be relatively low. Other than the makeup supplies and products required in order to do the job, there isn't much you'll have to pay for. However, if you are starting a storefront business you will have many expenses, which means you will need some working capital until the fees from your clients begin rolling in.

While you may be successful right from the start and exceed your own expectations, it is wise to be prepared for the possibility that it may take longer than expected for your business to bring in enough to support you. A standard rule of thumb is to have six months of living expenses set aside beyond your start-up costs.

Depending on the start-up costs you calculated in your business plan, you may find you have all the money you need to get started available to you. If your own resources won't cover all the things you would like to do with your business, you will need to look for financing.

One place to look for funding is from family members. They may be willing to invest in your business or give you a loan to help get started. To avoid any misunderstandings, it's wise to get any agreements in writing even (or especially!) with family members.

If you decide to approach a bank for a business loan, be prepared. In addition to your business plan, they will want to see a loan proposal that includes these five things:

- How much money you want

- How long you want the money for (i.e. the term of the loan before repayment)

- What you are going to do with the money

- How you will repay the loan

- What kind of collateral you have (these are assets you could sell to repay the bank if you don't have enough money to make the payments)

When you prepare this document, ask for a little more money than you need. No matter how good a business plan is, most people underestimate the amount of money they need. It is very difficult to go back to the bank and get more money when you've just gotten some. You can find some additional advice about financing from the resources in section 5.1 or **www.sba.gov/starting_business/startup/guide3.html**.

No matter where you go for money, be sure you're well prepared. Have an extra copy of your business plan available for the potential lender's inspection, and be able to speak clearly and concisely about your plans and goals. Keep these tips in mind when asking someone for funding:

- **Get an introduction or referral**. If you can get someone who is respected in the community to introduce you to a potential lender, it gives you credibility and a big advantage.

- **Be prepared**. Be able to discuss all aspects of your business plan, your long-range goals and your prospective market.

- **Be professional**. Shake hands, speak with confidence, and look the person you're talking to in the eye.

- **Dress to impress**. You're going to be a makeup artist, which means you must have a sense of style. Be sure you look the part.

- **Be receptive**. Even if you don't end up getting any money from a prospective lender, you may be able to get ideas and suggestions. Perhaps the person will have some pointers regarding your business plan or some suggestions about steering your business in a particular direction. Listen to the advice, and don't be afraid to ask questions.

Remember that if someone agrees to loan or give money to your business, they're doing so because they believe in you and what you can do. When you ask someone for money, you need to sell yourself and your ideas. Make sure you have a great sales pitch.

**TIP:** When you're just starting out, you will probably not be able to get a loan, line of credit or a credit card for your business without being backed up by your personal credit history. If you have problems with your credit, you may need to find a partner whose credit is sterling if you decide a business line of credit is necessary.

## 5.1.3 Choosing a Name

Some entrepreneurs love the prospect of naming their business, while others agonize over the task. Either way, the name you choose is an important part of what your business will be, so you'll want to put some thought into the process. While you can go as simple as "Jane Doe, Makeup Artist," there are many options open to you.

### Where to Start

Experts disagree about whether a business name should be vague, allowing an image to be built upon it, or concrete and informative, allowing potential customers to know right away what you're offering them.

Most experts do agree, however, that customers like names that are meaningful and easy to understand. At a minimum, your business name should: attract customers, be unique, and be available.

If you have the financial resources, you could hire a naming professional to help you choose the right name for your company. Known as name consultants or naming firms, these organizations are experts at creating names, and can help you with trademark laws. However, these services can cost thousands of dollars. For some free advice on what to consider when choosing a business name, visit **www.yudkin.com/generate.htm**.

## Get Creative

Here are some creative names of existing makeup artistry and cosmetic firms, just to get you thinking:

- Sweet Cheeks

- She She Cosmetics

- Pout

- Face It

- Too Faced Cosmetics

- Vanity

- Shades of Hue

When you've decided on a few names that meet all the requirements, let some friends and colleagues know what you're thinking of calling your business, and ask for their opinions. The decision is still up to you, of course, but the instant reactions of "real people" can be a good indication of whether you are on the right track or not. Some people get a group of friends together and brainstorm names. If somebody comes up with a really good one, you'll probably know it right away.

## The Legal Stuff

In most jurisdictions, if you operate under anything other than your own name, you are required to file for a fictitious name. This usually just involves filling out a short form and paying a small filing fee to your state or provincial government. You can find links to the appropriate government departments for filing your name at **www.sba.gov/hotlist/ businessnames.html**.

Before registering a fictitious name, you will need to make sure it does not belong to anyone else. You can do an online search of the federal trademark database to determine whether a name has already been registered. For good advice on trademarks and other matters to consider before choosing a business name, check out Nolo.com's Small Business Resources at **www.nolo.com**. You will have to click on the "Business and Human Resources" tab; then "Starting a Business"; then "Naming Your Business" to view the relevant information.

Business names don't have to be trademarked, but having them trademarked prevents anyone else from using the same name. Trademark laws are complicated, so if you want your company name trademarked it's a good idea to consult a lawyer with expertise in that area.

# 5.1.4  Legal Structure

A business can take several different legal forms. Which one you choose will affect how much it costs to start and run your business. Basically, there are four forms of ownership: sole proprietorships, partnerships, limited liability companies, and corporations. Let's have a look at what these terms mean, and what makes sense for the type of makeup artistry business you have in mind.

## Types of Structures

### Sole Proprietorship

If you want to run the business yourself, without incorporating, it will be known as a "sole proprietorship." The sole proprietorship is cheap and quick to set up, but it doesn't afford some of the legal protections of a corporate structure. You can report your business income on your personal tax return.

One drawback to this type of business is that you are personally liable for any debts the business incurs. If you are running a personal makeup service from your home, this is likely to be the appropriate choice.

## Partnership

If you want to go into business with someone else, the easiest and cheapest way is by forming a partnership. This might involve teaming up with another makeup artist, or other professionals who provide image services, such as a hairstylist. You could also plan to team up permanently with a photographer in a partnership arrangement. With this structure, both you and your partner are legally responsible for any debts of the company.

Partnership is all about communication. You may want to have an attorney set up a legal partnership, spelling out what each partner contributes to and takes out of the business. Talk with your partner and come to some firm conclusions about the points below. When you have agreed upon all points, put them into a written "partnership agreement" signed by both of you, which should cover:

- What tasks each of you will be responsible for

- How you will make decisions, and how you will resolve disagreements

- What percentage of the business each will own

- How you want the business to grow in the future

- What expectations you have of each other

- What happens if one of you wants out of the arrangement

## Corporation

You can incorporate whether you are working alone or with partners. Incorporation can protect you from being personally liable, and may make your business appear more professional to some clients.

However, it usually costs several hundred dollars to incorporate, and there are many rules and regulations involved with this type of business structure. Among other requirements, corporations must file articles of incorporation, hold regular meetings, and keep records of those meetings. Most new business owners consult with an attorney before incorporating.

### Limited Liability Company

A Limited Liability Company is a relatively new type of business legal structure in the United States. It is a combination of a partnership and corporation, and it is considered to have some of the best attributes of both, including limited personal liability. Talk with a lawyer to find out if a LLC is right for you.

## Registering Your Business

Once you decide on what form of legal structure you will use, you'll need to register it by filling out some forms and paying an annual license fee. Contact your municipal or county office for more information about registering your business, or check out the information on business licenses at the Small Business Administration's website mentioned earlier in this section.

Retail businesses that collect sales must be registered with their state's Department of Revenue and get a state identification number. All businesses that have employees need a federal identification number with which to report employee tax withholding information. If you are self-employed, you'll pay a self-employment tax to contribute to your Social Security fund. Contact the Internal Revenue Service or Revenue Canada office in your area for more information.

### Licensing Resources

Here are some websites to check out for more advice about structuring your business in the "starting a business" section at **www.nolo.com** or:

- *Proprietorship, Partnership, or Incorporation? (Canadian)*
  **www.cbsc.org/osbw/session5/busforms.cfm**

- *Quicken: Incorporate Your Business Online*
  **http://quicken.incorporating.com**

## 5.1.5 Insurance

Sit down with an insurance agent and determine what kinds of insurance you need—and don't need. Professional makeup artists advise that you at least take out some form of insurance on your makeup kit, and your portfolio of work, especially if you haven't created a back-up of it. A portfolio can take years to build, and seconds to lose. Make sure all risks are covered, including it being lost or stolen while you are out.

**TIP:** While you can replace a makeup kit's contents, arranging to replace photos or tear sheets can be downright impossible in some cases, so you should also put your name, number and a cash reward notice in the front of your book. Sections 4.3.3 and 6.2.1 on Your Portfolio have more advice about keeping your work safe.

Also be sure to ask an agent about your auto insurance if you'll be using your personal vehicle for business purposes. If you're liable for damages in an accident that occurs while you're working, your business could be at risk. Ask about special coverage that protects your business in those types of circumstances. Other types of insurance to ask about include:

- **Liability Insurance.** Laws regarding liability change all the time, so be sure you get the latest information regarding them from your insurance agent. Nearly all businesses require some kind of liability insurance. If a client has a skin reaction to a product you used on them, you'll be glad you have this in place.

- **Property Insurance.** If you're working from home, you probably already have this type of insurance, although you should check to make sure it covers all your valuables. If your business will be located in a building other than your home, you may need an additional policy. If you rent space, you'll need property insurance only on the equipment you have in your office, while the owner of the building should pay for insurance on the property.

- **Disability Insurance.** If you become sick for an extended period or otherwise disabled, your business could be in jeopardy. Disability insurance would provide at least a portion of your income while you're not able to work.

- **Business Interruption Insurance.** In the event that your property or equipment is damaged or destroyed, this type of insurance covers ongoing expenses such as rent or taxes until you're up and running again.

There are other types of insurance, and many different levels of coverage are available for each type. An insurance broker (check the Yellow Pages) can advise you of your options and shop around for the best rates for you. You can also check out the National Association for the Self-Employed (**www.nase.org**) which offers reasonably priced insurance plans for self-employed people.

## 5.1.6 Taxes

Most experts will encourage you to consult a good accountant or tax lawyer to walk you through the complicated path of business taxes. You'll be taxed differently depending on the structure of your business.

- If you're a sole proprietor in the United States, you'll be taxed as an individual. You'll simply file a Schedule C with your personal tax return. You might be eligible for investment tax credits and other tax advantages, so you definitely want to talk to someone who can tell you exactly what you're entitled to.

- Partnerships are taxed the same way as sole proprietorships. The income or loss from the business is passed on to the partners, who include it on their personal tax returns.

- Corporations pay taxes on earned profits.

If you're a sole proprietor with no employees or pension plans, you don't need to have an employer identification number, which is used for tax purposes.

Partnerships and corporations do need such numbers, for which you'll need to fill out IRS form SS-4. You'll also need to file a form to figure out how much social security tax you'll pay. An accountant can help you with all of these steps. Canadians need to work out how much they pay to the Canada Pension Plan.

If you're used to working for someone else, you may be in for a bit of a surprise concerning the social security tax. When you're employed, your employer pays half of the tax and you pay the other half. When you're self-employed, however, you need to pay the whole thing, and it can be daunting. You'll need to figure in the extra tax when you set your prices. If you have employees, you'll have to pay half of their social security contribution, plus withholding taxes and perhaps federal and state unemployment taxes.

You are required to charge state or provincial tax on all taxable purchases, and in Canada, you are required to charge GST on many goods and services as well. Your state or federal government's small business office will help you with this, and will explain how you go about making your regular payments of tax collected to the state and federal agencies that require them.

You will also need to deduct income tax from your employee's paychecks, and pay that amount to your state, provincial and federal government. And of course you'll need to pay income tax for yourself, too.

Here are some websites to visit to help you learn more about taxes.

- *Canada Revenue Agency*
  **www.cra-arc.gc.ca/menu-e.html**

- *Internal Revenue Service: Small Business/Self-Employed*
  **www.irs.gov/businesses/small/index.html**

- *Canada Business Service Centres*
  **www.cbsc.org/osbw/session5/taxes.cfm**

# 5.2 Setting up Your Business

Now that you are aware of some of the logistics of starting a business, it's time to think about setting up shop.

## 5.2.1 Choosing a Location

The location you choose will be based on the type of business you are planning to run. If you are starting small with limited funds, working from home will likely be the best option. In most cases, you will be required to go "on-site" to do your makeup application, such as to a client's home, hotel room, etc. so you might not even need a home office in many cases, though it will be smart to have some space available for if and when you need it.

Obviously, this is a service that a salon or spa can't easily provide, which is an advantage for you. You can also choose to rent space out of a salon or spa, where you would service their existing client base as well as your own, or set up a storefront of your own. Let's look at the pros and cons of each.

## Work Out of Your Home

When you are just starting your makeup business, you may choose to work out of your home for several reasons. It is cost-effective, and working from home allows you to start small and build your clientele gradually. Working out of your home also gives you the option of balancing a family life with your work.

Another big plus: you can deduct from your income taxes a percentage of your mortgage payment and property taxes (or rent) and a share of utilities and maintenance costs. There are various methods for determining those calculations, but by far the easiest—and most acceptable to the IRS—is to use an entire room for your business and to use it for no other purpose.

In the United States, IRS Publication 587 has information on how to compute the calculation and file the deduction. It is available online at **www.irs.gov/publications/p587**. You can also see section 5.1.6 of this guide for more information on taxes.

When deciding to set up a home-based business, make sure you have all the space you will need to conduct business. You will need:

- A large desk, preferably with enough space for a phone, your computer, catalogs of makeup and accessories, and plenty of writing room

- A comfortable and appropriate chair for clients to sit in while you apply their makeup

- Storage space for supplies and tools, like an airbrush

- Proper lighting to view your makeup application

- Room to expand to accommodate a part-time assistant or perhaps a bookkeeper

- A couple of guest chairs, and, if space and money permit, a conversation or waiting area with comfortable chairs and table to consult with clients before the makeup session begins

Remember that you're starting a makeup artistry business—not an accounting firm. Have some fun with your space, and make it warm and inviting. Here are some tips for creative and economical decorating:

- Be creative with fabric for curtains. Make coordinating pillow covers, or have someone make them for you.

- Create a mood with lighting. Soft light from table and floor lamps is much more appealing than fluorescent lights (although be sure you have the lighting you need to apply makeup!)

- Look for one-of-a-kind items, such as a great vase or candle, to create interest and give your office a focal point.

- Choose a couple of nice pieces of art for your walls.

- Add some personal items, such as interesting photos or the candy dish that's been handed down to you from your grandfather. These items give warmth and personality to your space.

- You'll need to have a filing system to keep track of your clients, but that doesn't mean you need metal or heavy oak filing cabinets. Check out secondhand furniture shops for filing alternatives.

You should also consider any local zoning laws that might be in place. Most areas won't have a problem with a home-based business that adds only a few cars a day to the street, but most will prohibit you from posting any kind of sign. To find out the rules in your area, look up "zoning" or "planning" in the local government section of your phone book.

## Work Out of a Salon or Spa

Booth rental salons or spas arrange with self-employed image service providers for them to work out of their retail space. As a makeup artist in this situation, you will work alongside nail technicians, hairstylists and estheticians. You rent a "booth" and pay rent weekly or monthly to the owner of the space.

You provide your own makeup supplies and tools, and set your own rates, becoming a subcontractor within the salon. The renting makeup artist keeps all the money from the services he or she provides, minus the rent payment.

The benefits of this kind of arrangement include getting walk-by clients or at least the notice of passers-by, and client-sharing with other image service providers. It is less risky than opening your own storefront right off the top, and can be a good way to build a clientele if you would like to open your own makeup service shop one day.

There are many salons that offer this kind of arrangement. Here are some considerations when choosing one. Make sure you get any agreement with the owner in writing!

- Do they offer a one or two week free trial period? Many salons and spas will give you a chance to "preview" the atmosphere and clientele for free, to see how you fit in and how business is in that location.

- What is the location like? Is it in an upscale neighborhood where people are more likely to need full makeup services? What is the walk-by traffic like?

- How long has the salon been in business? Does it have a good reputation?

- How much on-site storage is available? You don't want to lug in a full makeup kit every day if you don't have to.

- What is the current client base? What demographic information can the salon provide about them? Does it match your target market?

- When you meet the other contractors in the salon or spa, are they having a good day? Are they cheerful? Are they busy? Are they friendly?

- Is there anyone else at the location who typically does makeup? If so, how is work distributed?

- Can you sell makeup products to your clients?

- Is there a receptionist on site who will take bookings for you, or at least take messages? Is coffee provided? A debit and credit card machine? A suitable waiting area? A break area for you?

- Can you leave your chair empty and go home if not busy? Some salons and spas will prefer you to maintain a full-time presence, while others will be more flexible.

# Set Up Your Own Storefront

If you have the funds and the clients, you can also start a makeup service business with your own storefront. Setting up your own storefront is a good option if you want to have complete control over your business, but it's also a lot of work and involves a bigger initial financial investment. Don't let that scare you: It's completely doable, and owning your own makeup service center brings a lot of rewards.

Since there are many types of places to do business, the location you choose will, in part, determine the type of business you do. Here are a few options to consider.

Shopping mall locations offer benefits such as frequent walk-by traffic, mall promotions, marketing, mall security, a recognizable location, and plenty of parking. Drawbacks include extended hours (stores in a shopping mall are usually required to be open whenever the mall is), the relative distance a customer will have to travel to reach your shop once they leave their vehicle, and the need to participate in mall-organized promotions that may or may not fit with your own marketing plan. In addition, rents may be higher than at on-street locations.

Downtown or on-street locations offer easy access to your store, walk-by traffic, and a recognizable location, as well as the ability to set your own hours. Drawbacks include less parking, the possibility of damage or vandalism, and a less-predictable stream of customers.

Office buildings and hotels often have retail space on their main floors. Advantages include a steady clientele from the hotel or offices, in-building security, and parking. Disadvantages include less street-front visibility, and potentially higher rents.

Other things to consider when you are looking at potential locations include:

- Is it big enough to meet your needs?

- Is it so big that it will be expensive to heat or cool?

- Is it within a block or two of an established competitor, such as a salon or day spa that offers makeup services?

- Is it in an area with many homes, with residents who might be interested in having makeovers or using your services for special events?

- Is it near a large hotel, a function hall, or a church where weddings are often held?

Look for a place that is convenient to get to from your home and that gives you quick access to any services you may need, such as your bank, makeup suppliers, or even a good coffee shop. It should be a place you'll like coming to each day!

If you set up a retail space, note that you'll also need a sign to identify your business to your customers. It should be large enough to be easily read from the street or sidewalk, and simple enough to be recognized. It should announce your shop's name and perhaps have a simple image on it. Professional sign companies offer design and manufacturing. Check your local Yellow Pages under the "Signs—Commercial" category.

There are of course many more details to opening a storefront than this, including signing a lease, decorating, purchasing large equipment like chairs and mirrors, hiring staff, paying rent, keeping the books, etc. There are resources listed at the end of this guide to help you out in starting a small service business such as this.

## 5.2.2 Equipment and Supplies

If you are setting up space to apply makeup or consult, you will need equipment and supplies to run your business that go above and beyond the makeup and sponges described in section 2.1. Here is a list of considerations for your work space.

# Telephones

As a makeup artist, you will depend on your telephone, both for booking appointments and for talking with suppliers and customers. You can keep your regular line if you are a small business, but a dedicated business line will open the door to Yellow Pages advertising, which can help your business get off the ground.

You may also want a cell phone, a dedicated computer line (DSL), or a cable Internet connection. Later on, you may need an extra line for an employee or just an extra line for yourself if you find you must be on the phone with a supplier and a customer at the same time.

As your business grows, you may also find that you need to hire a receptionist to answer phones and book appointments. In your line of work, customers may quickly get annoyed if a live person isn't available to take their call.

# Fax Machine

Clients might want your rate sheets faxed to them to help them decide if they want to hire you. You may purchase or rent a fax machine. Pay a visit to your nearest office supply outlet to find out about the different types available.

# Cash Register

If you set up a storefront or are doing a lot of fast-paced business, you may need a cash register. You can find out about the different types of cash registers available by paying a visit to your local business equipment retailer. Some cash registers are stand-alone—that is, they are not connected to any online service, and you must process credit and debit card transactions separately. Some are online, which means you will have to have a dedicated phone line or Internet connection for them. Others can be connected to your computer system to allow for up-to-date accounting.

If you're just starting out, it makes sense to keep your system as simple as possible. You can always upgrade later, but investing in an expensive, possibly too-elaborate system from the very beginning can tie up money you could be using for other purposes. Some common brand names of cash registers are Sharp, NCR, TEC, Casio and Samsung. To learn more about cash registers available for sale, try the Cash Register Store online at **http://cashregisterstore.com**.

## Credit/Debit Card Machine

When you set up your business bank account with a visit to your bank's business services representative, you'll have the option of leasing a credit/debit card machine in conjunction with your account. Your bank will offer technical support for this piece of equipment and will help you make sure it's working properly.

## Computer

A computer is a wise investment, whether you want to design your own flyers or ads, generate invoices, update a website, or email portfolio images to clients. A home-based business might need your basic computer, while one for your store would likely need to have additional features and programs. The staff at a computer store or your office supply store can give you more information about specific programs and help you decide which ones are best for you.

## Digital Camera

If you want to have an online portfolio you can update with your latest work, or be able to email clients samples of past work, a digital camera will help. You can do this with a regular camera and a scanner, but you might not get the picture quality that you would with a digital camera. Prices on digital cameras have decreased and will continue to come down, so you should do a little shopping around before you buy one.

## Client Chair

This is where your client will sit while you apply their makeup. A good feature to have would be an adjustable height so you can look them right in the eye no matter how tall or short they (or you!) are. The chair should be comfortable enough for the client to tolerate long or complicated applications. Choose a chair that is easy to clean for makeup drops and spills.

# Lighting

You'll need to be able to see in fine detail when you are applying your makeup, so a variety of types of "clean" lighting (lighting that doesn't cast hues on the skin) is best, including overhead lighting, task lighting, and as much natural light as possible. You can also walk a client outside to check how the look will be outdoors if that is the purpose of the application.

# Office Supplies

Office supplies, such as receipt booklets and pens, are easy to find and can be purchased at a variety of locations. Staples **(www.staples. com)** and Office Depot (**www.officedepot.com**) are competitively priced, and may deliver if you buy in quantity. And don't overlook online shopping, which is becoming increasingly popular.

# 5.2.3 Employees and Contractors

If you're starting your business small, then you won't need to immediately deal with employees or contractors. Down the road, however, chances are you're going to hire someone, such as a receptionist, bookkeeper, or an assistant. You might choose to hire these people as employees, or you might bring them on as contractors. Let's examine the difference between the two.

# Employees

An employee is a person you hire to perform specific tasks for a specific amount of time during each pay period. You pay your employee a mutually agreeable amount of money at regular intervals in exchange for his or her services. Employees might be expensive, but when you need them and find good ones, they become your company's most valuable assets.

You may also extend benefits to an employee, such as vacation leave, health insurance, life insurance, disability insurance and retirement benefits. You'll need to pay payroll taxes on behalf of an employee, such as local, state and federal withholding taxes, social security taxes and federal and state unemployment taxes.

Regulations concerning payroll taxes, unemployment and worker's comp pay vary within the United States and Canadian provinces. Before you hire someone as an employee, it's a good idea to get some additional information concerning regulations, taxes, and other factors. For more information, visit the following sites:

- *Canada Business Service Centres*
  **http://bsa.cbsc.org/gol/bsa/site.nsf/en/su13296.html**

- *U.S. Internal Revenue Service*
  **www.irs.gov/businesses/small/**

- *U.S. Department of Labor*
  **www.dol.gov/dol/compliance/compliance-majorlaw.htm**

So how do you go about finding a good employee when you need one? Think of the same ways you would look for work, such as the classified section of your area newspaper, working with an employment service, or seeking help on an online site such as Monster.com. You may also want to consider searching for an employee through an industry association or website, such as those listed at the end of this guide.

## Contractors

Some business owners prefer to work with independent contractors rather than permanent employees. An independent contractor is a person who agrees to perform a particular job for a fee. It's understood that the contractor is not a permanent employee, and will stop getting paid when the agreed-upon work is completed or when your agreement with the contractor otherwise ends.

When you hire a contractor, you don't have to pay Social Security, unemployment taxes, or workers' compensation. This can save an employer almost one-third of the costs of a permanent employee who gets benefits.

The single most important thing to remember when hiring a contractor is to make sure you and the person you hire have the same understanding about the work to be done, when the work must be finished and how much you'll pay for the work.

Be sure that the person you're hiring is reputable by asking for the names of others for whom the contractor has worked. Never hire a contractor until he or she has signed a written agreement detailing services to be performed, delivery dates, amount of pay, and other details.

## 5.2.4  Keeping Track of Your Finances

If you are one of those people who seldom keeps track of the checks you've written, now is the time to make a change, at least as far as your business goes. Here are some tactics to use to keep track of your business income and expenses.

Open a business account at a bank, trust company, or credit union, even if you are using your own name to do business. Use this account only for paying business bills and your own salary, which you then deposit into your personal account.

Get checks that generate a carbon copy, and avoid using electronic payments. You want to create a paper trail so you are able to prove your deductions at tax time, create balance sheets that your vendors or other financial institutions may request from time to time, and see at a glance where your money has gone.

Also, keep track of your accounts receivable, accounts payable, and other transactions in a ledger book, which you can get at any office supply store, or use an electronic bookkeeping package. The most popular bookkeeping software for small business is Quicken. For under $100, Quicken's Premier Home and Business program can help you prepare invoices, manage your accounts, and generate reports from your records. You can find it at an office supply store or online at **www. quicken.com/quickensw**.

Also carry an envelope so you can keep receipts for everything you buy for the business. Be sure to file these receipts at night in the appropriate folders in your file cabinet. No matter how you design your system, make sure it works for you and that you can find receipts for anything at any time without calling in a psychic to help you figure out where you put it.

Finally, keep two additional ledgers—small enough to carry in your purse or briefcase—so you can log mileage or other travel expenses, and everything you spend during the day—but remember to keep personal and business expenses separate.

# 5.3 Marketing Your Business

If your client list and reputation are going to grow, you must be actively committed to marketing. Marie Augustine, a 35-year veteran of makeup artistry based at the chic Alex Roldan Salon in West Hollywood, California, where the clientele includes Emmy and Oscar winners, confirms this. "You can't succeed [in this business] unless you go out there and promote yourself," she says. "You can have all the tools, but if you don't have the motivation, it won't do anything for you."

This chapter looks at the following ways to promote your makeup service:

- Choosing a target market

- Assembling promotional materials

- Building a website

- Strategic partnering and networking

- Advertising

- Publicity and promotions

## 5.3.1 Choose Your Target Market

Before you start trying to sell your services to prospective customers, you should decide which types of clients you want. These are your target markets, the people who will help you establish your reputation; they will be at the heart of your marketing effort.

Novice makeup artists are often tempted to say they want any client who is willing to pay. Avoid that temptation. Instead, develop your client base around the services that are most suited to your talents and interests. Indeed, client prospects are more likely to respond positively to you if you position yourself as a specialist who understands the makeup needs of particular situations.

Some markets to consider may be:

- Teenagers/young women

- Brides

- Working women

- 40-somethings

- New moms

- Plastic surgery patients

- People with skin problems

- The elderly

Your target market will depend on the area of specialization in makeup artistry you have identified, such as makeup for special events, or for photographic portraits. For example, if you want to focus on doing makeup for weddings, you might market to wedding planners and salons that do bridal packages. We'll explain how to build these "strategic partnerships" later in this section.

Once you have decided who your target markets are, you can prepare materials and plan marketing activities that will most appeal to those groups. As you get more experience, you may decide to go after new target markets, or your business may naturally evolve to focus on particular types of clients. However, starting with some specific target markets in mind can help you focus your efforts and save you both time and money.

## 5.3.2 Promotional Materials

There are a variety of promotional tools that can help you spread the word about your new business. All of these tools should showcase your talent as a professional. Your most important promotional tools will be your business cards, your brochures, and your makeover portfolio, as well as your website, which we'll look at afterwards.

# Business Cards

Since you are in a creative industry, you have a lot more freedom in the style of business cards that you choose. Always have business cards with you to hand out and whenever you have the opportunity, tell people you meet, "I am a professional makeup artist!"

The business cards you select will help convey the image of your company, so give some thought to what you want. Your card should say enough about you to give people a sense of what you can do for them. Include your specializations, your website address so they can get more information, and consider a special offer, such as: "Call today for a free makeup consultation."

Pass your business cards out whenever it is appropriate. Give them to your friends, your relatives, people you meet at social functions, the people behind the counter at your local coffee shop, your dentist, your mail carrier. Mention that you are a makeup artist when handing out your card, so that people will look at it later and make the connection. When you send letters to people, stick a business card in the envelope. Make sure that you carry at least three or four business cards in your wallet or purse at all times.

If your start-up finances are limited, you might want to consider getting free business cards from VistaPrint (**www.vistaprint.com**). They offer color business cards on heavy paper stock, and a number of different designs are available. In return for the free cards (all you pay is shipping, which starts at around $5) they print their logo and "Business Cards are free at VistaPrint.com" on the back of the card near the bottom. If you don't want anything printed on the back, you can get their premium cards for only $29.95 plus shipping, which is still a value price. You can have a graphic artist design a business card for you with one of your images on both sides and send it to VistaPrint to get printed for little expense.

Another company that offers quality business cards and stationery at reasonable prices is Design Your Own Card.com (**www.design yourowncard.com**). The company offers templates, fonts, and logos to choose from and can have your business cards on your doorstep within a few days.

# Brochures

You can leave some brochures with the companies with which you do a lot of business, as well as mail them out or hand-deliver them to potential clients. It's a good idea to create a brochure even if your business is located in a spa or salon. That will help cement your identity with customers, and they offer a way for your customers to share your information with their friends.

Your brochure should contain your company name and contact information, including your web address. It can also include:

- A list of the services you provide

- Photographs of people you have made up (see the note on model releases below)

- The benefits of hiring a makeup artist, such as looking your best, feeling good about yourself, making sure you feel confident at an event

- A photograph of you

- Some testimonials from satisfied customers

Spend time on the copy and layout of your brochure, working with a designer if necessary. Consider using color to liven up the design of text or designs that you select. You can save money by asking for help from college or art-school students who can use your marketing project as their school project. Be sure you spell-check and grammar check everything. Also check your phone number, email address, and other contact information carefully to make sure clients can reach you.

Your brochure can be folded in three, with printing on both sides of the sheet, or you can simply print a one-page flyer that can also be pinned up on bulletin boards. If you are printing only a few copies of your brochure, you may be able to find nice paper at your local office supply store that you can run through your printer.

If you aren't able to produce brochures on your home computer, or if you need hundreds of brochures (for example, if you are participating in a wedding trade show), it may be faster and cheaper for you to have your brochures professionally printed. Check the Yellow Pages under "Printers," or use the printing services of your local office supply store.

The larger your print order, the more you save on per-unit costs, so don't be intimidated by numbers. If you're starting from scratch, you'll be surprised at how quickly you'll be able to burn through 1,000 brochures when you tally all the potential outlets for distribution, such as civic clubs, conventions, trade shows, direct-mail packages to the media, counter displays at beauty salons and health clubs, and other places.

## Model Release Form

Whenever you publish photos of your clients—whether on your website or in print—be sure to have them sign a model release form, which gives you permission to use the images in any of your promotional materials without remuneration. Most people are happy to have their image used in such a positive way, but there may be exceptions. Asking gives them the opportunity to say they'd rather not participate. Here is a sample model release form you can use.

---

### Sample Model Release Form

I hereby give (insert your name) permission to use my photograph taken of me on (insert date) at (insert location) for promotional, online or commercial purposes. I am of legal age.

_____

(Print Name)

_____

(Signature)

_____

(Date)

---

# 5.3.3 Your Website

A website gives prospective clients the opportunity to learn about your services 24 hours a day, seven days a week. It is a marketing tool that is always open for business, and with today's technology-savvy consumers, a website is often the first place a potential customer will go to get more information. Websites are relatively inexpensive to build and maintain, and allow you to update your work samples on a regular basis.

## What to Include

- Your professional bio

- A business email address to contact

- A mailing address (preferably not your home)

- A selection of images of your best work only

- Simple text descriptions of your services

In your bio, let your clients know who you are, what you do and what you can do for them like no other makeup professional out there. This is also a good place to add information such as your educational background, years in the business and other information that adds credibility to your business.

If you include a photograph of yourself to make your pitch more personal, a headshot, which is just of your face and/or shoulders, is better than a full-body shot, because it avoids situations in which the viewer might make judgments about your makeup design or abilities based on what you were wearing in the photograph.

A good way to get additional ideas for content is to visit the sites of other designers by doing an Internet search for "makeup artists".

Many makeup artists use technology on their website that shows "before" pictures "morphing" into "after" pictures, Flash design (where images move, appear, or disappear on your screen) and a portfolio of images that can be clicked on one by one to be enlarged. In an image-centered business, the look of your website matters quite a bit.

# Technical Considerations

Setting up and maintaining a website does take time, particularly if you've never done anything like it before or don't consider yourself particularly computer-savvy. If you have no idea what's involved, here's a list of what you'll need to get started:

- A modem to connect to the Internet

- An Internet Service Provider (ISP)

- A web host, to host your pages

- A domain name

- HTML software like Microsoft FrontPage to make your web pages

- FTP (File transfer protocol) software to upload your web pages from your computer to your web host

If this seems like a lot, don't be put off. Much of it can be done inexpensively, so that you can be online for less than $150 per month after your initial building and start-up costs.

Almost all ISPs offer free web hosting service. However, these usually have space limitations, and will bombard visitors with pop-up ads and other advertisements that might turn off prospective clients. For a small monthly fee you can host your site through a service company, register a domain name and get your site listed on search engines so that clients can find you. One such company is GoDaddy (**www.godaddy. com**).

You can find out about other, similar companies by visiting Webhost Magazine's website at **www.Webhostmagazine.com**. Webhost Magazine offers free, unbiased consumer reports on domain name registrars and web hosting companies. It also has a tutorial guide you can use to educate yourself about everything you need to know when it comes to the Internet and setting up a website.

Ipswitch (**www.ipswitch.com**) is the leading supplier of FTP software and provides good customer service for their product.

To get traffic to your website submit it to the most popular search engines, including Google at **www.google.com/addurl.html**.

TIP:   Include your web address on every piece of literature that you send out, your mailing envelopes, stationery and business cards.

## Hiring a Web Designer

While creating your own website can be fun and rewarding, it can also lead to some unfortunate surprises that will cost you time and money if you've never constructed a website before. For example, Microsoft FrontPage is easy to use, but some ISP software is not compatible with FrontPage, so you need to check this before you begin building your site.

Further, once the site is up and running, you're going to have to make updates. A website is never done, it merely changes form. If you're not updating your content, you're not moving forward. A simple website design and construction will usually cost you a few thousand dollars. This might be a good area to arrange to trade makeup application for services.

## 5.3.4   Strategic Partners

Referrals are a great way to get clients, and one of the best ways to get referrals is to develop a network of "strategic partners" who will refer business to you... and vice-versa. You need to approach businesses and service providers who are likely to encounter people looking for makeup services, and ask them to refer future business to you.

## Who to Contact

Some strategic partners you can approach as a makeup artist would include the professionals below. You can add to this list based on your specialization and interests, as well as the nuances of what your community has to offer.

## Fellow Image Service Professionals

- Hair stylists

- Estheticians

- Nail specialists

- Fashion stylists

- Dermatologists

- Plastic surgeons

- Other makeup artists

## Consultants

- Wedding planners

- Image consultants

- PR firms

## Media Professionals

- Portrait photographers

- Modeling and talent agencies

To find strategic partners in your area, your first stop will be the Yellow Pages. You can make a list of people or companies nearby, and then approach them to set up a meeting. A call is better than an email, which is easy to delete.

Attending industry functions is a great way to meet people and introduce yourself and your services to a large group of people. Use the tips on networking that follow this section to find diverse groups to join and network within. You can also approach professional organizations (e.g., the International Association of Image Consultants) to find out who is accredited and working in your area.

# What to Say

When you contact these professionals, explain that you are a professional makeup artist who is newly in business in the area, and ask if they have clients who are ever in need of makeup services. The answer should be yes (unless they are just not interested). Ask if they have 15 minutes for a meeting sometime soon to look over your portfolio. You should arrive at meetings you set up prepared, with your portfolio and your makeup kit in case you are asked to do an application on the spot.

If they already have a makeup artist they refer business to, it may be beneficial to find out if they ever get swamped at certain times of the year when accommodating high school proms, weddings, or the Christmas season. You could ask to be the "second" or "assistant" makeup artist they call in for back-up at their busiest times.

When you are arranging partnerships, you have to think in terms of what the person or company you are approaching might need. You can tell them:

- That you would like to help them offer added value to their service by having a talented, professional makeup artist on call.

- That you have a base of clients that is growing, and would like to be able to refer clients to them.

- That you will pay them a commission or referral fee for any business that comes through them. (NOTE: There are no firm guidelines for the amount of a referral fee. It can be whatever you negotiate with a particular strategic partner, and might be a percentage of what you earn from the referral, such as five percent to 20 percent, or a flat fee.)

- That you are available to do free makeup consultations for their clients, e.g., for four hours, once a month.

- That you will do the first three clients for free, to see if they like your work.

Once you have a network of strategic partners in place, you will save a lot of money trying to advertise and get clients, since they will largely be coming to you by word of mouth. This is one of the best and most effective ways of promoting an image service business such as makeup application, in addition to networking, as explained below.

# 5.3.5  Networking

The starving artist is poetic in books but stinks when you're living it. Finding work as a new makeup artist may seem tough at first, but once you make one good contact and continue to network the circle outward, you will be amazed at how quickly one job leads into another.

To be successful, clients need to know that an artist is out there. Two keys to networking are that it is "informal" and "mutual." This type of marketing includes meeting and interacting with people informally at social and business events.

While some of the people you meet may have an immediate need for a makeup artist or know someone who does, in many cases you are laying the foundation for future business. By establishing relationships through networking, you can be the one people think of when the holiday season comes around, or when a relative announces her engagement to be married.

## Networking Clubs

A networking club can be a great way to meet people who might be able to help you get work. Some of these clubs are general business groups, but many have a target group of clients and include one member from different industries (such as insurance, financial planning, law, professional photography, real estate, or the entertainment business).

Each member of the club is expected to bring a certain number of "leads" to the meeting each week or month. Fees vary, but they can be as low as the cost of breakfast once a week, so you may find that it's a worthwhile investment. Be aware that you may eventually be required to serve on the executive board. In addition to marketing opportunities, joining a networking group may give you access to discounts on services provided by other members of the group.

To become a member, you are usually either recommended to the group by an existing member, or you might approach the group and ask to sit in as an observer for a meeting or two and get accepted from there. Most groups will allow a trial period before demanding that you join. You may be asked to give a short presentation about your business and describe what business and personal skills you can bring to the group.

The types of participants will differ with every group, so don't settle for the first one you visit. Make sure the members represent the kind of very busy people with reasonable incomes who might become clients for you, or who would know others who could benefit from your services.

One way to find a networking club is through word of mouth. Ask people you know in the entertainment industry or at salons or spas in your area. You can also look for networking groups online. Business Network International (**www.bni.com**) has more than 2,300 chapters in cities around the world.

## Membership Organizations

Another excellent way to network is by joining associations that prospective clients may belong to. Some examples include:

- Civic and service clubs, such as Rotary Club or Kiwanis Club

- Business organizations, such as your Chamber of Commerce

- Clubs that attract the wealthy—for example, golf, polo, yachting, and country clubs

Membership fees may vary from $20, to hundreds or even thousands of dollars if you want to join an exclusive country club or private golf club. The more expensive clubs usually require current members to introduce you and put you up for membership, so you may have to join some less exclusive clubs in order to meet people who might also belong to the more expensive clubs.

Many less exclusive clubs will let you attend a few times for a nominal fee so you can decide if you really want to join. You can find organizations by asking your friends and colleagues what they are involved in. You can also find them in your local telephone directory or online. Here are a few to get you started.

- *Executive Women International*
  **http://www.executivewomen.org**

- *World Chamber of Commerce Directory*
  **http://www.chamberofcommerce.com**

- *Rotary International*
  **http://www.rotary.org**

- *Kiwanis Club*
  **http://www.kiwanis.org**

If you simply attend club functions without getting involved, the value of the membership will not be as great as if you truly pitch in. What sorts of things can you do to help out and gain the attention of others whose good will can help your business grow? Here are some suggestions:

- Serve on a committee

- Write articles for the association newsletter

- Volunteer to help out with the organization's events

- Run for election to the executive committee

## Other Groups to Consider

As mentioned earlier, there are also online industry-specific member-ship groups that may be helpful in finding clients. You can find these listed in the resources at the end of this guide.

Aspiring makeup artists can also meet with actors at theater groups. Many actors have a favorite makeup artist or two who prepare them for award shows, appearances, special occasions, and for work on the stage or film. Developing relationships with actors and models can lead to regular work in a semi-professional niche.

# 5.3.6 Advertising

While networking can be a particularly effective way to get business for your makeup business, you may also need to invest in some paid advertising, especially when you are first getting your business off the ground. Here are some possible advertising routes for you to pursue.

## Yellow Pages

You have probably used the Yellow Pages many times, but before you buy an ad for your makeup business, you should carefully investigate the costs compared to the potential return. Make sure that your desired clientele is the kind of market that would find a makeup artist in the phone book—it wouldn't be everyone's first stop in their search for a quality makeup application.

To minimize your risk, you might want to consider starting with a small display box, such as a 1/8 page ad. If you can get your hands on a previous year's edition, compare the ads for makeup artists from year to year. If you notice others have increased or decreased the size of their ads, this can give you an indication of what might work for you. Also, if you are doing informational interviews, you can ask makeup artists how well Yellow Pages ads have worked for them.

> **TIP:** Some localities also have "pages" or "books" of other types. These are limited to smaller geographic areas than, for example, a whole state or city. Check into that possibility, as well, especially if you don't want to travel great distances to find clients.

You can design the ad yourself, have the Yellow Pages design it for you, or hire a designer. If you are interested in advertising, contact your local Yellow Pages to speak with a sales rep. Check the print version of your phone book for contact information.

## Direct Mail

Your use of mailed advertising will depend in part on the operations concept you settle on. One use of direct mail would be to do a mailing of your brochure to people who have recently purchased cosmetics.

ZIP-coded mailing lists can be rented from list brokers, or you can use a list of contacts and clients that you put together yourself over time while you work at a salon or spa.

If you are running a smaller, more personal business, contact-management software is fairly inexpensive and can be programmed to alert you to clients' birthdays and anniversaries. Sending birthday and holiday notices is a mark of the personal touch associated with personal services, and if they are sent well enough in advance, you may find yourself doing their makeup for that event.

## Magazines and Newspapers

Magazine advertising can be expensive, and it usually needs to be run repeatedly to be effective. It has been estimated that many people need to see an advertisement three to seven times before they buy!

If you choose to buy advertising, it will probably be most cost-effective to place ads in small local magazines or newspapers. You can also consider local specialty magazines that cater to wealthy women, or whatever happens to be your target market.

The publications you advertise in will usually design your ad for an additional cost, and give you a copy of the ad to run in other publications. Here are some tips for effective advertising:

- Make your ad about your customers. Explain how they can benefit from your services rather than just listing the services you provide. (Saying "You will look fabulous" is better than saying "I can do your makeup for you.")

- Make them an offer they can't refuse. Your ad should describe a service or special promotion that makes you stand out from your competition. It should also include a call to action (i.e. saying "Call today" or including a coupon that expires by a certain date).

- Make sure you're available for people who respond to your ad. If someone wants to talk to you but keeps getting your voicemail, they may give up.

- Make long-term plans for your advertising program. Chances are that running an ad once won't give you as much business as you would hope. Develop a long-term advertising strategy and stick with it.

# 5.3.7 Publicity and Promotions

When a business gets publicity in a magazine article, newspaper story, radio, or television talk show, it can result in a tremendous amount of new business. Here are some ways makeup artists can get publicity for free.

## Press Releases

A press release is a brief document that you submit to the media (print, TV, radio, and online) in order to gain publicity for your business. Editors prefer to see a press release as a single page (under 500 words) and written as if it were a news story.

Most magazines and newspapers publish contact information for their editors. Newspapers may have dozens of editors, so make sure you send your submission to the appropriate one. For example, you would probably want to contact the Business Editor for launching your new business, and the Lifestyle Editor if your specialty is doing makeup for wedding parties.

Here are some tips for writing a good press release:

- Make sure the press release is newsworthy. For example, you could write about a new trend in makeup that all the celebrities are wearing.

- Give your press release a strong lead paragraph that answers the six main questions: who, what, where, when, why, and how.

- Include your contact information at the end of the press release so reporters and readers can get in touch with you.

You can find numerous online resources to help you write a press release including *Inside Secrets for Writing the Perfect Press Release* at **www.publicityinsider.com/release.asp**.

---

## Sample Press Release

For immediate release
October 15, 2005

### Makeover Expert Available

Expanding on the success of her personal makeup business and makeover parties, makeup artist Patricia Bryant of Sexy Salon in Wichita, KS is now available for expert commentary on personal appearance and skincare issues.

"The explosion of media attention to grooming is nothing short of phenomenal," says Bryant. "Every time an episode of *What Not to Wear*, *Extreme Makeover*, or *Queer Eye for the Straight Guy* airs, we're inundated with calls from women who have decided to get serious about their presentation."

Bryant reports a significant rise in calls from younger people. "We help them individually or in group settings," Bryant says. "We find that the more we explain, the more questions they have. It's important to give them good information."

Bryant is available for interview by telephone and is willing to appear in broadcasters' studios. Use the email address or the telephone number below to contact her.

Sexy Salon is located at 15552 Hill Street, Wichita, KS 99999, 000-000-0000; email: pbryant@sexysalon.com.

### ###

---

# Write an Article or Column

One of the best ways to establish yourself as a makeup expert is to write articles or a column for a newspaper, magazine, or newsletter. While it can be tough to break into large daily newspapers, there may be an opportunity to write for smaller newspapers or local magazines.

You could write on any topic related to makeup or makeup application, or you could volunteer to answer reader questions. The length and frequency of your column will depend on the publication's needs. You might produce a weekly 500-word column for a local newspaper, or a monthly 1,000-word column for a newsletter or magazine.

Remember to give your readers real information. This won't detract from the value of your services at all. Those who use the information and never call you would never call you anyway. Those who call you will do so because you enticed them—you gave away a little of what you know, and enticed them with how much more you could do.

You will probably have to write the first column or article and show it to the editor, or as an alternative to writing an article, you could call the editor or send him or her a brief "pitch letter" to suggest an idea for a story. If you want a few pointers on writing pitch letters, visit the Publicity Insider site at **www.publicityinsider.com/pitch.asp**.

Make your pitch letter as interesting as possible. To do that, you'll have to provide a hook—the element of your story that will be of interest to readers. For example, you might suggest that the publication do a story about how giving a makeover to a single mom down on her luck helped her feel great about herself and enabled her to get a job. Then follow up a week later with a phone call to see if they are interested.

While it is not necessary to submit photographs to a daily newspaper editor (most newspapers have their own photographers), photographs may help attract the editor's attention. They might also be published in a smaller magazine, newspaper or newsletter that doesn't have a photographer on staff. If you send photos, remember to make sure you have signed model releases from the people in the photos as well as the photographer's permission.

## Television and Radio Talk Shows

If you've always wanted to be an on-air personality, here's your chance. The best shows for makeup artists to appear on are morning and afternoon talk shows, as well as shows that cover celebrities, which tend to run in the evening.

Phone the appropriate producer at the local stations and let them know that you would be happy to appear and provide your expertise for their audience. You will probably be asked to send some information; this is where your promotional materials come in handy.

After you've sent them or dropped them off, give the producer a couple of days to look them over and ask for an appointment. Producers are often bombarded with local folks who think they have something to say, so be sure to use your best "hooks" to grab the producer's attention.

Make your pitch touch on events that are going on in the community, or seasonal or global happenings that are timely. Offer a makeup twist on a traditional topic—is it January 1st? You can suggest how a professional makeover can be part of a New Year's resolution. Get creative, and be persistent. It might be your tenth pitch that works, after the first nine are ignored with not a phone call.

## Give a Speech

You may be able to connect with group members and get new business by being a speaker at a breakfast meeting, luncheon, or workshop. The topic you speak on can be anything related to makeup artistry that members would be interested in. For example, a women's group might be interested in hearing tips on the differences in applying makeup for day wear and evening wear.

While you probably will not be paid for your presentation, it can be an excellent opportunity to promote your business. Your company's name may be published in the organization's newsletter, it will be mentioned by the person who introduces you, you can distribute business cards and brochures, and you will be able to mingle with attendees before and after your presentation. You may get a free breakfast or lunch too!

To let people know that you are available to speak, contact the local community organizations mentioned earlier in the section on networking, and ask friends and acquaintances if they belong to any groups that have presentations from speakers.

If you feel your speaking skills could be better, there are a couple of relatively painless ways to get comfortable talking to large groups. You can hire a speaking coach, or you can join Toastmasters, a national organization that helps people develop their speaking skills. To find a Toastmasters chapter near you, you can check your local phone book, call their world headquarters at 949-858-8255, or visit **www. toastmasters.org**.

## Teach a Class

Teaching a class can be a great way to earn extra money, establish your reputation, and meet prospective clients. You don't have to have a degree to teach adults—just lots of enthusiasm and knowledge of your subject.

The first step is to review the current catalog of continuing education courses offered by local colleges, high schools, and other organizations that provide adult education classes in your community. Call and ask for a print catalog or ask if the classes are posted online. Once you have reviewed the current list of courses, come up with some ideas for new classes that aren't already offered. (They already have instructors for any courses that are in their catalog.)

Once you have an idea for a new course, call the college or organization and ask to speak with whoever hires continuing education instructors. They will tell you what you need to do to apply to teach a course.

## Do Workshops or Makeover Parties

If you'd like to start presenting makeup events to people, consider designing and putting on a group event, such as your own workshops or seminars, or makeover parties.

You will need to choose a date and time (evenings are usually best) and a location, such as a meeting room at a hotel or conference center, or a private home. You will then have to decide how much to charge, if anything. For workshops, consider making the fee comparable to other continuing education courses offered in your community.

When preparing your marketing materials, remember to focus on communicating all the benefits of attending. As well as the information, benefits of attending may include: a fun night out, a chance to network, or personal advice from an expert. Other information you might include in the marketing materials for your course or parties are:

- Who should attend

- When and where the event will take place

- Your credentials

- Testimonials from past clients

- That attendance is limited (you can only handle so many people at a time!)

- How to get more information, including your phone number and website

- A call to action such as "Book now!"

Brochures with this information can also be used to market group events to the public. The ideal brochure is one that can double as a poster that you can post around to get publicity.

Keep your events enjoyable and informative, and ask attendees to spread the word, or offer a referral discount for full service makeup business. The hostess should also get a discount on a full-service makeup application in the future. You can also consider partnering with other image professionals to put on a full "makeover" event that includes makeup, hair and wardrobe advice, complete with a photographer to take a picture of the results.

## Trade Shows

If you specialize in doing makeup for weddings or other special events, you may be able to find prospective clients at public trade shows such as bridal trade shows. Renting a booth at a trade show to market yourself can be an excellent way to find clients. Be sure to bring along your portfolio, and consider doing a few free makeovers to show off your talents.

The cost to be an exhibitor will vary depending on the particular show, the location, the number of people expected to attend, and the amount of space you require. It may range from as little as $50 to $1,000 or more. To cut costs, you could partner with another non-competing exhibitor and share a booth space.

Before investing in a trade show booth, attend the event if possible or speak to some past exhibitors. While you may find a $100 booth at a wedding show is a good investment to market yourself as a makeup artist, $1,000 spent on an industry trade show booth could give disappointing results. (Trade shows are often used to raise awareness rather than generate immediate sales.)

When setting up your booth you should bring business cards, your company brochures, and your portfolio for display at your booth. When you speak with prospective clients, talk about your approach to doing makeup. For instance, at a wedding expo, you might talk about a time when you helped put a bride completely at ease on her wedding day and relate how thrilled she was with your work.

To arrange consultations and discuss possible bookings, bring an appointment book or calendar of events you already have on the books. This information is very important to know if you are a one-person operation and have already booked jobs for the coming months.

You can find out about upcoming shows by contacting your local convention centers, exhibition halls, or chamber of commerce. Many shows now have their own websites and provide registration information as well as site maps and logistical information.

TradeShows.com (**www.tradeshows.com**) lets you search for events by industry, type of event and location. For most events, you can then click on a link to find out contact information. Here are some links to bridal expos, some of which may be in your area:

- *Great Bridal Expo*
  **www.greatbridalexpo.com/default.asp**

- *Wedding Day Expositions*
  **www.weddingdayonline.com/shows/welcome.htm**

- *Brideworld Expo*
  **www.brideworld.com/events.htm**

- *Northwest Wedding Showcase*
  **www.nwweddingshowcase.com/weddingshowcase/**

- *Bridal Show Producers International*
  **www.bspishows.com**

# 5.4 Working with Clients

If you've been effective at your marketing efforts, you'll start getting calls for work. This section deals with turning client prospects into paying clients... and then getting paid.

When you work with private clients you are most likely to be doing it for one of two reasons. First, the client may be looking for makeup for a special occasion, such as a wedding or prom, or for a glamorous portrait or promotional headshot.

Alternately, the client may be looking for consultation on everyday makeup. Perhaps they are new to wearing makeup, are bored of their current look, or have recently had plastic surgery and want to know how to show off their new features. In some cases the client may have had an injury or developed a skin condition that they want to learn to camouflage. In any case, this involves teaching the client a bit about how to use the products themselves.

## 5.4.1 The Initial Consultation

Whether the person you're meeting with is a potential client, you need to be both personable and professional. The first contact may come by telephone. If you're at a salon or a retail outlet, you can take the call and set up the appointment. If you're a sole proprietor and don't have any support staff, you're probably used to answering with a simple "Hello." But you will get a professional edge if you get into the habit of answering with your name, as in, "Pat Bryant, good morning."

Be prepared to answer questions about your services, such as whether you do aesthetic makeup, body makeup, or other work, and your fee structure. Your immediate objective is to set up a meeting to make a presentation of your portfolio, though you may be asked to send samples of your work in advance. Confirm a definite follow-up date while you're still on the phone, and send out any requested information in a timely manner.

For individual clients, you may have to meet at their homes. Try to get as much advance information about what the occasion is, when your service will be needed, and so on so you can be prepared for the meeting.

You don't necessarily have to show up in a suit and heels, but you should not dress too informally either. Bring your portfolio or laptop so you can show the prospect your credentials and track record. Let the prospect talk, and ask clarifying questions, as detailed below.

Not only will the answers to these questions help you determine what type of makeup style to apply, but answering them will also help your client feel at ease and will help you develop a rapport with each other.

If for some reason the meeting doesn't result in a commitment, you should still send out a follow-up letter thanking them for the meeting and wishing them the best. The prospect may still turn into a client at some future time.

## 5.4.2 Makeup for Special Occasions

Doing makeup for a special occasion is an opportunity for you to help a client look and feel her best, giving her the confidence to fully enjoy her special event. Your role as a makeup artist in this situation is to determine the most flattering application for your client's particular look and style. You should strive to enhance and flatter the person's natural appearance, bringing out her own beauty and diminishing any flaws her face might have.

In many cases, and especially with bridal work, it is a good idea to do a test-run of the makeup application in advance of the event. This gives you and the client time to come to an agreement on a look, or try a few looks she can choose from. You can charge a consultation fee for this test-run, or build it into your overall price. We'll go over setting fees later in this section.

For makeup for a special occasion, ask the client:

- What kind of makeup do you usually wear?

- Do you want to try something different from your usual? How different?

- Do you want a subtle look or a dramatic one?

- Will the event take place during the day or at night?

- What do you plan to wear?

- How will your hair be arranged?

- Will you be indoors or outdoors?

- Will you be photographed before or during the event?

For most special events, it is especially important that you pay close attention to skin tones and colors, ensuring the makeup looks as natural as possible, because your client will be in close proximity to others, so their makeup will be viewed from close up.

When you do makeup for special-event photography, you will need to talk with both the client and the photographer before you get down to work. You will need to find out what type of film the photographer is using, whether he is using any kind of filter on his lens, and what the lighting will be like. In general, soft, subdued lighting is used for glamorous effect, while more direct lighting is used for an energetic or character effect. Here are a few more tips to keep in mind:

- Be on time—the time for the event will be fast approaching, and your client may already be stressed out or nervous

- Know in advance how many people you will be making up

- Ask about skin and coloring in advance so you can bring the right products

- Find out if you will be working alongside a hairstylist

- Get them comfortable—offer sips of water, especially if the application will take a while

- Ask to see a photo of the dress and veil, as well as the bridesmaids dresses

- Find out what the groom is wearing

- If possible, do a "test run" of everyone's makeup in advance, and take notes of the products you used

## 5.4.3 Doing a Makeover Consultation

Often, a client will come to you seeking your expertise about what sort of look might work best for him or her. These individuals might be searching for an entirely new look or simply want to enhance or fine-tune the look they already have.

First and foremost, you will want to determine what the client is hoping to achieve through a makeover or makeup application. The person's answers to the following questions should help you learn what they are looking for.

- Why are you seeking makeup advice?

- What types of makeup do you usually wear?

- What are your favorite makeup brands and products?

- Which celebrities, actors, or musicians wear makeup well, in your opinion?

- What part of your current look are you happiest with?

- What part would you most like to change?

- Are you hoping for a dramatic change or a subtle one?

- How would you describe your personality?

- What are your favorite colors and styles to wear?

Makeup artist Florence Johnson cautions makeup artists not to go overboard in accommodating the bad aesthetic judgment of clients who may have an idea of what they want—but an idea that won't serve them very well and that they won't like if you follow through on it.

"You have to be the professional," she says. "Try to find out the clients' image of what they want, but do something that is going to conform to their face. You're not a maid. You've got to have that attitude. We're going to tell you what's good. We're the pro."

## 5.4.4  Setting Your Fees

When you work with private clients, you can charge your clients hourly, or by the service. Which you choose is up to you, and depends on what your market will bear. When it comes right down to it, the only rule is that you can't charge more for your services than clients believe they are worth. Some markets may be willing to pay a makeup artist $500 an hour, while others wouldn't go over $50 an hour.

You need to consider what your competition is charging for similar services. It's best to stay in the same range as your competitors, unless there's something about your services that sets them apart from those of other makeup artists.

You'll also need to think about the kinds of profits you want to make, and how many hours you are likely to work in a week. Remember that you need to make enough money to cover your expenses and pay yourself enough to live on. If you are only working 8 hours a week, and you need $400 a week to live on, you need to charge a minimum of $50 an hour, plus expenses.

## Charge by the Hour

Setting an hourly fee is usually based on a profit margin you have in mind. You need to cover the cost of the product you will use, a percentage of the overhead of your business, as well as an hourly rate for your talent and time.

For example, you could charge $15 per hour for a flat product fee, $10 an hour for your overhead (all the items in your expense budget, as explained in section 5.1.2), and $40 an hour for your time and expertise, for a total of $65 an hour. Of course, you wouldn't explain it to clients this way, but that's how you would come to a figure. If you want, you can bill clients separately for the products you use, and leave them with the client at the end of your application.

One drawback of charging by the hour is that when clients know they are paying for your time, they may expect you to hurry up AND do a great job. As an artist, you'd prefer not to have someone breathing down your neck while you do your thing.

Although there are fluctuations beyond these ranges, most consultation professionals charge anywhere from $40 to $200 an hour.

## Charge by the Service

Many makeup artists who work with private clients set a rate sheet for certain services they perform frequently. For example, you might charge for each of these services shown below.

| Sample Fees | |
| --- | --- |
| **Service** | **Fee** |
| Initial Consultation | $50 |
| Bridal Makeup | $200 |
| Bridesmaids | $100 |
| Glamour Makeup | $100 |
| Makeover Party (up to 5 people) | $500 |
| Consultation Only | $50 per hour |

Although these fees are reasonable in some markets, they are listed only as an example. You will need to find out what such services go for in your area by contacting the competition and requesting their rate sheets, or visiting other makeup artists' websites to compare.

## 5.4.5 Arranging Payment

Regardless of what rate you set your fees at, you want to be sure that you'll get paid in a timely manner. Unfortunately, many small-business owners find that collecting what they're owed can be challenging, even downright unpleasant. The most important thing is to arrange for payment before you perform any service.

### Type of Payment

You should know that being able to accept credit cards comes with a price. You'll pay either a percentage of every credit card payment, or a monthly fee, depending on what arrangements you make. Still, many clients will expect to pay with credit cards, and it could jeopardize your business if you're not able to accept them.

To accept Visa or MasterCard, you will have to work with a bank to get an account set up, or you can check out an online site, such as Yahoo!

Small Business which can get you set up with a merchant account at **http://smallbusiness.yahoo.com/merchant**. You can also accept payment through PayPal at **www.paypal.com**.

Personal or business checks are another method of payment, and generally a safe way for you to get what's owed to you, provided you see some kind of identification.

## Writing an Invoice

In most cases, you will get paid for your services right away. However, sometimes you may need to bill a client. To do this you need to create an invoice, on which you'll list the services that have been provided, the agreed-upon fee for the services, and other pertinent information.

---

### Sample Invoice

**(Your Letterhead)**

**To**:         Carla Client
123 Main Street
Sunday, California 91234
(678) 555-1234
carlaclient@clientmail.com

**Date**:      March 1, 2006

**Basic Fee**:  $100 per hour

**Services**:   Makeup consultation (1.5 hours) =   $150

**Products**:   One tube of Sacha lipstick =       14

                                   ————

                        **Total Due**:   **$164**

Payable immediately on receipt

---

Also include special payment instruction, such as that payment is expected within 30 days.

If a client doesn't pay within the time requested on the invoice, you can send another invoice, noting that payment is expected with a shorter time, perhaps five or 10 days. This gives your client a reminder and a chance to quickly make the overdue payment.

# 6. Freelancing as a Makeup Artist

Who hires freelance makeup artists in the professional media? Lots of people, fortunately! You'll be approaching:

- Key makeup artists

- Makeup department heads

- Photographers

- Artistic directors

- Fashion designers

- Modeling agencies

- Celebrities

- Magazine beauty or fashion editors

- Ad agencies/companies

- Production companies

Finding work in media and the entertainment industry is a matter of persistence and patience. "You need calloused knuckles, cauliflower ear, and multiple faxes," explains Marvin Westmore, a member of the legendary Westmore makeup family in Hollywood.

It's true—finding work in this business may require you to make dozens or even hundreds of telephone calls, and you may need to start out working part time, a day here and a day there, or even providing makeup services for free under certain conditions. And even when you land a great gig, chances are it will be a short one, then it's back to looking for work. However, this is the type of work most makeup artists aspire to. It's challenging, rewarding, and puts you into daily contact with the exciting world of Hollywood, top models, and other celebrities.

This chapter is your guide to finding professional work, by first building a great portfolio that will get you noticed, then approaching the top photographers, fashion designers, agencies and unions who will launch your career on its way to stardom.

# 6.1 Getting Ready

Are you ready to start pursuing a career applying makeup for the professional media? Only you can say for sure, and you will want to do some self-assessment. This type of work frequently involves travel, and could require that you move to Los Angeles, New York, Vancouver, Toronto, or some other major center, as the small towns just don't have movie shoots and fashion shows every day. For these reasons, it is best if you have a nest egg of money tucked away, and have the freedom to follow the jobs if you want to do this kind of work.

If you think you are ready, it's time to start getting some professional experience. Your portfolio cannot be made up of bridal work, student films, or photos of your girlfriends... you've got to have professional quality work to show potential employers.

In the age-old conundrum of needing experience to find work, but needing experience to get experience, the makeup artist industry has found a unique solution. Makeup artists frequently arrange with photographers, modeling agencies, or the models themselves to work for free, in order to build a portfolio of work that will lead to paying gigs. This can be accomplished by testing, arranging TFP (free work in exchange for prints), working with small or independent companies, or assisting other makeup artists. We'll explain how the process works in this section.

# 6.1.1 Testing or Test Shoots

Testing refers to the process where new models are tested out in their first professional photo shoot. It is usually arranged between a modeling agency and a photographer. If the photographer later sells the work for publication, the model (and the agency) will get a portion of the payment. So essentially they are "testing" the new model's talent and marketability with a test shoot.

Here's where you come in. Since the photos are being taken on spec and neither party may ever get paid for them, agencies and photographers hire makeup artists who are willing to work for free to build their portfolio. Your ultimate goal would be to get tear sheets (published work) as opposed to just photographs of your work, which establishes your credibility. But any kind of experience is usually worth your effort.

In most cases, you will be hired for testing work by a modeling agency or a photographer, but you could also be enlisted by other contacts you've made: hairstylists, fashion stylists, or the actual model working on the shoot. Building a web of contacts in the industry you keep in touch with will help you get tipped off to future projects.

## Who to Test With

You will want to test with a variety of photographers and models in order to get a portfolio that reflects a broad range of work. Even within this range, try to have a coherency that reflects your style and your work.

To find modeling agencies and photographers to test with, start with the Yellow Pages. You can also check the same talent directories you would list yourself in, which you can find links to in section 6.2.4.

You will approach these professionals the same way as if you were looking for an informational interview, or even for paid work. You can send an email or make a phone call and explain that you are looking for testing work. If they are interested, set up a meeting to view their previous work (or models who work with them) and to discuss the terms of the arrangement. If they are too busy to meet with you but still seem interested, direct them to any samples of your work you have online, or offer to send them a digital portfolio.

In most cases, you will be working with a reputable agency and photographer, but to protect yourself, make sure you have a contract in place that stipulates how many photos you'll get for your portfolio, what size, and if you'll get a cut or at least a credit if the photos are sold.

## How Long Will it Take?

While it is an incredible career advancement tool, building a portfolio by testing is not a quick process. Professional makeup artists advise that it can take up to two years to build an impressive portfolio by testing. Of course, you can start this process part time before you commit to a full time career as a makeup artist. You can also speed up the process of getting experience by finding or arranging Time-For-Print (TFP).

## What About Film?

If you want to work in film and television, you'll go through a similar process building a reel, or set of clips from productions you've worked on. These days, you'll want it in a digital format. You build a reel of work by approaching small production companies, independent filmmakers, and local or public access TV stations about working for them for free.

According to makeup guru Marvin Westmore, filmmakers who are on very tight budgets sometimes contact makeup institutes seeking makeup students who are right out of school.

A recent online ad posted on the site of the Independent Film Project called for a crew for wardrobe, hair, makeup, props, set designers, and production assistants who "must be savvy and willing to work without a budget." Translation: No salary, and lots of hard work.

Westmore says that such projects are very common. "You get no money for them," he explains. "[Just] a credit here, a credit there. You take a low-paying job, and work your way up from there." You can read more about building a reel of work in section 6.2.3.

# 6.1.2 Time-For-Print (TFP)

TFP is an arrangement between a model and photographer, and sometimes a makeup artist, hairstylist and fashion stylist to take photos for mutually beneficial reasons. The model usually wants to get professional quality photos for her portfolio, while the photographers are often looking to try new ideas or test new equipment. Both the model and photographer get to keep copies of the photos, and agree that they can both use them for self-promotion. Thus, they are exchanging the model's "time" for the photographer's "prints".

The artist and stylists are the "middlemen" that make the shoot possible. They might be hired by either the photographer or the model to provide makeup and styling services for the event. While TFP is most common in print work, makeup artists who want to work in film will go through a similar process with actors and filmmakers to build a "reel" or videotape of their work.

If you can't find TFP work, a makeup artist can also approach models and photographers to arrange their own TFP for the purpose of growing their portfolio. If you are arranging or paying for the shoot, you should have a reasonable level of creative control, so use this to your advantage. Don't get caught up taking traditional head-shots or far-away shots you can't use—have your photos tell a "story" in a series of frames. Change clothing, change locations, and be creative with your ideas, so when you put them together they will be eye-catching and unique.

## How to Find TFP Work

You can look for TFP work by approaching models and photographers, and asking if they ever do TFPs, or have some set up. Realistically, it will be easier to set up TFPs with photographers and models who are just starting out, but try to get the best ones you can, so you get good quality photos. If they have an artist already enlisted for this type of work, you can ask if you can be on site to assist him or her.

To find models and photographers, use the talent directories listed in section 6.2.4. You can also state on any talent directory listing you put up that you are available for TFP, so that they can contact you as well. Contact information for photographers and modeling agencies is also listed in section 6.3.

To find up-and-coming photographers, you can also try contacting the local college's photography students, but be sure to see a portfolio of work first so you don't waste your time on someone who won't be able to produce portfolio-quality shots.

Also, beware of photographers who seem to do little else than TFP work. Not being able to publish their own work is a sign that this is not a professional "photographer", but someone who likes to meet and take pictures of models as a hobby. This is not the kind of work you want to present, and could put you and your model into contact with dangerous or undesirable people.

The Worldwide Alliance of Makeup Artists has a bulletin board where makeup artists can list themselves available for TFP projects. Others in the industry can advertise for makeup artists to do TFPs with them. Visit **http://groups.msn.com/WorldwideAllianceofMakeupArtists/ jobstfp.msnw**. You can also find some international work (most of the work is UK-based) at **www.whoistesting.com**.

## Create Your Own TFP Work

To do this, you would still contact models and/or photographers. Write to or call them and politely inquire whether they would be willing to arrange a TFP with you, and refer them to any previous work you have available. It is up to you whether you want to arrange TFP projects with up-and-coming people in the industry, or find ones who are already established, as there are advantages and disadvantages to both.

If you work with established individuals, you will probably have to pay them their usual day rate, and might also be responsible for hiring anyone extra you need to do the shoot. The trade off is that you will get top-quality prints or clips, good-looking models, and someone who won't skip town with your prints. They might be harder to convince to work with you, though.

If you work with someone else who is just getting started, you may be able to arrange to work for free and get your prints in exchange. In rare cases you might even get paid. However, be forewarned that you might then be working with B-quality models, or a photographer who doesn't know how to use lighting properly, or a filmmaker who is doing a cheesy piece of work.

## How to Find Good Help

To convince a legitimate model or photographer to be a part of your TFP project, you have to let them know you are professional and organized, and speak in terms of what benefits them.

Think about what each person might be motivated by. To get a model on board, he or she needs to know that your photographer does good work. Have one lined up, and direct him or her to their website, or list their credentials. They will also be happier if there is a good chance the work will be printed, or that it will help them make contacts and advance their career. They will also want prints for their portfolio, so if this is possible, let them know.

To convince a photographer to work with you, try approaching someone who does a completely different kind of photo work, but is well respected in that area. It's a long shot, but they may be harboring thoughts of changing specialties. You could also ask if they have areas of their portfolio they feel are out of date, or if they have any new equipment or techniques they want to try out.

A photographer might also be motivated to work if you've lined up a professional model, or even a new model who is talented and beautiful, but as yet undiscovered.

Here are some more tips to getting good models and photographers without having to pay, or pay much.

- Research their work in advance to see what kind of work they do, and if it is not in line with the project you have planned, offer to do a bit of both. Maybe you want some up-close head shots, but your photographer does themed body shots. Arrange with the other parties to do both in one day, and you both get what you want.

- Know what you have in mind before you contact them. Have a concept or unique idea for the shoot, so they can see it complementing their existing portfolio. Set time parameters, too: half day, full day, or a few hours, how many shots you think will be taken, and how many prints you'll need.

- Have as many of the other details arranged as possible, such as a location tentatively booked, other team members (hairstylist, fashion stylist, model, photographer) ready and in place. If they feel like they have to do all the work, you won't get to do the project.

- Ideally, it would be great to have a buyer lined up for the pictures, although this might be tough for you to arrange yourself. Everyone is looking for a tear sheet they can add to their published work. If you get any leads on photo projects that might pay, jump in and offer to arrange everything yourself, and then you don't have to ask the other team members to work for free.

## Pitfalls to Avoid

TFP work is a great way to get experience in makeup artistry, but you can also waste time and money working with the wrong people. Horror stories abound of the model who never showed up, the fashion stylist who showed up with only two outfits—both in the wrong size—and the photographer who never gave anyone the prints. Make sure you do your homework by:

- Looking over their previous work

- Asking questions about the shoot if it's not your own (location, purpose)

- Asking for pictures of the models in advance

- Asking for references

- Asking what you are going to get in return, and when

- Making sure you will get to see and choose from all shots taken

- Asking for a deposit before you do any work

If everyone plays their part well, you will get great pictures. If one person in the team tries to outshine everyone else, it tends not to make for good pictures.

There is an excellent article online at **www.makeupmentors.com/html/tfp.php** about pitfalls to avoid in this practice, such as blemished models, irresponsible or untalented photographers, and adult/pornography work (unless this is your niche). It includes a list of questions to ask the person who hires you for the project. At **www.makeupmentors.com/html/testingform.php** you can find a sample contract for all parties involved to fill out if you arrange things yourself.

## 6.1.3  Assisting Other Makeup Artists

Your initial contact with future employers is likely to come in the form of assisting established artists. You might refresh the makeup, clean brushes and run errands. While the pay is usually not high, this is a good way to break into the makeup business, particularly for print work. You will learn invaluable lessons about lighting, makeup application and "shoot" politics.

And you may even get paid! Pay for assisting usually ranges from $75 to $300 a day. The "star status" of the makeup artist you are assisting affects your day rate, as does the client you are working for, but the connections you make and the information you glean about lighting, technique and work environment make assisting a plum job no matter the day rate.

### Why You Should Be an Assistant

Being a good assistant can help kick-start a career. This job gives aspiring artists an opportunity to experience what the job is like without the pressure of doing everything alone. It's also a wonderful opportunity to learn from a senior member of the profession, so ask a lot of questions.

A capable assistant will establish a reputation and can work for many different artists. If the assistant is talented, these key artists may begin sending work to him or her. Every makeup artist has a time in their life when they get a double-booking. Since they can't be in two places at once, guess who they're going to recommend? Their talented, trustworthy, hardworking assistant.

One of the contributing authors for this guide, Todra Payne, got her first celebrity job because an artist she assisted on several projects had two celebrity bookings for the same time. "She called me and told me step-by-step how to do the makeup the client liked. The celebrity trusted me because of the good things her regular artist told her about me," Payne says.

"Whenever the other makeup artist was not available, the celebrity always called me. I got to meet her family, hang out in her house, and even give input on the color choices for her kitchen! It was a nice little gig every now and again in addition to my other work."

## What an Assistant Does

It's rare that an assistant will get to create a look or even touch a face beyond applying powder on their first or even second time assisting a star makeup artist. Your duties will vary depending on the number of people needing makeup. With music videos there are so many people that you may get to do extras or you may be assigned powdering duty. Below is a list of things you will be asked to do as an assistant.

- Running to the store for last-minute products

- Applying lotion, self-tanner, glitter, etc. to models' arms and legs

- Prepping models' or actors' faces with moisturizer

- Powdering on set

- Cleaning work area and makeup brushes

- Staying behind on the shoot to powder while the lead makeup artist rushes to another booking

- Packing and unpacking the artist's kit on travel jobs

When you arrive at the job, introduce yourself to the lead makeup artist, and allow him or her to introduce you to the rest of the team. If it's a runway show, everything will be fast-paced and hectic so don't take it personally if the makeup artist is quick in explaining the look you are to copy and which models are yours.

> **TIP:** When assisting another makeup artist, use the opportunity to talk with the photographer's assistant who is probably putting together a portfolio of his or her own work. This is a great way to find work with someone who is showing promise in the field!

Try to determine how comfortable a makeup artist is with having you "around". Some would prefer if you were in the background cleaning brushes and getting coffee. Others will want you at arm's length when needed. If you're not sure, ask, but always have the supplies you need on hand, in a hip apron for quick and easy access.

## Finding an Artist to Assist

Finding a makeup artist to assist is relatively easy if you are in a fashion Mecca like New York or Los Angeles. The joke in New York is you can throw a rock in any direction and hit a photographer, and the same can be said about makeup artists. But you don't want to assist just any makeup artist; you want someone with star power. She or he has to be working consistently and doing the major gigs, like national fashion magazines or runway shows for top designers.

Top makeup artists are found at agencies like Celestine in LA and Jed Root in New York. (You can find a list of agencies to contact in section 6.4.3.) Take a day trip to your local bookstore and sit down with every major fashion magazine from *W* to *Vogue* (along with a cappuccino) and do your research.

On the editorial pages near the center of the magazine, there will be fashion spreads—these are not the advertising ads. Look in the folds of the magazine and you will find a little treasure: the names of the team that worked on the shoot. It will say something like "*Makeup: Clare McShane for Trilese*".

Pay attention to the artists and the agencies that are credited numerous times. These are the agencies with the connections to keep their artists working. Try calling the top agencies on your list and ask if any of their artists are in need of an assistant.

**TIP:** In New York, the best time to call agencies is just before the 7th on Sixth fashion shows. Every artist who has secured a spot as the makeup artist on a designer's runway show will need at least five assistants to help create the look on 20-30 models. Those are good odds!

Some of the agencies may ask you to come in. If you have a portfolio, bring it with you. Dress slightly trendy but not too crazy. Look professional; nothing overtly revealing or sexual. Resist acting like a diva or bragging about how great you are as a makeup artist—they are looking for someone who can take direction and fade into the background if necessary.

The agency will keep your contact info on file, but it doesn't hurt to call about once a week and ask if they have any openings. Once you get a "yes", get all of the details about who you will be assisting, time, place, and who the client is, and follow the tips on being a great assistant that follow this section.

You can also try to get assistant work from any networking contacts you have made. If you meet with or interview a makeup artist you respect and find you "click with" right away, you can conclude or follow up your meeting with a request for work. Ask if they would be willing to take on an assistant, and make it clear that you are willing to do menial or even unrelated work in exchange for a chance to help them on the job. If they don't have any work, ask them for a referral to someone who does.

If they tell you to keep in touch for future work, call every so often, but not to the point of pestering them. Take cues from how they respond to determine if you might assist them in the future. If they aren't willing to share their time, someone else will be!

There is also a website called Makeup Mentors that offers on-the-job training for aspiring makeup artists under the guidance of established and successful artists. This free program provides lists of assistants and mentors. Artists looking to become assistants can sign up at **www.makeupmentors.com**.

## Expert Advice

Emmy-award winning makeup artist and contributing author Eva Jane Bunkley explains what an up-and-coming makeup artist can do to convince a big-league pro to take them on as an assistant:

> To convince someone to take you on as an assistant you must have the attitude of a servant. Not in a bad way, you just must be willing to take the passenger seat, even if you feel that you are a better 'driver'. There is nothing worse than someone who is supposed to be assisting trying to take over in front of a client. You have to be humble.
>
> You must also be reliable (which includes being on time) and trustworthy. There is a proper etiquette to follow when assisting that includes not trying to promote your own business on a job that you got through the artist that you are assisting. You should absolutely never give your information to the client without the approval of the artist that hired you to assist them. That is both rude and back-stabbing.
>
> Be teachable—able to take instruction, even if you don't agree. Take on a role of submission, as this is a part of professionalism as an assistant. Carrying another artist's bags should not be beneath you if you truly want to be of help to them.
>
> Let that artist know: "I don't expect to be paid," "I will be as quiet as a church mouse, I just want to observe you," and, "I will help you in whatever way I can!" Of course, never do anything that is outside of your code of ethics or will make you appear negatively in the eyes of the client.

# 6.2 Promotional Materials

While you are gaining experience working for free in the makeup industry, you should also be acquiring prints, clips, or even programs from shows with your name on them. You will use these images and clips to build your promotional materials from, and use them to find and keep yourself in work. Your main promotional materials will be a portfolio, a comp card, and if you are doing "live" makeup, a demo reel of clips.

# 6.2.1 A Professional Portfolio

A portfolio is an 11x14 or 12x15 presentation folder that has between ten and fifteen full-page photos of your professional or published work. You'll use your portfolio to show anyone who is interested in your work what you are capable of. It takes a few years to build a solid portfolio that will get you steady work as well as respect in the industry. While you may have a portfolio of bridal or makeover work from earlier in your career, this kind of work is not sufficient to get work in television and film or fashion.

## It Must Be of Professional Quality!

This is important, as many people in the industry will be unable to get past the look of an amateurish photograph to see the great job the artist did on the makeup.

## What Agents and Clients Look For

An excellent portfolio that will catch an agent's or client's eye has great images that show the artist's creativity and a wide variety of makeup techniques. There should be images involving different ethnicities and skin types and tones as well. This will show that an artist can do a wide range of makeup requirements, and help you avoid being "typecast" for only one kind of work. Ideally they will be published work, and you can say where they appeared.

Photographs also need to reflect the artist's knowledge of what is going on in the business. Agent Mary Goodman from the Seattle branch of Celestine Agency suggests that artists should know what is currently in fashion as well as the classic looks that are popular. This keeps an artist marketable. Artists should not necessarily copy what they see in magazines or catalogs but rather emulate the spirit of what is being done and expand on it. This means an artist must work on as many different jobs as possible.

> TIP: If you have worked (or plan to work) in different media, you may want to have different portfolio books for each of them. For example, you might have one book of print ads, one book of runway work, and a digital file of film and/or TV work you've done.

It is important to update your portfolio continually as you work on different projects. When styles become outdated, they should be removed. Never include "fair" or "okay" pictures just to fill the book. A portfolio tells clients what a makeup artist considers to be his or her best work— you don't want to send the message that "average" is the best you can do.

As mentioned earlier, once you have put together a portfolio that you are happy with, consider insuring it, and try to get duplicate copies of tear sheets and photographs the first time around. You will be out of work if you lose this proof of your ability.

You can carry your portfolio in your pocket or on a laptop—in digital form. If you scan your photos and put them on a CD, you can leave it with prospective employers for them to review at their convenience. Make sure that the photos are scanned at a high-quality resolution, and are not full of lint, etc. Another cheaper option is to prepare a comp card, as explained below.

## Resources

The Internet is a great resource for aspiring makeup artists when it comes to creating a portfolio. Many successful artists have websites that display their portfolio pictures. You can visit these sites to get an idea of the images that are working in other artists' portfolios.

- *Award Studio Media Makeup*
  **www.mediamakeupartists.com/artists/bookings.asp**

- *The Portfolio Network*
  **www.theportfolionetwork.com**

## 6.2.2 "Comp" Cards

The images in your portfolio can also be made into leave-behind promotional cards, often called "comp cards" (short for composite) or "promo cards". The advantage of a comp card over a business card is the amount of space that you have to display your craft and thereby, sell yourself as an artist.

The cards have an attention-grabbing image (or a few) along with the makeup artist's contact information. Comp cards frequently have two sides, portraying one striking image on the front and three or four more on the back. These cards can be left behind after meetings with agencies, studios, producers, agents, and photographers. They can also be sent out or displayed for advertising and self-promotion.

The size of your card can range from the size of a large postcard to 4 1/4" by 5 1/2" (half the size of a letter-sized sheet of paper) to a folded 8 1/2" by 11". They are generally printed on cardstock, and can be glossy or matted. Your comp cards should be in color so that prospective clients can see your makeup color choices. The goal of your comp card is to display your very best work and give your contact information. It should not appear cluttered and your makeup should be flawless!

Your comp card can show a variety of looks but your main photo should represent what you want to be known for most. For instance, if you are wanting to work in print and film, you want a clean beauty shot on the front of your card. If you work in a variety of areas, you may want to have more than one comp card printed. You may also want to show different ethnicities to demonstrate your versatility as an artist. You can show the dramatic and the fantasy as well, but remember a good makeup artist knows when to pile it on and when not to as well.

> **TIP:** Don't waste space on your comp card by showing full body and 3/4 shots like a model would. You deal in faces only, and your images should be close-ups of faces.

It is perfectly okay (and expected) to have computer-enhanced or retouched photos on your card. A good graphic artist will be your best friend! Their prices can range from around $30 to $60 per hour, but they are worth every penny. Some photographers will retouch photos before they even give them to you, so always ask if they do. With so many photographers shooting digital now, a lot of them are well versed in PhotoShop.

While the front of your comp card should have at least one image, your name, and perhaps your contact information and specialty, the back of the card should include some more detailed information. In particular, it's a good idea to add a short bio that details your unique approach to makeup artistry. Other information to add to your comp card might include:

- A list of photographers and/or celebrities you have worked with

- A list of media your work has been featured in

- Your website and a short paragraph on what viewers will find there

- A list of any training you have been through or awards you have received

Don't choose a font that is too fancy—your name and contact information should be clear and easy to read. Having a voicemail number that does not change and always contains your current contact information can keep you from losing jobs due to change of home or cell phone numbers. Check with your local phone company to see if they offer this service.

If you are picked up by a talent agency to represent you, they may have a specific format into which they will incorporate images that you provide them with.

It is good to have both business cards and comp cards. Comp cards are more expensive to print, so you may be more selective as to whom you hand them out to. But the more you put into the hands of the right people, the more business that you are likely to generate.

You can also leave some of your comp and business cards at businesses that people who would use your services would frequent. Photo labs, costume shops and bridal boutiques often have display areas near the entrances to their business for just this purpose.

You can view sample comp cards online at these websites for companies that print them.

- *Comp Card Express*
  **www.compcardexpress.com**

- *Compcard.com*
  **www.compcard.com**

## 6.2.3 A Demo Reel

A demo reel is a video presentation showcasing your talents. A demo reel should be eye-catching and attention-grabbing; a combination of visual and auditory stimulation. Some clients may only look at the first few seconds, so the pace of the reel should be quick and should flow without breaks so that whoever is watching is more likely to watch from start to finish. A demo reel need not be any longer than three minutes. Around two and a half is a good length.

The beginning of the reel should start with a "slate." The slate tells the person who is viewing what they are about to see and how long it will last. For example:

> Demo reel of Jane Doe
> Professional Makeup Artist
> Time:  2:32 min.

The slate will stay up for no longer than 10 seconds; just long enough to read it. For the next two minutes and thirty-two seconds, the client will see images combined with movement and graphics and upbeat music.

A demo reel is particularly useful for a potential client who has never heard of you or had the opportunity to view your work. It can be used as a good buffer before a cold call. After you have found out who the person is in charge of choosing the makeup artist or if someone has expressed interest in you working on an assignment, a demo reel can put you ahead of your competition by bringing a sense of familiarity.

A demo reel can not only show projects that you have worked on, but you may also want to include footage of you actually working on a face. If you can hire a professional videographer, great—if not, rent, borrow or buy a digital video camera and have a friend with a good eye and a steady hand tape you working.

The video can consist of a combination of your print work that you have digitally saved or recorded using a video camera, music videos, television work, etc. Whatever you have hard documentation of can be included. Just be sure that it is your best work and truly represents your talents.

**TIP:** Try not to do things that will date your video such as saying, "Jane has been in the makeup industry for seven years." Rather, state, "Jane has been doing makeup professionally since 1999."

The editing process usually costs any where from $50-$100 per hour and can take as little as two hours or as long as two working days to produce, depending on the amount of "pre-production" needed by the editor. Give your editor tapes that are labeled and cued to where you want the footage taken. This will save the editor time and will save you money! You may also pay a little more if the editor uses a lot of time-consuming video effects in making your video. Discuss these issues up front.

Also discuss whether or not your editor will be duplicating your footage for you or if they can refer you to somewhere that will reproduce the "master copy" that the editor will provide you with.

Labels should be attached directly to the video itself, not just the cover; covers get separated! The label should state what it is, how long it is and your contact phone number. For example:

Demo Reel of Jane Doe
Professional Makeup Artist
Time: 2:32 min.
Phone: (123) 555-5555

You may want to have your reel produced in both DVD and VHS format. DVD is a more up-to-date format, but it is good to have both available. If it is a VHS tape make sure that it is cued to the slate at the beginning of the tape so that the person viewing the reel can just pop it in and enjoy. It can be frustrating to the person if they have to take time to rewind the tape.

Once you put together a good demo reel, it can serve you well for up to five years and by the end of producing it you may have spent only a few hundred dollars. Remember, this is a promotional tool to display your best work, so if your skills aren't fully developed, wait a while to produce your reel.

Continue to collect materials from each client that you will be able to include, and watch as your skills progressively improve with each face that you paint! Many insiders believe there's no need to invest in producing a reel of your work until you are being considered for a Department Head position.

## 6.2.4 The Internet and Talent Directories

In addition to building your own website as explained in section 5.3.3, many makeup artists post their resumes and portfolios online in talent directories so that work can come to them. There is usually a fee for your listing. This can be a great way to augment your job search, but should not be the only way you look for work.

Also, as the directories will be filled with competition, try to find a way to stand out from the crowd with a deluxe listing, and have a website that potential clients can click on right away to jump to your portfolio, or you'll probably be wasting your money. There are literally hundreds of online talent directories; here are a few to get you started:

- *Musecube*
  Free basic listing, additional features from $12-$260
  **www.musecube.com**

- *New Faces*
  Online portfolio for $160-$240 annually
  **www.newfaces.com**

- *Portfolios.com*
  Three levels, ranges from $10 monthly to $600 annually
  Free three-month trial
  **www.portfolios.com**

- *Resource Advantage*
  Annual listing for $12.95
  **www.rasource.com**

- *Talent Networks*
  $195-$495 annually
  **www.talentnetworks.com**

# 6.3 Where the Jobs Are

So you've got your portfolio beefed up with free jobs, and now you're looking for paid work. Where to begin? It depends on where your talents and interests lie.

By the time you are looking for paid work you will have worked for free in a variety of places, and started to get a feel for the type of work you want to pursue.

Here is some insider advice from our FabJob makeup experts on how to get a foot in the door in each of the following areas of work. Each section covers how to break in, what the work environment is like on the job, and tips to help you succeed.

## 6.3.1 Photographers

Every makeup artist eventually learns that photographers are at the top of the industry "food chain". Many clients hire photographers before the rest of the team, sometimes even before the model is chosen. Photographers have major hiring input, particularly if they are a big name like Patrick Demarchier or Gilles Bensimon.

Many photographers have a few hairstylists and makeup artists whom they are comfortable working with and trust with their models or clients. Making strong contacts with a few photographers can lead to a steady stream of work.

### How to Break In

In order to be a part of the team a photographer wants to recommend, you have to have worked with him or her on an earlier project, as an assistant to another artist or testing. If you see a photograph in a magazine that strikes you, check for the images' credits. It will tell you the photographer's name as well as the artist who worked on the model. You can also search for striking images in the photography directories listed at the end of this section.

Contact the photographer (you can often find the person's contact information by doing a search on the Internet), reference the image you saw, and offer to work on the person's next shoot for free. You may have to be persistent, but it would be worth it to have a stunning picture in your portfolio, more experience, and a good contact in the business.

As mentioned, another way to meet photographers is through modeling agencies. They compile lists of photographers they use for testing. Drop by one of the big names like Ford (**www.fordmodels.com**), Elite (**www.elitemodel.com**) or Next (**www.nextmodels.com**) and ask for their list. Most will have no problem passing along the names. Also leave a comp card if you have one, or a business card if you don't. They will pass your name along as well.

Contacting local art schools, colleges, and universities that teach photography is another way to make a connection. "You will find budding photographers before they move to New York," says makeup artist Tobi Britton. "Call modeling schools. Sometimes you have to be willing to drive to the next largest town."

Here are some directories of photographers you can search through to find someone local, and whose work reflects your own style and talent.

- *Global Photographers Database*
  **www.photographers.com**

- *Professional Photographers of America*
  **www.ppa.com**

- *American Society of Media Photographers*
  **www.asmp.org**

- *Editorial Photographers*
  **www.editorialphotographers.com**

- *Yahoo Photographers Directory*
  Includes Fashion and Celebrity, Portrait, and Weddings/Events
  **http://dir.yahoo.com/Business_and_Economy/**
  **Shopping_and_Services/Photography/Photographers**

## The Environment

Once a photographer is in the position to recommend you for a paid shoot, make him or her proud, because your attitude and talent reflects on them.

Meet with the photographer a few days prior to the shoot if possible, and discuss the logistics. Ask for a picture of the model or celebrity you will be shooting, and dialogue on the client's expectations. When the day of the shoot comes, you will be confident and prepared.

Use the extensive advice in section 6.1 on testing to prepare yourself for this environment, as well as the upcoming information on working with magazines, as the environment will generally be the same regardless of who hired you or if you are working for free.

As with other jobs, during the shoot itself you will apply, touch up and maintain the makeup. Your job is to make the person's face appear as natural and beautiful as possible. On jobs for magazines and ad agencies, photographers take Polaroid pictures or shoot in digital as a test before the real shoot begins, providing a way for you to see the results of your work immediately.

## Insider Tips for Success

- Professional photo labs post work boards where you can put one of your cards, or check for test photographers seeking makeup artists. Occasionally there will be small jobs posted on the board as well. In NYC, the photo district comprises 19th through 23rd streets between 5th and 6th Avenues. Start with Duggal's located at 11 West 20th Street. Lots of magazines and in-demand photographers use their services.

- A basic photography class can be a big help in learning what questions to ask the photographer to help you plan the correct makeup. The advice you get on lighting will be a huge help. If you've never taken a class, it's a good idea. Check out local colleges or continuing education centers for classes in your area.

## 6.3.2  Magazines

International fashion magazines are the "cream of the crop" for editorial makeup artists, with the lure of working with top models and celebrities, seeing your name in print and traveling to exotic locales.

To find work in this industry, editorial makeup artists have to be very good at what they do and have connections. Most makeup artists who are working with *Vogue, Cosmopolitan, W* and the likes have good agents who send their portfolios directly to the magazine for review. Section 6.4 will explain how to approach an agency for representation.

Getting a big-name magazine to meet with you without an agent will prove challenging unless you know someone on the inside. However, working with smaller, artsy music and alternative fashion magazines can provide tear sheets and valuable connections to someone who may move over to one of the big-name magazines in the near future.

## How to Break In

For work with smaller magazines, check out the page near the front of the magazine that tells you where the magazine's offices are located. Call them and ask to meet with the fashion or beauty editor to show your portfolio and discuss working with them in the future.

If this doesn't work, call back later and ask for contact information for the names of the photographers on their editorial pages. Call the photographer and see if you can show him or her your portfolio or test with them. They could be your "in" for work with the magazine.

There is high turnover in the magazine world, so every contact is valuable because you don't know where they will be working in six months. If you have a good connection with a smaller magazine, ask them if they know someone at one of the national magazines. You may meet the Beauty Editor for *Harper's Bazaar* because you were bold enough to ask for the introduction.

You can also try entering the magazine world through a back door. Become an editorial assistant or even a receptionist at one of the national magazines. It's not glamorous, but you will be in the industry and in a prime spot to network.

For leads on in-house work at a magazine, look at the classifieds in *Women's Wear Daily* (**www.wwd.com**) magazine.

Also, Media Bistro is a website with job listings in the media industry, including fashion magazines. You can find everything from internships to administrative positions, and degrees are not always needed. A recent job posting simply wanted someone with "good communication skills and a polished look". Doesn't that sound like you? See their job listings at **www.mediabistro.com/joblistings**.

## The Environment

Most magazine work is straight beauty makeup, nothing complicated like you would find in film. You are there to make the models or celebrities gorgeous. It's that simple.

Once you land a magazine booking, ask the magazine for a "call sheet," which will list all of the details of the shoot, from grungy rock bands to leggy Brazilian models in swimsuits. Ask to see the models' composite cards or a promotional picture so you can get an idea of skin tones and features. Find out if you'll need to hire an assistant. Will you be required to do body makeup or hair? Ask if there are any special makeup needs like glitter, glycerin, feathers, body jewels, etc.

Shoots take place in the studio, on mountains in Iceland, and everywhere in between. Studio shoots allow for more control of environment but travel shoots are adventurous and fun. And even if it rains the first three days of your beach shoot in Hawaii, you are still paid your day rate.

When you arrive on the shoot, introduce yourself to each person on the team and look at the clothing, lighting and set. Polaroid or digital test shots will be taken before the actual shoot begins to check lighting, colors, positions of models/props and so forth. Check these shots for anything that needs to be changed about your makeup before shooting begins.

Normally, you will have about 30 to 45 minutes for each model's makeup. Some makeup artists take longer, but it's to your advantage to be quick but skilled. Your workday on a shoot can be anywhere from three to ten hours. As a rule, location shoots take longer because of travel and set-up time. An eight-hour day is common.

## Insider Tips for Success

- Be prepared for questions like "do you have a nail file, nail polish remover, bandages, breath mints, etc." Most makeup artists carry such items in their kit as a courtesy, although these items are not directly related to their craft.

- Magazines have a day rate that they will quote you, but this doesn't mean you can't negotiate for more.

- Besides makeup, you may be asked to lotion or oil body parts… sometimes this gets into strange territory. If you're not comfortable with the parts needing lubrication, politely hand the cream to the model and have her or him do it.

## 6.3.3  Music Videos

Compared with movies and television, music videos are one of the newer opportunities for makeup artists. Makeup artists tend to either love doing music videos or hate it. Some of the conditions are the same as they are for television and film—particularly the 10-18 hour days—but there are other nuances of the work environment that put videos in a realm of their own.

### How to Break In

Getting work in this medium boils down to having your name out there in the major magazines and networking in the music industry. Also, many video productions are not union-regulated, so this is a good type of work to break into if you want to eventually do TV or film. Many of the makeup artists working in videos have agents that push them. So how does a "newbie" break in?

Record labels often source out the making of major music videos, so a production coordinator or producer usually makes the hiring decisions. You can find production companies using the same resources that will be listed in this section under TV and film work. Make sure that the production company specializes in music videos, though.

According to Jesse Valentine at De Facto, a hip photographer's agency that also reps makeup artists: "The way to break into videos is to assist an artist who is doing video work." Find out what agencies near you rep artists who work on musicians. Agencies will quite often list their artists' bios on their website, so make a note of any artists who list a lot of singers or bands. These are the artists you can express a preference to assist when you contact an agency.

Approaching small record labels with your portfolio and a composite card to leave behind may be the best way to get a few videos on your reel or resume before going after the big fish. Most small record companies don't have the money to hire a famous makeup artist but can afford a couple of hundred dollars for someone just starting out.

You might offer to do makeup for free or at a low rate to gain experience. Many groups who don't have the financial backing of a major label will be glad to use your services in exchange for shots for your portfolio. It's also easier to get to be the lead artist on videos than it is for film and television, particularly if the recording artist isn't a big name yet.

Pick up an independent music magazine, or a local entertainment weekly and flip to the music section to find some small record labels. Their name will often be in brackets after a mention of the band or performer, particularly if there is an "indie" chart of hot new songs. Many small record labels will also take out ads to promote several of their artists at once, and the ads will include their contact info. A record store that carries independent titles might also be able to supply you with some leads.

Even if the labels, bands or artists are not "big" enough to make a video yet, you can offer to work on publicity shots or album covers. If you are their makeup artist of choice, they may recommend you to bigger acts they open for, or will stick with you when they make it big and are ready to shoot their first video.

You can list yourself as a freelance makeup artist at the Music Video Production Association's website at **www.mvpa.com**.

## The Environment

Like films and TV, there's a hierarchy of makeup artists on set, though the chances are good on a video shoot that the lines will be blurred when it comes to duties. If there are twenty-five dancers on set sweating off the makeup after every take, no one cares about who's the lead and who are the assistants.

There are usually three categories of people you will make up on a music video set: principal talent, principal extras, and extras. The key makeup artist is hired primarily to work on the principal talent (the star of the show), but on lower budget sets you may be required to care for everyone and pay for an assistant out of the sometimes meager budget provided.

"I have artists who are commanding between $1,800 and $5,000 a day," says Jesse Valentine of the De Facto agency. "Assistants are paid $150 to $300, but sometimes they make the connections to get their own work in the future." When working directly with small labels the highest rate you're likely to encounter is about $500, often paid in cash.

## Insider Tips for Success

- If you are working as the key artist on a video shoot, you will most likely benefit from hiring an assistant so that one of you can stay with the "talent" on set and one can stay in the trailer if needed to do additional faces that may arrive.

- If you work with a music celebrity on a film or print project, make sure you network with them so that they think of you when it comes to their next video.

## 6.3.4 Catalogs and Advertisements

Catalogs and advertisements are where the big money is spent. For print work, these are the highest-paying categories. The makeup artists hired to do ads for products that appear in magazines are normally well-known names in the industry. It's almost like catalog and ad work is given out as a gift to veterans in the industry.

One added element in commercial work is the advertising agency. Often they work as the liaison between the company who is advertising something and the production company, art director or photographer creating the commercial.

## How to Break In

The best advice for getting this kind of work is to make sure your name is in print every chance you can, and assist. Catalog houses and ad agencies love to see portfolios with beautiful editorial tear sheets, especially creative "international" work, much of which is actually shot in New York.

This is also an area where photographer contacts come in handy. Many an art director will ask the photographer whom he would like to work with. It's always someone he's worked with previously and believes to be talented and professional.

For TV commercials, either the advertising agency or the production company might hire you. If you're really gutsy, you can go right to ad agencies like Young and Rubicam (**www.yr.com/yr**) or Saatchi & Saatchi (**www.saatchi.com**) and visit the creative floor (providing you can get past security) with the hopes of dropping off your book for an art director to peruse. Have cards in the pockets. Ask when you should come back to pick it up, and try to get a name of who will be looking at your book. You can call later to verify that the person actually viewed it. This is a long shot, but it's worth a try.

Also, the Association of Independent Commercial Producers has a small job board at their website at **www.aicp.com**.

## The Environment

On the set or shoot, the client is the most important person in the room. He or she is the representative for the company whose products the commercial, ad or catalog promotes. You may or may not deal directly with the client, but they will judge your work. Not surprisingly, some clients are very easy to work with and defer to the expertise of the creative minds on the job, while others would prefer to have a hand in everything.

Commercial work involves striking a balance between meeting the director's or photographer's demands and those of the client. If you find yourself in conflict, be pleasant to the client and then ask the director or producer of the spot to make the call. It is their job to come to a mutually acceptable vision.

TV commercials may be only 15, 30 or 60 seconds long, but don't let that fool you that it will be quick and easy work. The length of a commercial shoot is based on the complexity of the shoot, the amount of locations required and the number of actors involved.

The makeup for catalogs and ads is pretty much the same as for magazines, sometimes even easier. The makeup in most advertisements is very low-key. It's important that the product and the brand name are the focus. The same is true of catalog work. The client cares about showcasing the clothing, but wants the model to look pretty also.

Catalog and advertising shoots can last eight hours or four days. You will be paid a day rate instead of an hourly rate. Here again, the range can be enormous, but the low end is around $500 a day, and the high end is up around $5,000 a day, or more.

## Insider Tips for Success

- When you are showing your portfolio to an art director for ad work, don't have too many over-the-top makeup shots. It's rare that Bayer aspirin will ask you to dip their model in blue body paint.

- The hair and makeup should never stand out in either of these work categories... unless you are doing an ad for a makeup or hair product company!

# 6.3.5 Runway Shows

There is a lot of glamour surrounding the big runway shows like New York's 7th on Sixth. Twice a year legends in the fashion industry like Oscar de la Renta show their fashion creations alongside newer talents like Stella McCarthy.

For a makeup artist, runway shows are a combination of theater and editorial work. On one hand you are working with the top print models who are on covers around the world, but on the other, your job is to join forces to create a show that is very theatrical in nature.

## How to Break In

Most makeup artists who have the pleasure of creating the look for the well-known designers are working heavily with the fashion magazines. This type of job would normally come from a personal relationship you have with the designer or the director who is putting the show together, or through your agent. Sometimes they are also national makeup artists for a particular brand of makeup (as explained earlier in section 4.1.3). This happens when a makeup brand is sponsoring a show.

Call the agencies in New York (that's where the fashion work is, and the agencies that work with it) that represent star artists like Laura Mercier and Pat McGrath and ask if you can come in and speak to someone about assisting for the upcoming shows. Makeup artists can get pretty busy during Fashion Weeks and may be desperate for an extra set of hands. If you are willing to travel, say so.

While working as an assistant, you should try to speak to some up-and-coming designers who may use you as their lead artist the following year. Always have a card of some sort to hand out at the shows. It's a long-term investment in your future that may pay off.

Even if you aren't working at them, if you want to work in fashion, attend as many fashion events as possible to network. Keep your eye open for trunk shows (exclusive fashion sales) where the designer is often in attendance, and make sure you get a chance to speak with him or her and tell them what you do. Bring your portfolio (or a mini-one, as explained in section 6.3.7) or a comp card. You can also get experience working on charity fashion shows, which will be advertised locally.

A back-door way to network in the industry is to work as a gopher or intern for a designer. This will get you into the environment, although it doesn't provide direct makeup connections. Look in the classified section of *Women's Wear Daily* (**www.wwd.com**), the fashion industry bible, to find out about intern positions. It's sold on any newsstand in New York.

There's no need to attend cosmetology school to work as a makeup artist in fashion, but workshops like the Runway Makeup Workshop offered at Fred Segal Beauty in L.A. (see section 3.3.3 on workshops) gives you tools for the trade. At $525 for a two-day seminar (you get $250 worth of beauty products to keep), it's an affordable way to take your craft to the next level. Fred Segal also runs an agency that represents makeup artists, which could be your ticket in.

## The Environment

The pace at the shows on the big day is crazy and fun. Small spaces, poor ventilation and lots of hair spray and cigarette smoke create quite an ambiance. But from start to finish it's about three hours of work. Most shows book about 30 models.

On the day of the show, assistants are expected to recreate the look the lead makeup artist shows them, or simply prepare them for application. Some makeup artists put new or unfamiliar artists closest to them so they can monitor their work, so don't be surprised if this happens— take it in stride.

At runway shows you may encounter snippy, exhausted models who are not always pleasant. Try to remember that they are doing several shows in a day, have numerous hands touching them and may have flown in from Paris last night and may be heading out on a plane in two hours for the shows in Milan. Jetlag and exhaustion can turn the sweetest model into Attila the Hun. It's not personal, so maintain your professionalism and keep your cool.

Pay on the big runway shows like 7th on Sixth is enormous, with rates up to $10,500 a day for a makeup artist designing the look for a big-name designer. Naturally, the rates can run considerably less for makeup artists working for brand-new designers showing their first collection in a rented space, like an art gallery or well-decorated basement. Assistants are paid about $150 a show.

## Insider Tips for Success

- It's important that you duplicate what you've been shown precisely. If you're not sure about something, ask. If shifting colors for darker skin tones are difficult for you, ask the lead makeup artist for direction or colors from her kit to use.

- The makeup artist may choose to do the model's makeup or ask you to do it, but then she or he will tweak it. It's important not to be offended when something you've done is changed, blended or taken off. As an assistant, you are there to learn.

# 6.3.6  Film and TV

Television and film makeup can mean anything from the predictable, low-key makeup for the evening news to SFX makeup in movies like Lord of the Rings. Because working behind the scenes in the entertainment industry to help the people in front of the camera look good is the glamour job of makeup artistry, it is one of the hardest to break into full time.

It took star makeup artist Toy Russell about five years of project work at ABC-TV as a production assistant before she became what Dick Cavett wryly referred to as "my makeup man." But that was a full-time job that lasted for as long as *The Dick Cavett Show* was on the air. On the other hand, there are as many ways in as there are makeup artists, and the rewards can be enormous.

There's lots of work out there for non-union makeup artists in film and television, but the big budget, name-making jobs are always union. That means makeup artists working on a film or TV show have to be a part of the International Alliance of Theatrical Stage Employees union (IATSE), whose requirements will be explained later in this chapter.

One of the only ways you can get work on a big-budget film before you are union is by the power of "star request," in which the star of the production specially requests that you come to work for them. More information about becoming a celebrity makeup artist will be coming up soon.

## How to Break In

You won't find work in this industry by sending out resumes or emails. Try to arrange to meet with directors, makeup department heads, or production companies and show them your portfolio of work. Don't worry if you don't have a "demo reel", as most industry insiders realize that this comes in time. Be politely persistent in your approach.

Marvin Westmore, founder of Westmore Academy of Cosmetic Arts, says, "There can be any number of individuals on a major film who are individually or collectively involved in the hiring of a makeup artist: the producers, the director, the production manager, actor or actress. It's all in who you know and how much pull they have and you have. The secret of being employed is to network constantly."

You can track available jobs through a number of trade resources that list contact information for production companies and executive per-sonnel, including *Hollywood Reporter* (**www.hollywoodreporter.com**), *Variety* (**www.variety.com**), and *Below the Line* (**www.btlnews.com**). Subscribing to the *Reporter* or *Variety* can be very pricey, so people tend to buy one or the other at newsstands only when they need it.

*Below the Line*, which follows the fortunes of the crew (makeup is a "below-the-line" expense) rather than the industry or the latest deal, is modeled on Variety but is a little less expensive.

Working on student films is a great way to get on-set experience and network with potential employers. Choose excellent film schools or colleges like NYU and UCLA, so the people you work with will be more likely to move on to bigger and better things. Students from film schools also contact the top makeup schools to request artists for their projects, so keep in touch with anywhere you choose to study at and let them know to refer you for this type of work.

With the tremendous growth of the cable industry, there are more jobs than ever before for makeup artists. Even home repair and design shows have makeup artists to work on the hosts and the cast members.

Contact your local cable company and ask if you can come in for a meeting, or assist the current artist. Cable companies will sometimes have a public access station right in your local area. Note that a small budget usually means a trade out. You won't get paid (or paid very much), but you can get a copy of the show in exchange for your makeup services.

Makeup artistry for television news is usually contracted out to an individual makeup artist. You can call your local stations to find out who does the makeup for the news anchors, and how can you contact them. Ask if they would mind you coming out to observe them, or if they would be willing to possibly take on an apprentice. Offer to work the early morning shift and you may be more likely to break in.

Another source for work is the job boards and online communities created for employers and crewmembers working in film and television. You can search for current jobs, post a resume, and chat with others in the industry. Try searching any of these:

- *Crewmarket*
  **www.crewmarket.com**

- *Backstage*
  **www.backstage.com/backstage/index.jsp**

- *Mandy.com Film and TV Jobs*
  (Search for makeup jobs under "crew")
  **/www.mandy.com/index.cfm**

- *Independent Film Project*
  (Has a "Networking Center" with production jobs listed)
  **www.ifp.org**

- *Association of Independent Video and Filmmakers*
  **www.aivf.org/index.html**

Once you have worked enough small projects to get into the union, a great way to get your foot in the door for major films and television is to put yourself on the day-check list. This is a list of available makeup artists who are hired to assist a Department Head for crowd scenes, making up extras. The job can last one day or several. Treat this as a chance to assist, and follow the tips and suggestions listed in section 6.1.3 on being a great assistant to make this work lead to more. Keep in touch with the union to make sure your name is at the top of the list.

According to Michael Key at *Makeup Artist Magazine*: "An excellent way to meet the makeup artists who are working in film and television with the clout to hire you is to attend trade shows like the International Makeup Artist Trade Show, held in L.A. and London."

Michael Key and the folks over at *Makeup Artist Magazine* sponsor the International Makeup Artist Trade Show, and he's right. It's an all out feast for a new makeup artist wishing to make contacts and learn amazing techniques for stage and film. The key speakers and workshop instructors are award-winning makeup artists with incredible talent and skill. Bring your portfolio, a resume and cards to leave behind. You'll find a link to more information about this trade show at the end of this guide.

# The Environment

New makeup artists work under another makeup artist known as the Department Head. This makeup artist designs the look of the characters, does research, and maintains continuity. He or she is also the person who hires the assistant artists; and sometimes there will be up to 50 makeup artists working on a film! The pecking order is Department Head, First Assistant or Key Makeup Artist, Second Assistant and so on.

By the time you meet with an actor, you should have already read about his character, seen a picture of him, and learned something about what he is wearing. Do a trial run to see if the makeup looks right and is comfortable for the actor. The trial run will also help you to gauge how long the makeup will take to apply and when the actor needs to be called to have his makeup done.

Respect your "call time" or the time you are asked to be at the shoot. Carry a city map in your car and download directions from the Internet so you can plan your route in advance. Being late is unacceptable in this business. Once you get to the shoot, locate the Department Head or producer and ask where the makeup room is so you can go and set up immediately, and find out what the schedule for the day will be.

Once the makeup is done for any given shoot, you will take continuity shots to make sure that everything looks the same from one take to the next, and that it is appropriate to the action, the time of day and the events that are taking place in the script. If you are working on a multiple-day shoot, you should take a picture of each actor to refer to the next day. Keep a copy of the script with you as a guide.

Finally, keep your energy high and prepare for long days. You are usually well fed on a movie shoot, but bringing snacks and water along is a good idea, just in case. Stay energetic and positive.

This type of work is freelance, which means that you have a job for the length of the movie or video shoot. A typical workday is ten or more hours for film or television and call times can be as early as 3:30 a.m., especially for the morning news. You may be in a warm studio abuzz with activity or you could be standing in a foot of snow someplace remote and very cold shooting a scene over and over again. It's all in a day's work.

Working on a television show is a full-time salaried position. If you work on a pilot, the show may or may not be "picked up" or chosen by the network. Once the show is on the schedule and shooting, you will be contracted to work for the season. One season is normally 13 episodes and if the show continues, contracts are renegotiated at that time.

News makeup is one of the more demanding forms of artistry because of the early morning hours and quick turn-around times required. A high level of skill is required as well, because a lot of the shots are close up.

> **TIP:** It is rare, but some stations in some markets require that you be a "licensed" makeup artist in order to work with them. Since there is actually no state-backed licensing for makeup artistry, what this translates to is becoming a licensed cosmetologist or esthetician.

Assignments for TV commercials are typically a few days, whereas television movies shoot approximately 20 days. Series shoot for six to nine months and feature films can require three months to two years of shooting.

If you are day-checking, don't assume your work is finished until you are told it is. If you don't show up because you figured the regular makeup artist would be back the next day, and he or she is not, your supervisor will not be impressed, and you won't work for them again.

As of this writing the rate on a union television show or film pays a minimum of $38 an hour for Department Head, with many DHs making much more. A second artist gets at least $35 per hour.

In addition, some productions (but not all) provide what is called a "box rental", which is to be used for incidental makeup supplies that are not covered by the makeup production budget. The box rental is generally around $30 per day.

## Insider Tips for Success

- There is often a lot of "hurry up and wait" on a film or TV set. The lights and camera need to be moved and readjusted each time a new shot is done. You should be the one waiting—do not make the director wait on you! The same goes for dallying just to tack extra time onto your time card—clean up and get on your way when the day is through.

- If you are on a movie shoot it may run hours or even days over what was originally planned. Although you are not obligated to work that extra time, it is much better to make yourself available by blocking out extra time for a job. Always try to avoid double-booking yourself or canceling a job. If you cannot do a job that you've booked because of illness or emergency, always offer to provide a replacement.

- If you start work on a show that is already running, make sure to familiarize yourself with the show. Watch past episodes, speak with current employees and do your homework about the actors' likes and dislikes. When the filming is taking place, you should follow the action rather than gabbing with the other artists.

- Film and TV work can involve working with a lot of other makeup artists. Be friendly and non-competitive—you are on the same team, and one of these people might be able to hire you or refer work to you in the near future.

# 6.3.7 Celebrities

Many celebrity personalities and movie stars travel with their own makeup artists. Some even have the makeup artist written into their contract so if the actor is hired, the makeup artist automatically gets hired too, something known as "star request".

According to the makeup artist and hair stylist union (IATSE), a "star request" applies to a non-union makeup artist who has a verifiable record of having worked with a celebrity on several projects prior to being asked to work on a union production. This means a celebrity can be the catalyst to a makeup artist receiving an invitation to join the union and work on big-budget films!

Everyone knows that meeting a celebrity is 99 percent luck, but you can increase your odds by networking in the right crowds, and being in the right place... and hopefully at the right time.

## How to Break In

Publicists and celebrity personal assistants can represent golden opportunities for a makeup artist to find work. Especially if you live in New

York or Los Angeles, you will probably come in contact with publicists and CPAs at some point in your travels. These are the people who can recommend you to their celebrity, so treat them like stars themselves.

Because of the nature of their work, they are discreet about what they do, but the key is to tell everyone that you come in contact with that you are a makeup artist. Somebody is bound to be in a position to introduce you to a celebrity who may need your services.

Believe it or not, amazing connections are made while working in free-standing makeup stores located around the city. One makeup artist interviewed for this guide shared this success story:

"I got a celebrity gig when I was still working behind the counter in a chic little makeup shop in Manhattan. I didn't have an agent or anything, not even a portfolio. I had a great rapport with one of my clients in the store. As it turned out, she worked for Harrison Ford. I was standing in his kitchen doing makeup a week later. It was very surreal."

SoHo, a very fashionable section of Manhattan, is home to many of the freestanding makeup stores visited by models, makeup artists and beauty editors. Stores like Face Stockholm (**www.facestockholm.com**), Make Up For Ever (**www.makeupforever.com**) and Helena Rubenstein (**www.helenarubinstein.com**) have a reputation for having great makeup artists who are doing editorial work alongside their store gig.

Celebrity personal assistants dash into stores to pick up products for their clients, or sometimes the clients go to the stores and get their own products. Several screen beauties have been sighted at Face Stockholm on Prince Street trying on their infamous Wicked lip gloss. To get a position at one of these intimate little boutiques, bring your portfolio, dress in trendy black clothes and head to SoHo. Half the battle is being personable and fashionable. But keep your future aspirations to yourself. It's better to say how much you love makeup and sales...You love sales!

If you decide to go the store route, make a smaller copy of your portfolio (4x6 or 5x7) and carry it with you all of the time. If you meet someone that may become a client, take your lunch break, cigarette break or whatever you can get, and go outside of the store where you can whip out your picture and cards. Be more than a body they met in a makeup store—make an impression.

Once you've worked for one celebrity and she or he likes your work and your personality, you will be called back. Even better, you will be recommended to friends. Usually the first job with a celebrity will be for a night out on the town or a party they are attending. Most celebs have someone they regularly use for print that may not be interested in running over to the house to do a 30-minute application that will not make it into the portfolio.

After several personal appearance makeup jobs, the celebrity may decide you would be great to do makeup for print or product endorsements when their regular isn't available. This will help your career immensely. Tear sheets of a well-known face are worth twenty-five tears of a cute, but nameless model.

## The Environment

Most celebrities are understandably cautious about new people because they are always in the public eye. Be professional, warm and friendly, and make sure that you respect their privacy. You are going to encounter details of their private life the general public would kill to hear. Don't betray that trust by gossiping or revealing "tidbits".

Some of the responsibilities of being a personal celebrity makeup artist include doing their makeup for film or television work as well as for any live or broadcast appearance. Prior to appearances you will meet with them to review the travel itinerary, what they will be wearing, and what look they want to project—formal, casual, sexy, etc.

Celebrities are used to being made up and may have very particular opinions on the products and techniques they want you to use. The person you work with will probably have her own ideas about what colors are right for her and what makeup is best suited to her skin. She may have had cosmetic surgery done that needs to be camouflaged, or have particular ideas about which features she likes to have accentuated.

## Insider Tips for Success

- Always make the design of the makeup a joint effort when working with a celebrity. Their job requires them to know what makes them look good and what doesn't. Respect their input, but also don't be afraid to make suggestions. Your ideas might lead to a gradual update or change in the celebrity's image which can enhance his or her career—and yours.

- Try to get a sense of how chatty or invisible your celebrity wants you to be. If they are rehearsing an acceptance speech or trying to relax before a big event, your chit-chat might not be appreciated. Their threshold may vary from day to day, so try to be intuitive.

## 6.3.8  Theater

The opportunity for work in theater exists all across America. You could be hired by a repertory theater company, a touring show, a Broadway show, an opera or dance company, or the actual theater venue.

Unlike film and print, which rule the two coasts, regional theater can allow a makeup artist to enjoy working in their field without moving. Many smaller cities have local chapters of the hair & makeup artist union. Of course if your dream is to be in the big leagues, Broadway is the place.

Makeup artists who work in theater tend to have a broad-based educational background, including a theoretical interest and an understanding of period and current fashion in addition to makeup and technical skills.

### How to Break In

Theater makeup artists do not have agents, nor does the union actively pursue work for their members. It's up to you to network and knock on doors. By the way, Broadway is all union. No exception. There's plenty of non-union theater work out there... just not on Broadway. More about applying to the union is explained in section 6.5.

Before you meet the union criteria of hours worked, you will be limited to non-union work. Find it by checking industry magazines with casting calls for actors so you know what shows are being produced.

In New York, check out *Backstage* (**www.backstage.com**) and *Playbill* (**www.playbill.com**). In L.A. look for *Variety* (**www.variety.com**),

*Hollywood Reporter* (**www.hollywoodreporter.com**) and *Drama-Logue/ Backstage West* (**www.backstage.com**). These can be purchased at any newsstand.

You would be most likely be hired by the person who designed the makeup and who would supervise its application, usually called the Department Head. The best time to try to meet Department Heads is about 1 ½ hours before a show they are working on opens. For example, if a show is scheduled for an 8:00 p.m. showing, try to be there around 6:30 p.m.

You can call and ask if they've hired a makeup artist for the production, and offer to assist if they have. It may be a way to get some non-union productions on your resume and build up hours towards joining the union.

"A makeup artist who was working on *Phantom of the Opera* encouraged me to move from my hometown in Ohio to New York City to pursue my dreams on a larger scale," says Whitney Adkins-Mvondo, who as of this writing was touring with *Les Miserables*. "I was already working in regional theater in Ohio and I was part of the union. Once I moved to NYC, I beat the pavement with my resume. I went to theaters every day and met with every Department Head that I could," she explains. Adkins-Mvondo has also worked on *Cats*, *Showboat*, *Rent* and many other Broadway productions.

Working backstage at an amateur theater company or doing relevant unpaid work is a good way to get experience and make contacts that can lead to full-time work on more esteemed productions. Job shadowing and working as an assistant to a senior makeup artist for the stage is another way to gain insight, develop your portfolio, network, and prove your commitment. You can use the Playbill website to find an amateur or community theater company near you. The webpage is **www.playbill.com/theatrecentral/sites/category/2032**.

In the beginning your resume will be all amateur work, but that's okay. Simply put the name of the show and what you did. It also helps to have a portfolio of your work, but it's not as vital as it is in print or television. In some cases even playbills of productions you worked on will suffice, but also try to snap a few pictures during full-makeup rehearsals, with permission, of course.

Once you have your pre-union hours worked, the best way to get work is to be on the union's list of availability for "swing work". Swing work is the theater industry's equivalent of day-checking. It is day-to-day work given to a makeup (or hair) artist, usually because the regular artist is sick or on vacation.

You can "swing" several shows at a time to ensure you are working regularly and making contacts quicker. "My first break came with *Cats*. I was called in for swing work and one job led to another. I was very fortunate," says Whitney Adkins-Mvondo.

# The Environment

Theatrical makeup artists are mostly used to design the look of characters. She or he comes in during what is known as "tech time", brings sketches and teaches the actors and hair artists how to do the makeup for each character. When the show opens, the actors do their own makeup. Then the hair artists "police" the work by ensuring they are doing the makeup for their character exactly the same each night. For this reason, employers in the theater often seek makeup artists with hairstyling skills.

In theater work, the reality is there are many more openings for hair than makeup. "Hair work is about 85 percent of Broadway jobs, while makeup is only 15 percent. I can do both, but not on one show. The union requires me to choose one or the other," says Adkins-Mvondo. If you really only want to do makeup, go after the shows that are makeup-heavy, like Disney's *The Lion King* or even Cirque du Soleil, a colorful fusion of circus and theater. They tend to hire separate hair and makeup artists.

Broadway shows book makeup artists on one-year contracts that state the terms of employment; however you are free to leave at any time to go to another show. Industry courtesy dictates a two-week notice before leaving a show.

# Insider Tips for Success

- If you can do both hair and makeup, maintain separate resumes. If you did a show regionally that was not union-regulated, chances are you did both. It's okay to put the same show on both resumes.

- A theater makeup artist interviewed for this guide advises, "You have to have the confidence to go to the shows and ask to meet with the Department Head. Don't be timid. Believe in your work and do a good job. One person will tell another person and soon you'll be living your dream."

# 6.4 Joining an Agency

Is an agent essential for every makeup artist? No, but most top artists will have an agency representing them. Your credibility as a makeup artist is boosted one-hundred-fold if you can flash a composite card with the name of a prominent artist agency across the front.

Your legwork is cut down significantly, as an agent or booker simply picks up the phone and has a messenger whisk your portfolio over to *Elle* magazine, and then everyone at Elle is eager to see your portfolio because your agent has told them about this talented new makeup artist now on the company roster. Having an agent also frees you up from some of the less desirable parts of freelancing, like negotiating pay and collecting money owed.

One prominent makeup artist interviewed for this guide reveals: "Agent fees are well worth it. They get you work that would take years to get on your own. And they fix messes you make when you're an inexperienced artist. Once I ate most of the food in a mini-bar in a hotel on a booking out of town. I didn't understand the concept of mini-bars [you pay for] and $20 M&Ms.

"When I tearfully told my agent I'd eaten most of the food and the champagne in the mini-bar, he fussed at me pretty badly, but somehow got the client to pay for it. I would have made very little on that one-day shoot if he hadn't fixed the mini-bar incident. He never let me live it down, though. It was a source of constant amusement."

## 6.4.1 What an Agency Will Do

Having an agent is a whole new world experience for the lowly makeup artist who has worn holes in pair after pair of sneakers beating the pavement and knocking on doors. For example, a good agent:

- finds artists work

- promotes their artists in the industry

- may update portfolios for their artists

- meets with clients

- bills and collects for services

- schedules jobs

- negotiates rates and expenses

- drops in on your job to make sure everything is going well

In return for these services, most agents receive a percentage of the job fee (usually 15 to 20 percent) as well as a fee from the client who has booked the job. For many people, not having to worry about being paid or about talking money with clients is well worth the agent fees.

All of your accounting and client tracking is done by the agency. At year-end you are presented with a 1099 for taxes. All you have to keep track of are the costs you incur for makeup and other tools, which are tax-deductible.

There are other perks to being listed with an agency. Beauty writers contact the agencies and ask for makeup artists to interview for beauty articles that are posted on websites or placed in magazines. It's free publicity.

The coveted agency spots also bring with them tons of free makeup. Cosmetic brands want makeup artists to mention their product in print or interviews, so they send it out to the agencies for artists to try. Sometimes hundreds of dollars worth of products are sitting in neat little goody bags at the agencies—one for each artist listed with the agency.

## 6.4.2 How to Choose an Agency

A makeup artist needs to have total confidence in his or her agency. Good communication is essential to a successful partnership. An agent should be up-front and honest with the artists he or she works with. The person should be able to thoroughly explain how he or she works so that you understand what is expected and what you will get in return.

To decide which agency to choose, talk to working artists to find out who they work with, and if they are happy with their agents. Big-name clients can also assist in this research. Representatives of these companies or successful photographers can often recommend agencies they have worked with and had positive experiences with. Word of mouth is a great way to find a good agency or specific agent, and to avoid those that aren't as good.

When looking for an agent, remember it's a partnership that needs to work for both of you long term. Even as an assistant, think ahead. Is this an agency I'd like to rep me? Do the artists I assist seem happy with this agency? Are they working the types of jobs I want to work?

Once you have found the names of agencies near you (a sampling is listed below), you can research them further on the Internet to find out if they are accepting new artists in the type of makeup artistry you are interested in. Even if an agent is not currently accepting new artists, he or she may keep your information and contact you when there is an opening.

Most likely you will have an easier time if you ask to assist an artist they already represent. It's less risky for an agency to take on a new assistant versus a new makeup artist. Many of them don't want to take the time to develop a new artist, but an assistant is an asset.

There's no law that says you can't assist artists from several agencies. It's a smart idea to keep all your options open. One agency may offer you a coveted spot on the real artist list instead of the assistant list sooner than you think. At that point, they will likely get you to sign an exclusivity agreement that you will be represented only by them.

An agency may charge a lot of incidentals, such as postage and messenger fees, back to the artist. When your portfolio needs new sheets to hold your tears the agency will order them, put them into your portfolio and bill you for them. You will not get a call asking if they may charge you for anything. You will simply get a tally sheet with the charges taken out of your check! Ask what will be billed to you, and pay attention to these incidentals. They add up, especially if you're not working, but your book is going out all over the country.

> **TIP:** Keep your own updated list of magazines, celebrity contacts and photographers you work with. If you change agencies, your new agent will ask you for this info to contact your clients and let them know your new "address", and your old agency may not be too eager to provide it.

# 6.4.3 Agency Contact Info

For many agents, an email message or telephone call is enough to get the ball rolling. Then a sample of what work you have done is all that is needed. It doesn't take long for an agent to know if the artist is a good match with the agency and the clients with whom they work. If the agent is taking on new artists and feels that your work meets the agency's standards, the agent may invite you in for a meeting.

Getting into an agency is slightly easier than it was even five years ago because many now have "open calls," which are days that they designate for meeting with makeup artists looking for representation. And there's also been a crop of new agencies springing up all over NY and LA, challenging the old establishment.

Don't be disappointed if when you show up for your "meeting" a receptionist says, "leave your book over there on the pile." That happens sometimes. Be polite and go have a snack while the agents look over your portfolio. Always have a duplicate of your book in case it is lost. This rarely happens, but better safe than sorry.

Here are some of the better-known agencies that represent makeup artists in North America. While their offices are on the East or West coasts, the actual work may take the artist to other locations, so don't think that because you don't live in New York you can't get an agent. The agency will tell you where you need to be to work.

- *Artists by Timothy Priano*
  Location:   New York City, NY
  Phone:      (212) 925-5996
  Website:    **www.artistsbytimothypriano.com**

- *Artists Untied*
  Location:    San Francisco and Los Angeles, CA
  Phone:       (415) 957-0500 (SF); (323) 933-0200 (LA)
  Website:     **www.artistuntied.com/artistuntied.html**

- *Celestine Agency*
  Location:    Santa Monica, CA
  Phone:       (310) 998-1977
  Website:     **www.celestineagency.com/**

- *Cloutier Agency*
  Location:    Santa Monica, CA
  Phone:       (310) 394-8813
  Website:     **www.cloutieragency.com**

- *Contact*
  Location:    New York City, NY
  Phone:       (212) 290-0230
  Website:     **www.contactnyc.com**

- *De Facto*
  Location:    New York City, NY
  Phone:       (212) 627-4700
  Website:     **www.defactoinc.com**

- *Exclusive Artists Management*
  Location:    Los Angeles, CA
  Phone:       (323) 436-7766
  Website:     **www.eamgmt.com**

- *Fred Segal Agency*
  Location:    Beverly Hills, CA
  Phone:       (310) 550-1800
  Website:     **www.fredsegalbeauty.com/agency/**

- *I Group*
  Location:    New York City, NY
  Phone:       (212) 564-3970
  Website:     **www.igroupnyc.com**

- *Jed Root*
  Location:    New York City, NY
  Phone:       (212) 226-6600
  Website:     **www.jedroot.com**

- *Magnet*
  Location:    Los Angeles, CA
  Phone:       (323) 463-0100
  Website:     **www.magnetla.com**

- *See Management*
  Location:    New York City, NY
  Phone:       (212) 966-0071
  Website:     **www.seemanagement.com**

- *Stock PhotoCrew*
  Location:    Los Angeles, CA
  Phone:       (323) 766-1733
  Website:     **www.stockphotocrew.com**

- *The Crystal Agency*
  Location:    Los Angeles, CA
  Phone:       (323) 906-9600
  Website:     **www.crystalagency.com/**

- *The Rex Agency*
  Location:    Los Angeles, CA
  Phone:       (323) 664-6494
  Website:     **www.therexagency.com**

- *Zenobia Agency*
  Location:    San Francisco, Los Angeles, and nationwide
  Phone:       (415) 621-7410 (SF); (323) 937-1010 (LA)
  Website:     **www.zenobia.com**

# 6.4.4  What Agencies are Looking For

In many cases, it is essential for a makeup artist to have a strong portfolio to show agents. This means that the artist often needs to be in the business for a few years building a good portfolio before he or she can find an agent.

A good book with tear sheets from magazines or editorials serves as proof that the makeup artist is not only talented but has also been hired by other clients. The better the book, the more work an artist will be able to get. Most agents won't mind if the portfolio has photographs from test shoots, as long as the pictures are high-quality tear-sheet look-alikes.

Don't go in with before-and-after photos, bridal work, or poor quality shots. In an interview with MakeupMania.com, makeup artist Marietta Carter-Narcisse advises new makeup artists to be honest if they don't have quality professional portfolio work. She tells readers: "Say, 'I don't have a portfolio, what do you think is the first step for me to take in getting one together?' Inquire about advice for starting out. The worst thing you can do to yourself is approach an agent with mediocrity." You can read the complete article online at **www.makeupmania.com/ greenroom/interviews/marietta_cnarcisse.cfm**.

For some agencies, artists need to be skilled in both hair and makeup. Agencies in larger markets, however, will accept artists that strictly do makeup.

Finally, if an artist is talented enough, some agents will take them on and work with them despite not having a great book yet. They will be hired as assistants or trainees, and may work for free. Once the makeup artists build up their portfolios, they can get paying work.

Mary Goodman at the Celestine Agency (listed earlier in the contact info) told FabJob that she will help exceptionally talented artists who are just starting out in the business. They will meet with a new makeup artist and offer advice, insights, and direction to help them figure out the best way to launch their careers. "I believe in perseverance," says Mary. "If someone has the talent, they will prevail, and I'll definitely help them do that."

# 6.5 Joining a Union

The makeup and hairstylist union is a division of the International Alliance of Theatrical Stage Employees union (IATSE), which regulates work conditions and pay rates for its members. The general office for IATSE is in New York City, but local chapters are set up in several U.S. cities and Canada. Contact information is listed below.

## 6.5.1  Should You Join?

For most makeup artists working in the entertainment industry, their objective is to get a union, or "organized," job, which gets you not only union minimum or higher pay but also the benefits that go with it.

As a member of a union, you also have access to leads for other union projects. You also have access to the protections and work rules that union membership brings. Union membership also offers health benefits and 401Ks to their members at a rate that is lower than individual health plans. And of course, if there are ever "issues" that seem unethical on a shoot, the union steps in on behalf of its members.

There are two schools of thought about union membership. Obviously if you want to see your name roll across the screen of a big-budget film produced by Paramount, there's no debate—seek union membership. But union membership is not a necessity to find work. After all, being invited to join the union in the first place is based on a number of hours obtained working on non-union productions.

Television news organizations, television production stations, music videos and even some film productions will hire non-union makeup artists. Most of the major production studios are located in Los Angeles and New York City, but there are a number of local production companies that produce locally broadcast shows and that need makeup artists.

The point is, don't think that you are limited because you are not a part of a union. There are many companies that will hire non-union artists that display a high level of professionalism.

## 6.5.2  Union Requirements

According to the L.A. chapter of IATSE, Local 706, if you work a total of 60 days a year for three years on a non-union job, and get a letter from the productions you worked with, you can apply for union membership.

Another way to get into the union is to work just 30 days during a year with a production that was originally non-union but later becomes union. Again, ask for a letter from the production company stating that you worked with them, and have copies of your pay stubs to show.

Once you present the proper documentation, there's an initiation fee of approximately $4,500 (the amount differs for each local chapter). Half is due when you join and the rest is due 18 months later. There are also dues (minimal amounts like $150 a year) and a percentage that is taken from your paychecks.

The makeup artists and hair stylist union requires hairstylists to have a current cosmetology license to join the union, however this is not a current requirement for makeup artists. 706 also requires that makeup artists pass a color-blindness examination. Be aware that these requirements are subject to change, so for complete details, visit their website listed below.

If you are on the East Coast, the general IATSE office listed below will provide a mailed copy of the Local 798's regulations upon request, or you can call them once you are asked to work on a union-regulated project to see if they will admit you based on the project. Call them at the number listed below, as they don't have a website.

Canadians can contact the office closest to them (Toronto or Vancouver) for up-to-date regulations. Visit the websites listed below first to review the procedure, as the offices are busy and won't give general information over the phone.

## 6.5.3  Union Contact Info

- *International Alliance of Theatrical Stage Employees (IATSE)*
  Location:    1430 Broadway
               20th Floor
               New York, NY 10018
  Phone:     (212) 730-1770
  Website:   **www.iatse-intl.org/about/welcome.html**

- *I.A.T.S.E. Local 706, West Coast*
  Location:    11519 Chandler Blvd. N.
               Hollywood, CA 91601
  Phone:     (818) 984-1700
  Website:   **www.local706.com**

- *I.A.T.S.E. Local 798 - East Coast*
  Location:   152 West 24th Street
                 New York, NY  10011
  Phone:      (212) 627-0660

- *I.A.T.S.E. Local 891, Vancouver, BC*
  Location:   1640 Boundary Road
                 Burnaby, BC V5K 4V4
  Phone:      (604) 664-8910
  Website:    **www.iatse.com**

- *NABET 700 – Toronto, ON*
  Location:   100 Lombard Street
                 Suite 203
                 Toronto, ON M5C 1M3
  Phone:      (416) 536-4827
  Website:    **www.nabet700.com**

# 6.6  Getting Paid

Billing clients for your work really isn't as intimidating as it may seem at first. When a client has hired you without an agency, you will negotiate your own rate up front. Working with an agency frees you from this process as they negotiate rates and call clients to remind them of payments.

## 6.6.1  Deal Sheets

Ask the client to fax you or provide you with a call sheet, which gives pertinent information like call time, location, client, etc. You can set your fee based on this information and the general pay ranges provided later in this section, or the client will simply make you an offer.

Typically payment is negotiated as an hourly rate, a half-day rate or a full-day rate. Overtime is typically charged when a session exceeds eight hours (including a one-hour lunch break). Of course you can choose to negotiate different fees if you are starting out and want to offer your services at a lower rate.

Once you are in agreement, ask them to provide a "deal sheet," which simply states the terms of the work agreement. It will say how long the assignment is, how much you have agreed upon as pay, and client information. It is basically a contract of work.

If it has been decided that makeup costs are part of the production budget, you will be asked to submit your estimated costs ahead of time. Be sure to set a budget. Your costs will be up front, and you may not be paid for the project until 30 to 60 days after the completion of the project. As you purchase supplies, save all your receipts, put them in a labeled envelope, and then turn them in so you can be reimbursed.

On the actual day of the shoot, bring a typed voucher with the deal sheet details on it, and have someone on set sign it at the end of the day. This is the exact procedure artists from agencies use, so it will not be something out of the ordinary.

If you are working with a company you have never worked with before and are uncertain that you will be paid, you can also ask for 50 percent of your fee up front. This is a fairly common practice in the industry, and guarantees that you will receive at least 50 percent of what you are owed, in case the company defaults on their debts.

## 6.6.2  Sending Invoices

When the work is done, mail the client an invoice listing the fee along with any cost incurred for travel or specialty products purchased for the shoot. As mentioned, these details should also be discussed prior to the shoot so that they don't come as a surprise to the client.

Make copies of any receipts you may have such as cab fare, hotel accommodation or parking fees. If the job is not catered, sometimes the client will also allot a certain amount for lunch or dinner. Include copies of receipts from everything! Keep the originals for your records and in case the ones you mail get lost.

You can request payment within 30 days on the invoice, but some clients will still take 90 days or more to pay. Be persistent with the accounting department, but not nasty. You want the client to use you in the future.

If you have an agent, most times you will be paid when the agency gets the money from the client, but a few agencies pay their artists two weeks after the job, no matter what. Then when the client pays they simply keep the check. Some agencies charge fees for late payment, so clients are more apt to pay on time.

Agencies also get the client to cover the travel expenses up front in most cases. Airline tickets are delivered via messenger to the agency. A car service whisks you to the airport. You simply sign a voucher and forward it on to the client. It's virtually annoyance-free.

## 6.6.3  Typical Rates of Pay

- **Film, Video and TV**: In the film and video industry, the mean annual wage for makeup artists is about $88,000. A key makeup artist working for film or television may earn around $500 per day, and a highly experienced makeup artist working in these industries can command as much as $2,000 to $5,000 per day. Assistants are paid progressively less, depending on how low on the totem pole they are.

- **Print**: You'll be surprised to learn the bigger magazines aren't always the highest paying. Expect anywhere from $150 to $750 a day, with $200 being the typical rate.

- **Theater**: Pay for theater, like in most artistic industries, is negotiable. The union sets a minimum of approximately $100 a show, but artists can negotiate more. The average range is $900 to $1,000 per week for bigger shows (keep in mind that you may not be working 52 weeks a year). When you tour with a show a "per diem" (daily amount of cash) is added to cover hotel and food expenses. According to the U.S. Department of Labor and Statistics, the mean annual wage for all makeup artists in the field of performing arts (theater) is about $30,000 per year.

- **Celebrities**: Celebrity bookings can command $1,500 a day, and sometimes as much as $10,000.

- **Union Film and TV**: Compensation for makeup artists on union jobs in the TV and film industry is established by collective bargaining between the networks, studios, and production companies on one hand and the artists' unions on the other. Minimum rates and work rules are renegotiated with every round of contract renewal, so they will vary. As mentioned earlier, as of this writing the minimum union compensation for a makeup Department Head was about $38 per hour. A second (or key) artist gets about $35 per hour.

# 7.  Success Stories

Although you're near the end of the *FabJob Guide to Become a Makeup Artist*, hopefully it's also the beginning of your new life as a makeup professional. Being a professional makeup artist involves a lot of goodbyes, but just as many hellos. You'll meet many people, change their look, and sometimes alter their lives forever. Your hands and your vision will be powerful tools of change, as you'll read in the makeup artist Success Stories that conclude this guide.

At the end of your day, you'll clean all your tools and reorganize your makeup kit, making a list of any products you need to order, wash your smocks and towels and put them away, and store your kit and carry kit. Now take a deep breath. Because before you know it, you'll be off to work again.

Several successful makeup artists were kind enough to share their career stories with FabJob. We have included these profiles to inspire you and inform you how a career path truly takes shape. Each of these makeup artists has extended a friendly welcome to you as you join their ranks, offering insider tips to you to help you succeed.

# 7.1 Dyana Aives

Dyana with Jimmy Fallon of *Saturday Night Live*

Dyana Aives is a freelance makeup artist/hairstylist based in New York City. With more than 15 years in the industry, her specialties include fashion, editorial, catalog, commercial (print and television), runway, and music videos. Her print work has appeared in such publications as *InStyle*, *Surface*, and *Time Out New York*. She has also worked on the *MTV Music Awards* and the *VH1 Fashion Awards*.

Although Aives had family connections to get her foot in the door in makeup artistry, she decided to do it on her own. A former model for a swimwear company in California, Aives comes from a family rich with tradition in the beauty industry. Her aunt is Jeannie Van Phue, who was on the Emmy-award-winning makeup team on *The X Files*. "I have big footsteps to follow in," says Aives of her aunt, whose film credits include *About Schmidt*, *High Fidelity*, *The Mighty Ducks* and *Young Guns*.

While working on *Young Guns 2*, Van Phue asked Aives, who by then had trained as a makeup artist, to assist. "I was a little too stubborn. I decided I didn't want people to think the only reason I was on the set was because of who I knew," she says. "So I decided I wasn't going to do the movie route. I decided I wanted to do fashion."

A native New Yorker, Aives moved from California back home. "I figured if I was going to start from the bottom, I would start in the best place in the world for fashion—New York," Aives says. Her decision has provided her with a lifestyle she clearly enjoys. "What I love about my job is that I am doing photo shoots. My longest shoot is maybe six hours," she says. "I go in, do my stuff, get out, and I get my check."

It has been eight years since she made the decision to return to the East Coast. In that time, the highlight of her career was working on the VH1 Concerts for New York, a fund-raiser after the September 11 terrorist attacks. Working with Jon Bon Jovi, Kid Rock, and the Backstreet Boys, Aives knew she had reached a high point in her career.

"Basically, it was two days of non-stop celebrities.... I realized that I was getting to be around people that I would pay to hang out with, [but I was] getting paid for it," she says.

Aives doesn't regret her decision to make her own way in the industry, although she admits that connections can help. "There are makeup artists who have gotten jobs before me because of someone they knew. But there are some purists like me who want to do it on technique and skill level," she says.

At first, Aives found modeling agencies in the phone book and offered to work for free, hopeful that it would lead to paying work. This process, known as testing, is common for photographers, models, and makeup artists. "You are basically working to get really good prints in your book," she says. "You start out at the bottom of the barrel with the girl no one wants to shoot. As you progress and your skill level gets better, you get a little recognition and you start to get the better girls that the modeling agency has to offer."

One of the photographers Aives tested with eventually was published, which meant her work was featured. "Then I was doing smaller magazines that no one had ever heard of, but as the publications increased, I moved up to the next level," she says. "It was like a snowball effect."

Aives suggests newcomers use the Internet. "[My work is featured] on about 120 websites. I posted my work on Portfolios.com and Newfaces. com; basically anywhere I could post free work," she says. From these sites, she connects with clients and photographers. Another useful Internet site is Resource Advantage (**www.rasource. com**), which lists photographers, stylists, hair and makeup artists, and agents for print photography. These sites, she says, are a good place to seek a photographer with whom you want to build a relationship.

"Get with a good photographer. That's key, especially with freelancing," she says. "You want to look for a photographer whose style you want to emulate. Don't go to the biggest photographers you can find. The same goes for finding an agent.... Take it down a notch. You find your level, (work) with everyone on your level and pray that someone there will get you to the next level."

# 7.2 Tara Anand

Tara Anand has built up an impressive resume during her 17 years as a makeup artist in the fashion industry. The London, England native now directs the Artists Within School of Makeup (**www.artistswithin. com**) in Calgary, Alberta.

Her work has appeared in such well-known publications as *Allure, InStyle Weddings, Marie Claire, Flare, Chatelaine, Canadian Living, Avenue* and *Fashion Magazine*. Anand has also worked on fashion shows and commercials as well as television slots and as a national artist for Laura Mercier cosmetics. She has done makeup for many beautiful people including Jennifer Lopez.

Anand began her professional career as a hairdresser but she knew fairly quickly that wasn't her passion. "I loved watching the makeup artists in the salon and at shows, and found that I became more and more interested in makeup," she says. "The whole fashion industry had always appealed to me; it was just a matter of time before I found what part of it I loved and was good at."

Anand says she spent a lot of time early in her career volunteering and working for free. She worked at makeup events in department stores, at charity fashion shows and other such events. "I made myself as available as possible and put myself in the right place at the right time," she says. She realized that she had to spend money to make money. "I would fly myself out to shows or events that I knew would further my career."

Anand stays on the cutting edge of her industry. "I try to push myself, to try new things, mix different products together," she says. "I love to do creative shoots just for my enjoyment and to test myself. To take an idea and put it all together with the photographer, hair person, stylist and model is pretty gratifying."

Education in this field is a career-long venture, although that doesn't always mean the learning needs to come in a traditional setting. "I am always aware of other artists' talents and styles, and always try to take something from everyone I work with," she says. "I believe that you can never stop learning or bettering yourself."

As with any industry, a makeup artist who is new to the field has to start at the bottom and work their way up, Anand says. "You have to start doing anything and everything, much of it is for free. The more your work and face is seen, the more confidence someone hiring has in you."

Networking is key. Anand suggests newcomers attend various fashion events, find out who hired the artists, offer your services for the next event they put on, and then follow up with it.

"A makeup artist needs to get their portfolio together," she says. "This is where trading work for pictures comes in as it can get expensive to pay a photographer to do each shot." Work with up-and-coming photographers for free, she says. This is a way of getting your work around and becoming known in the fashion circuit. "That way when [the photographers] are hired for a job they think of hiring you as the makeup artist," she adds.

Connecting with a photographer can be as simple as putting a notice up at a local art college where photographers are looking for artists to work for free or for a low fee. "Once the portfolio is ready it is a matter of showing it to various advertising agencies, artist agencies or photographers," she says. "Persistence is the key—the more you remind people who you are, the more likely they are to think of you when hiring." She also suggests putting together a comp card and constantly sending it around.

Anand says it is vital to treat every job with the same dedication and enthusiasm as you did your first one. "Remember there is always someone else who wants it as badly as you," she stresses. "I have always followed this and have remained at the top for many years now as I never get lazy and think I'm better than everyone else."

There are several pitfalls newcomers can avoid, according to Anand. You should be prepared for each job, she says, by finding out what is required beforehand and practicing the look if needed. "Never experiment or try anything new for the first time on a job," she says. "And be on time, always."

She says the best advice given to her as a newcomer was a simple strategy. "You can do anything you set your mind to," she says. "Make a plan and follow it until you get to where you want to be."

# 7.3  Tobi Britton

Tobi Britton is a celebrity makeup artist and owner of The Makeup Shop (**www.themakeupshop.com**) in New York City. Tobi has shaped the faces of hundreds of models and actresses, and taught the art and craft of makeup design and application to hundreds of professional makeup artists. When not working in the film, television and fashion entertainment industries, Tobi can be found in the Makeup Shop's Professional Training Center passing on her knowledge and skills to people eager to learn.

Britton's career as a makeup artist has spanned an illustrious 22 years. During that time, she has reached the top of her craft, even working for U.S. Presidents Richard Nixon and Bill Clinton. But her goal wasn't always to work in this industry.

Britton studied acting in college, where she took a class in theatrical makeup. Her career as a makeup artist began as a way to support herself in New York City while she tried to break into acting. "I figured that would be my day job while I pursued being an actress," she explains. "It turned out I was pretty good at it, and I started getting jobs."

Britton began doing print work. She built up a portfolio by testing with photographers then joined the local branch of IATSE, the labor union that represents technicians, artisans, and craftspeople in the entertainment industry, and says she hounded the head of the local union to give her a shot.

"Every time I got a new picture, I would show it to him," she says. "Obviously, today there are so many makeup artists, I wouldn't recommend doing that. But I believed in what I was doing, and I had a vision."

Her break came when the union leader helped her get hired as an extra artist for CBS News. "At the time, that was the most amazing thing that ever happened to me," she says. She began getting work on television commercials and eventually did a three-year stint on *The Cosby Show*.

Britton's career eventually moved toward teaching. She opened The Makeup Shop in New York City in 1991. She offers classes in many aspects of the field, including fashion, runway, airbrush, television, and film. She still works as a makeup artist, mainly doing print work for magazines.

Britton suggests new makeup artists pick an area to focus on, but says they should be open to other opportunities. "I always tell people to sit down and think, if a fairy godmother came down and said you could be any kind of makeup artist—and forget about your life situation and everything else—then what would you do?"

She advises having business cards made to set things in motion. "Do it, even if you just put your name and then 'makeup' underneath it, if you aren't confident enough to put 'makeup artist.' You can meet people in all different places. You could be sitting next to a photographer on the subway."

But don't leave it up to fate. Use the Yellow Pages to seek out photographers. "In every place there are photographers who do portraits and weddings," she says. "This isn't going to get you a professional portfolio, unless you are doing bridals, but it is good practice, and you usually get paid for it."

The Internet is another resource, but Britton says to use care when going this route, especially if you are not working in a major market. Meet the photographer in a public place—like a coffee shop—and ask to look over his or her portfolio, even if you have nothing to show in return, Britton says. See how current the work is and the caliber of the models used.

"You want to make sure you are safe," she says. "Trust your gut, and know that people are always full of promises. They might tell you that the next big shoot they get they will pay you for. If you do it on 'spec' (meaning you'll get paid if the photographer sells the work), don't [have any expectations about getting paid]."

Contacting local art schools, colleges, and universities that teach photography is another way to make a connection. "You will find budding photographers before they move to New York," she says. "Call modeling schools. Sometimes you have to be willing to drive to the next largest town."

Experience is key, and even working with unknown photographers and models has its upside. Sometimes a job will simply mean that you get familiar with being on a shoot. "People work for different things," Britton says. "Obviously the end result is that you want to get paid. But in the beginning, you want to make sure you are not wasting your time. You are either going to get experience; experience and a picture; or experience, a picture, and money."

Decide what is important to you, Britton stresses. "You don't have to have the goal of being the top makeup artist in New York," she says. "You can have a goal of being the biggest makeup artist in a small town—that's okay too."

# 7.4 Thecla "TC" Luisi

Thecla "TC" Luisi has more than 15 years experience as a freelance makeup artist in New York, Miami, and Los Angeles. She has worked in almost every area of the field, including print, music videos, album covers, commercials, TV shows, reality TV, films, special effects, and runway shows. The talent she has worked with includes the likes of Frankie Muniz, Paul McCartney, Angela Lansbury, Burt Reynolds, Roger Clemens, and Salt-N-Pepa.

A licensed makeup instructor, her film and television credits include: *A Better Way 2 Die*, *The Versace Murder*, A&E *Biography*, Discovery Channel, History Channel, and *America's Most Wanted*. Her print credits include *People Magazine*, *Ocean Drive Magazine* and *Modern Bride Magazine* to name a few. Her commercial work includes Nickelodeon Kids, Discovery Kids, Kodak, Kleenex, and Close Up Toothpaste. She also worked on over 40 music videos including being the head makeup artist on *Sex U Up The Way You Like It* by LFO and *Expect the Unexpected* by Dog Eat Dog.

Luisi started dabbling in beauty at a very young age, applying makeup to her stuffed animals. By the time she was 8 years old, she had graduated to playing with the makeup kit of her aunt, a Broadway actress. Eventually she took charge of her friends' makeup and costumes for Halloween.

Luisi attended a New York dance conservatory, where she learned every aspect of backstage work. "It helped me understand lighting, and that is an asset to this day," she says. "You can have a fabulous beautiful face, incredible makeup, and an incredible photographer, but if you don't have incredible lighting, it won't matter. I always tell people, if they can, they should take a lighting course in college or a photography course."

She now has more than 15 years experience as a freelance makeup artist. During a recent two-week period, Luisi worked for both A&E and ABC, and then did a catalogue cover shoot. "I am one of those types who likes to do it all," she says. "I enjoy it, especially special effects. Some people find one area they like, but what suits my personality is the variety."

Luisi has worked for several cosmetic retailers. She was a resident makeup artist in a Chanel boutique. That job had an added bonus: the ability to build up her makeup kit. "All of the money I made went back into my kit," Luisi says. And often, she adds, retail vendors give their resident artists a certain amount of free products.

Luisi advises that newcomers to the field who live or want to work in a major city look up the resource guide for that city at 411Publishing.com (**www.411publishing.com**), a reference tool for film and video production. Be familiar with the local branch of IATSE, the labor union representing technicians, artisans and craftspersons in the entertainment industry, she adds. Criteria to join union branches differ from state to state and experience in the field is necessary.

To get experience, be persistent, and be willing to work for free. "If you are calling a photographer to test with, they probably already have someone they are working with," Luisi says. "You can't take it as rejection if they don't respond. It is a numbers game—the more people you contact, the more likely someone will give you a shot." Go in person, and meet with photographers so they have a face to put with a resume, she advises.

Luisi developed a relationship with a photographer this way. He eventually hired her to do three catalog shoots. "Then I had professional shots to put in my book," she says. She also worked for three years doing free makeup for a fitness show. She always kept notes for every job. "Then when the pictures came back or the television show came on, I would know how the makeup I used looked in that lighting."

Self-education is critical. Luisi suggests studying fashion magazines' websites where they list the cover shot's photographer and makeup artist. Know your favorite makeup artists and photographers, she says. "If you want to work in film, know your favorite directors and know who did the makeup in the movies you love." Rent DVDs of movies that featured makeup you admired, she adds. "You can freeze-frame that, and you have a perfect image to look at."

Luisi says if you can't afford to go to school but you are a disciplined person, there are many opportunities for self-education. "There is enough information out there," she says. "The rest is practice. You have to do as many faces as possible. After the first 100, you start to get good. After the first 1,000, you develop your own style."

# 7.5 Davida Simon

With 20 years working as a makeup artist in film, television, and photography, Davida Simon's client list looks like a "who's who" of the entertainment industry. She has worked with Natalie Cole, Jodi Foster, Lisa Hartman, Lauren Hutton, Anthony Hopkins, Heather Locklear, Susan Lucci, William H. Macy, Demi Moore, Brad Pitt, Bonnie Raitt, Kiefer Sutherland, Vanessa Williams, and sports superstars John Elway and Patrick Roy.

It wasn't always star power that fueled Simon's career. She began as a makeup artist in a salon, which lead her on a path to Hollywood's elite. "Through the salon, I met some models because the salon was doing hair shows," she explains. "Through some of the models, I started doing testing with photographers. Though no money changed hands, everyone got photos and got practice."

Through this arrangement, Simon formed relationships with photographers who hired her for print work. She started by doing makeup for a cover shoot for *Oui* magazine and then did an album cover for Arista Records.

From there, Simon started working for Vidal Sassoon. "Working with him gave me a lot of opportunities," she says. "I was able to do a lot of advertising for him, and I worked with him and his wife on their TV show."

After that, Simon decided to go the freelance route. She had the opportunity to work for ABC in Century City, California, in the photo gallery department. "I started doing hair and makeup for actors on television series for their promotional shots," she says. "With that I met actors who asked me to do movies."

Simon also has done print shots for well-known magazines as *Rolling Stone*, *Mademoiselle*, and *Playboy*. She has worked in television on such shows as *48 Hours*, *Days of Our Lives*, *Boy Meets World*, *NBC Nightly News*, and *The Tonight Show*.

Simon says the business has changed since the 1980s and early '90s when she started. At that time, people had one niche they worked in: television, film, photography, or commercial work. Now all that has changed.

"I will do anything," she says. "In order to be a makeup artist today, you need to know it all, from one type of job to another, including… special effects. You need to know how to create a real character."

With the plethora of makeup schools out there, you need to do some research before you enroll anywhere, says Simon. "See what the schools are offering and see who their instructors are," she says. "There are some schools who bring in guest instructors who are Academy Award-winning makeup artists. Those are the schools I would go to, ones with working makeup artists."

Self-education is important as well. Simon keeps a massive research library. For example, along with fashion magazines from the 1930s, she has a 1930 high school yearbook. "Sometimes it is not what glamorous people look like that you need to know," she says, "but what the real people of that time period looked like."

Garage sales are a great way to build up your library, according to Simon. "I have old Time-Life books from the '50s, '60s, and '70s," she says. "*National Geographic* is a great magazine to hold onto."

Simon also collects makeup books that feature topics ranging from Kabuki (Japanese) style and Latino beauty to theatrical makeup. She even has some paramedic books on file. "You have to be observant," she says. "If they say, 'Dirty them up,' what does that mean? If you have to create a gunshot wound, you need to know what one looks like. You want to be as real as they will let you be."

One of the highlights of Simon's career was working on the 1990 Emmy award-winner for outstanding miniseries, called *Drug Wars: The Camarena Story*. Before applying any makeup, she studied photos of the real Enrique Camarena, an undercover DEA agent who was kidnapped and murdered in 1985 by Mexican drug lords. Filming took place in Los Angeles and Spain.

"It was challenging," she says. "We had three scripts, and we went back and forth in time. There were a lot of torture scenes, so I had to do a lot of torture makeup and to know that really happened [is difficult]. It was very interesting, and I had to do a lot of research. You want to be as authentic as you can be…that is what makes it rewarding."

# 8. Resources

## Consumer Fashion Magazines

- *Vogue*
  **www.style.com/vogue**

- *Elle*
  **www.elle.com**

- *Cosmopolitan*
  **www.cosmomag.com**

- *Allure*
  **www.allure.com**

- *Fashion Magazine*
  **www.fashionmagazine.com**

- *Women's Wear Daily*
  **www.wwd.com**

# Makeup Industry Publications

- *Makeup Artist Magazine*
  **www.makeupmag.com**

- *Cosmetic News*
  **www.cosmeticnews.com/index.htm**

- *Cosmetics Magazine*
  **www.bizlink.com/cosmetics.htm**

# Makeup Information Websites

- *Makeup 411*
  Includes breakdowns of how stars achieved certain looks
  **www.makeup411.com**

- *CosmeticsCop*
  Reviews products on the market
  **www.cosmeticscop.com**

- *iVillage Makeup*
  Tips from a respected source
  **http://beauty.ivillage.com**
  (Click on "Makeup")

# Professional Organizations and Tradeshows

- *UK National Association of Screen Make-up Artists and Hairdressers (NASMAH)*
  **www.nasmah.org.uk**

- *Canadian Network of Make-up Artists (CNoMA)*
  **www.cnoma.com/index.htm**

- *International Makeup Artist Tradeshow*
  **www.makeupartistshow.com**

## Chat Groups and Message Boards

- *Makeup Artist Network*
  **www.makeupartistnetwork.com/messageboard/
  messageboard.html**

- *Makeup Artist Online Career Center*
  **http://p203.ezboard.com/bmakeupartistnetwork**

- *Makeup Artist Magazine Message Board*
  **www.make-upboard.com**

- *Worldwide Alliance of Makeup Artists*
  **http://groups.msn.com/WorldwideAllianceofMakeupArtists/
  general.msnw**

## Cosmetics Manufacturers

These are by no means all the cosmetics manufacturers in the world, as there are many more than can be listed here. These are mainly the companies that have been mentioned in this guide for one reason or another, and the most well-known brands.

- *Bobbi Brown*
  **www.bobbibrowncosmetics.com**

- *Clinique*
  **www.clinique.com**

- *Cover Girl (Procter and Gamble)*
  **www.covergirl.com**

- *Estée Lauder*
  **www.esteelauder.com**

- *Lancôme*
  **www.lancome-usa.com**

- *Laura Mercier*
  **www.lauramercier.com/site/**

- *Lorac Cosmetics*
  **www.loraccosmetics.com/makeup.htm**

- *L'Oreal USA & Maybelline*
  **www.lorealusa.com**

- *I-Iman Cosmetics*
  **www.i-iman.com/cosmetics/index.html**

- *MAC Cosmetics*
  **www.maccosmetics.com**

- *Max Factor (Procter and Gamble)*
  **www.maxfactor.com/index.jsp**

- *Prescriptives*
  **www.prescriptives.com**

- *Revlon & Almay*
  **www.revlon.com/corporate/corp_jobs.asp**

- *Sacha Cosmetics USA Inc*
  **www.sachacosmetics.com/index.htm**

- *Sephora*
  **www.sephora.com**

- *Shiseido*
  **www.shiseido.co.jp/e/index.htm**

- *Shu Uemura*
  **www.shuuemura.com**

- *Smashbox*
  **www.smashbox.com**

- *Stila Cosmetics Inc.*
  **www.stilacosmetics.com**

- *Trish McEvoy*
  **www.trishmcevoy.com**

- *Ulta*
  **www.ulta.com/control/storelocator**

## Stage and Screen Makeup Manufacturers

- *Alcone*
  **www.alconeco.com**

- *Ben Nye Company Inc.*
  **www.bennye.com**

- *Cinema Secrets Inc.*
  **http://store.yahoo.com/professionalsecrets**

- *Graftobian Makeup Company*
  **www.graftobian.com/index5.htm**

- *Joe Blasco*
  **www.joeblasco.com/blascoschools/cosmeticsnew**

- *Kryolan Corp.*
  **www.kryolan.com**

- *Make-up International Ltd. (Face-to-Face)*
  **www.make-upinternational.com/catalog/index.php**

- *Mehron Inc.*
  **www.mehron.com**

- *Manic Panic*
  **www.manicpanic.com**

## Corrective Makeup

- *Dermablend*
  **www.dermablend.com**

- *Covermark*
  **www.covermark.com/pages/home_en.html**

# Online Makeup Retailers

- *Cosmetics Superstore*
  **www.cosmeticbag.com**

- *Drugstore.com*
  **www.drugstore.com**

- *Makeup Artist's Choice*
  **www.makeupartistschoice.com**

- *MakeupMania*
  **www.makeupmania.com**

- *Sally Beauty*
  **www.sallybeauty.com**

# Books about Makeup

- *Bobbi Brown Beauty*, by Bobbi Brown

- *Classic Make-up & Beauty*, by Mary Quant

- *Face Forward*, by Kevyn Aucoin

- *Fine Beauty*, by Sam Fine

- *Making Faces*, by Kevyn Aucoin

- *Makeup for Theater, Film and Television: A Step-By-Step Photographic Guide*, by Lee Baygan

- *Stage Makeup*, by Richard Corson

- *Stage Makeup Step by Step,* by Rosemarie Swinfield

- *Stage Makeup: The Actor's Complete Step-By-Step Guide to Today's Techniques and Materials*, by Laura Thudium

- *The Complete Make-up Artist 2E : Working in Film, Television, and Theater*, by Penny Delamar

- *The Technique of the Professional Makeup Artist*, by Vincent J-R Kohoe

# Videos

The following videos are full of useful makeup tips and are available at Amazon.com.

- *Pamela Taylor's Professional Makeup Course*

- *Step-by-Step Makeup Videos - Bridal Makeup Made Easy*
The step-by-step series also includes a number of other titles such as anti-aging techniques, women of color, sexy eyes and luscious lips, etc.

# SFX Resources

- *Cinefex magazine*
**www.cinefex.com**

- *Fangoria magazine*
**www.fangoria.com**

- *Cinefantastique magazine*
**www.cfq.com**

- *Special Make-up Effects*, by Vincent J-R Kehoe

- *Special Effects Make-up*, by Janus Vinther

# Small Business Resources

- *SCORE*
The Service Corps of Retired Executives has volunteers through-out the U.S. who donate time to mentor small businesses free of charge. Their site has helpful articles.
**www.score.org**

- *Small Business Administration*
The SBA is an excellent resource with advice on business licenses and taxes as well as general information on starting a business.
**www.sbaonline.sba.gov**

- *Online Small Business Workshop*
The Canadian government offers an Online Small Business Workshop which includes information about taxes, financing, incorporation, and other topics.
**www.cbsc.org/osbw/workshop.cfm**

- *Nolo.com*
Nolo is a publisher of legal information presented in plain English. Their website also offers free advice on a variety of other small business matters.
**www.nolo.com**

- *Seven Steps to Starting Your Own Business*
Start-upBiz.com offers helpful step-by-step business advice plus helpful links.
**www.startupbiz.com/7Steps/Seven.html**

# More Fabulous Guides

Find out how to break into the "fab" job of your dreams with FabJob career guides. You can choose from more than 75 titles including:

## Get Paid to Help People Look Fabulous

Imagine having an exciting high paying job showing people and companies how to make a fabulous impression. **FabJob Guide to Become an Image Consultant** shows you how to:

- Do image consultations and advise people about: total image makeovers, communication skills, wardrobe, and corporate image

- Start an image consulting business, price your services, and find clients

- Select strategic partners such as makeup artists, hair stylists, and cosmetic surgeons

- Have the polished look and personal style of a professional image consultant

## How to Open Your Own Spa

Imagine having your own spa. You can learn how to start and run your own spa in the **FabJob Guide to Become a Spa Owner**. In this guide you will discover:

- Services you can offer (with information about makeup, facial, body, hair, nails, massage, hair removal, alternative care, and other services)

- Your options for buying an existing spa, franchising, partnering, or starting your own spa

- How to design your space, get equipment and supplies, find staff, and meet health requirements

- How to set prices for services and products

- How to market your spa to attract clients

**Visit www.FabJob.com to order guides today!**

# Does Someone You Love Deserve a Fab Job?

Giving a FabJob® guide is a fabulous way to show someone you believe in them and support their dreams. Help them break into the career of their dreams with the ...

- FabJob Guide to **Become an Actor**
- FabJob Guide to **Become a Bed and Breakfast Owner**
- FabJob Guide to **Become a Business Consultant**
- FabJob Guide to **Become a Celebrity Personal Assistant**
- FabJob Guide to **Become a Children's Book Author**
- FabJob Guide to **Become an Etiquette Consultant**
- FabJob Guide to **Become an Event Planner**
- FabJob Guide to **Become a Fashion Designer**
- FabJob Guide to **Become a Florist**
- FabJob Guide to **Become an Interior Decorator**
- FabJob Guide to **Become a Massage Therapist**
- FabJob Guide to **Become a Model**
- FabJob Guide to **Become a Motivational Speaker**
- FabJob Guide to **Become an Personal Shopper**
- FabJob Guide to **Become a Public Relations Consultant**
- FabJob Guide to **Become a Spa Owner**
- FabJob Guide to **Become a Super Salesperson**
- FabJob Guide to **Become a Wedding Planner**
- **And dozens more fabulous careers!**

## Visit FabJob.com for details and special offers